ND NIETZSCHE

Illuminating Modernity

Illuminating Modernity is dedicated to the renewal of faith in a world that is both Godless and idolatrous. This renewal takes the legacy of faith seriously and explores the tradition in the hope that the means of its contemporary development are to be found within it. This approach takes the historical crisis of faith seriously and makes sincere efforts to receive the strength necessary for a renewal. We call our way the Franciscan option. And yet, one of the greatest resources upon which we hope to build is Thomism, especially those hidden treasures of modern Thomistic thought to be found in Continental and phenomenological philosophy and theology.

The Franciscan option takes the history of faith seriously both in its continuity and in its change. It takes seriously the tragic experiences of the history of faith since the Wars of Religion and especially in late modernity. But it also takes seriously the rich heritage of faith. As Michael Polanyi argued, faith has become the fundamental act of human persons. Faith involves the whole of the person in his or her absolute openness to the Absolute. As Hegel saw, the logic of history is prefigured in the story of the Gospels, and the great and transforming experience of humanity has remained the experience of resurrection in the aftermath of a dramatic death.

The series editors are boundlessly grateful to Anna Turton, whose support for this series made a hope into a reality. We also owe a huge debt of gratitude to Notre Dame's Nanovic Institute for European Studies for giving us financial and moral support at the outset of our project. Many thanks to Anthony Monta and James McAdams for caring about the 'Hidden Treasures'.

BEYOND KANT AND NIETZSCHE

The Munich Defence of Christian Humanism

Tracey Rowland

LONDON • NEW YORK • OXFORD • NEW DELHI • SYDNEY

T&T CLARK

Bloomsbury Publishing Plc

50 Bedford Square, London, WC1B 3DP, UK

1385 Broadway, New York, NY 10018, USA

29 Earlsfort Terrace, Dublin 2, Ireland

BLOOMSBURY, T&T CLARK and the T&T Clark logo are trademarks of Bloomsbury Publishing Plc

First published in Great Britain 2021
Paperback edition published 2023

Copyright © Tracey Rowland, 2021

Tracey Rowland has asserted her right under the Copyright, Designs and Patents Act, 1988, to be identified as Author of this work.

For legal purposes the Acknowledgements on pp. ix–x constitute an extension of this copyright page.

Cover image: *Market in Marienplatz in Munich*, 1843, by Adam Heirich, Germany 19th Century. Photo by DeAgostini/Getty Images.

All rights reserved. No part of this publication may be reproduced or transmitted in any form or by any means, electronic or mechanical, including photocopying, recording, or any information storage or retrieval system, without prior permission in writing from the publishers.

Bloomsbury Publishing Plc does not have any control over, or responsibility for, any third-party websites referred to or in this book. All internet addresses given in this book were correct at the time of going to press. The author and publisher regret any inconvenience caused if addresses have changed or sites have ceased to exist, but can accept no responsibility for any such changes.

A catalogue record for this book is available from the British Library.

A catalog record for this book is available from the Library of Congress.

ISBN: HB: 978-0-5677-0316-3
PB: 978-0-5677-0320-0
ePDF: 978-0-5677-0317-0
ePUB: 978-0-5677-0319-4

Series: Illuminating Modernity

Typeset by Newgen KnowledgeWorks Pvt. Ltd., Chennai, India

To find out more about our authors and books visit www.bloomsbury.com and sign up for our newsletters.

In Memory of Rev. Dr. Paul Stenhouse MSC (1935–2019)

CONTENTS

Acknowledgements	ix
INTRODUCTION	1
Chapter 1 CARL MUTH (1867–1944)	19
Chapter 2 THEODOR HAECKER (1879–1945)	35
Chapter 3 THEODOR STEINBÜCHEL (1888–1949)	67
Chapter 4 GOTTLIEB SÖHNGEN (1892–1971)	91
Chapter 5 ROMANO GUARDINI (1885–1968)	117
Chapter 6 ERICH PRZYWARA (1889–1972)	143
CONCLUSION	169
Selected Bibliography	175
Author Index	183
Subject Index	187

ACKNOWLEDGEMENTS

I wish to thank Francesca Aran Murphy, Kenneth Oakes and Balázs M. Mezei for their invitation to contribute to the 'Illuminating Modernity' series and for their editorial assistance. I am also grateful to Anna Turton for shepherding another manuscript through the production process for Bloomsbury.

This book was in many ways an exercise in intellectual excavation work, unearthing 'treasure' from libraries and antiquarian bookshops in Germany and Austria. Most of the translation work I undertook myself, but I did farm out the most difficult books to Sebastian Condon. He deserves a medal for his translation of Przywara's book on Kant and sections of Przywara's *Humanitas*. Sebastian also helped by leaving much-needed books from the local Dominican library by an iron pig garden ornament for my collection at a time when all libraries were closed due to the pandemic. It is the second time in my life I have managed to get access to books by simply knowing Dominicans. The first time was in Poland in the final months of the communist regime.

Uwe-Karsten Kramm, an antiquarian bookseller in Stuttgart, heroically carted boxes of the journal *Hochland* to post offices in Germany during the 2020 lockdown, and when Australia stopped accepting parcels from Germany, my friend Maria MacKinnon accepted my German book purchases at her home in the south of England and rerouted them to Australia.

My friends Fr Juan Vélez who has written extensively on the thought of St John Henry Newman, Michael Daniel (an English Master at Camberwell Grammar) and Anna Silvas (a world-renowned Patristics scholar from a Romanian family, and who is thus by background multilingual) read drafts of each of the chapters and made some highly valued editorial suggestions.

Dr Greg Munro and Dr Jakob Knab who are both scholars of German history (in particular, in the case of Dr Munro, the history of German publications during the Weimar and Nazi eras and, in the case of Dr Knab, of the White Rose resistance leaders) each read sections of the manuscript and offered valuable expert advice.

My mother, Pauline, offered her office support services, and my husband Stuart listened night after night to stories of the latest discoveries and logistical problems.

I am grateful to all who helped to make this publication possible, and I hope that it will be a source of consolation and encouragement for its readers.

INTRODUCTION

The first half of the twentieth century witnessed a Catholic literary renaissance in France and England, and the conversions of notable artists and scholars around the world, including Germany. The generation of Catholic theologians who provided the inspiration for the Second Vatican Council (1961-5), or who were theological advisors (*periti*) at the Council – and some fell into both categories – was highly creative. Many of its outstanding names were, academically speaking, virtuoso performers.[1] Such as these do require raw talent, but also nurture within a culture that is already very mature, on a very high level. Just as champion racehorses are often associated with particular studs and trainers, and renowned prima ballerinas come from ballet companies with already legendary performers who in turn foster the talent of the next generation, so too with theology professors.

This book is about the intellectual milieu that produced the post-Second World War generation of German Catholic scholars who were so influential around the time of the Council and beyond. In particular, it seeks to profile six of the outstanding characters located in the Munich academies and intellectual salons in the first half of the twentieth century: Carl Muth, Theodor Haecker, Gottlieb Söhngen, Theodor Steinbüchel, Romano Guardini and Erich Przywara. The last two names on the list are already well known to graduate students of theology, although doctoral theses on their works are only now beginning to be written in English. Each one broke new ground in the respective fields of art criticism, translation work and social commentary, fundamental theology, theological anthropology, the *Christian Weltanschauung* and what might be called the 'gestalt' of Catholic theology, its overall form conceived as something more than the sum of its parts. They were working within a culture infused with the spirit of German Idealism.

---

1. Reinhard Hütter from the Catholic University of America is one of many authors to observe this fact.

For some dozen years (1933–45) they were united in their opposition to the Nazi regime, though two of the six, Muth and Haecker, were to die shortly before the 'Third Reich' experiment ended. Guardini is the best known of the six. He was one of the young Joseph Ratzinger's intellectual heroes. He was also admired by Karl Rahner who succeeded him in his Chair at the University of Munich in 1963. About two dozen of his 60 plus books are available in English translation, mostly those dealing with topics in spirituality, as well as his *Letters from Lake Como, Freedom, Grace and Destiny, The End of the Modern World* and *The Spirit of the Liturgy*. Notable anglophone scholars who have published books and articles about Guardini are Robert A. Krieg and Roland Millare, while the leading German language authority is Hannah-Barbara Gerl-Falkovitz from the Benedikt XVI *Pontifical Athenaeum* located at the Heiligenkreuz monastery in the Vienna Woods. Krieg is based at the University of Notre Dame in Indiana, and Millare comes out of the late Cardinal Francis George's Mundelein stable. The publisher Morcelliana has also embarked on a project to translate Guardini's *Opera omnia* into Italian under the direction of Gerl-Falkovitz.

Guardini was a major figure in German Catholic life throughout the first half of the twentieth century. Not only did he hold personal Chairs at the Universities of Berlin (1923–39), Tübingen (1945–48) and Munich (1948–63), he was also the patriarch of the German Catholic youth movement 'Quickborn' and an editor of its journal *Schildgenossen*. In 1962 he was awarded the Erasmus Prize, given to individuals who are deemed to have made exceptional contributions to culture, society or the social sciences in Europe. This civic recognition came just six years before his death in the cultural-earthquake year of 1968.

Erich Przywara, the only Jesuit in this line up, is known first and foremost for his approach to the *analogia entis* – a concept famously criticized by Karl Barth as an idea worthy of the anti-Christ. The Catholic University of America Press published James V. Zeitz's account of Przywara's *analogia entis* in 1982. More recently, Eerdmans has published three books on Przywara: *The Analogy of Being: Invention of the Anti-christ or the Wisdom of God?*, a collection of conference papers edited by Thomas Joseph White OP in 2010; *Analogia Entis: Metaphysics, Original Structure and Universal Rhythm*, a translation of Przywara's original work by John R Betz and David Bentley Hart in 2014 (the 115-page introduction by Betz is arguably the most user-friendly introduction to Przywara available in English); and *Reimagining the Analogia Entis: The Future of Erich Przywara's Christian Vision* by

Philip John Paul Gonzales in 2019. The University of Notre Dame Press has also published three Przywara books: Thomas F. O'Meara's *Erich Przywara, SJ: His Theology and His World* in 2002, Graham McAleer's *Erich Przywara and Postmodern Natural Law* in 2019 and *Church of the Ever Greater God: The Ecclesiology of Erich Przywara* by Aaron Pidel SJ in 2020. John R. Betz has also contributed a chapter on Przywara's *Analogia Entis* to the flagship volume of Bloomsbury's *Illuminating Modernity* series, *Christian Wisdom Meets Modernity*, edited by Kenneth Oakes. In Europe the Pontifical Faculty of the University of Warsaw is emerging as a centre of Przywara scholarship. Andrzej Persidok has published essays on Przywara's ideas on the supernatural in both Polish and Spanish, and Maciej Raczyński-Rożek has published two articles in English, one on Przywara's understanding of the Church as the realization of the nature of man and one on the *Analogia Entis* as a model of Catholic thinking in postmodern reality. Two of Pryzwara's syntheses, one on Augustine and one on Newman, whom Przywara regarded as the Augustine of his age, have long been available in English. However, these two synthetic collections, along with Przywara's publications on metaphysics and ecclesiology, represent only a small fraction of his literary output. No one has yet had the courage to translate his 903-page *Humanitas: Der Mensch gestern und morgen*, or his slightly less intimidating 408-page *Crucis Mysterium: Das christliche Heute*.

Humanitas examines the 'what is man?' question through the lens of a large number of German authors, literary, philosophical and theological, as well as other outstanding 'foreign' names like John Henry Newman, Paul Claudel, Fyodor Dostoevsky, Søren Kierkegaard, Simone Weil, Charles Péguy and, of course, Plato and Aristotle. In many ways this work, published in 1952, takes a similar form to Hans Urs von Balthasar's doctoral dissertation titled *Geschichte des eschatologischen Problems in der modernen deutschen Literatur* completed in 1928 and published in an expanded version as the *Apokalypse der deutschen Seele* in the years 1937-9.[2] Whereas Balthasar focused on the theme of eschatology in German Letters, Przywara focused on the theme of *Humanitas* but broadened the scope to include non-German writers.

2. Hans Urs von Balthasar, *Geschichte des eschatologischen Problems in der modernen deutschen Literatur* (Einsiedeln: Johannes Verlag, 1998) and *Apokalypse der deutschen Seele: Studien zu einer Lehre von letzten Haltungen*, 3 vols (Leipzig: Anton Pustet, 1937-9).

Crucis Mysterium, its title taken from the Latin chant *Vexilla regis*, is also largely an exercise in comparative theological anthropology. It begins by comparing the radicalism of Nietzsche's superman, driven by the will to power, with the radicalism of the act of self-surrender demanded by the spiritual exercises of St Ignatius. It then moves on to a comparison of Ignatian spirituality with Thomist and Carmelite spirituality, and an analysis of the differences between the Dominican theology of Aquinas and the Ignatian theology of Luis de Molina. These reflections on spiritual polarities are followed by a series of essays on the relationship between the world and religion in which several pairs, St John Henry Newman and Henri Brémond, Nicholas of Cusa and St Augustine, Plato and Aristotle, are juxtaposed. The final third of the work is dedicated to the spirituality of the Sacred Heart, Marian theology, the Nuptial Mystery, the mystery of the cross and questions about death. Przywara explains that the title *Crucis Mysterium* describes the unity of these investigations, 'each of the individual pieces somehow contains the whole of this image of the Church today, and yet all of them only aim towards it in the form of rays'.[3]

Alongside these two formidable tomes, and some shorter monographs, some eight hundred publications appeared between the years 1912 and 1962 under the authorship of Erich Przywara SJ.[4] These took the form of Festschrift articles for colleagues, book reviews, published keynote lectures and journal articles spanning the disciplines of theology, philosophy, political theory and literature. A list of the names of scholars who appear as subjects in the titles of these publications runs to more than four hundred entries.

Little has been written in English about the other four authors. Haecker is known as the German translator of the works of Kierkegaard and Newman, and as the person who introduced the White Rose martyrs Hans and Sophie Scholl to Newman's ideas on conscience. Both Sophie and Hans would be executed by the Nazis in 1943 for their opposition to their regime. Beyond this, publications about Haecker in English have tended to focus on his use of satire as a rhetorical device. An exception has been a small collection of journal articles by Helena M. Tomko on the place of Haecker in European literature in which she highlights his Catholic sensibilities. Gottlieb Söhngen is known to a

---

3. Erich Przywara, *Crucis Mysterium: Das christliche Heute* (Paderborn: F. Schöningh, 1939), p. 5.

4. See the complete list of eight hundred publications in L. Zimny, *Erich Przywara: Sein Schrifttum 1912–1962* (Einsiedeln: Johannes Verlag, 1963).

small circle of Ratzinger scholars as the person who supervised both of Ratzinger's theses – the doctorate and the *Habilitationsschrift* – and his name is well known among Barthian scholars for his treatment of the *Analogia Fidei*, which Barth much preferred to Przywara's *Analogia Entis*. The journal *Pro Ecclesia* has published two English translations from Söhngen on the *Analogia Fidei*, both by Kenneth J. Oakes. Outside of the worlds of Barthian and Ratzinger scholarship, however, Söhngen's publications have not been investigated in the anglophone world. The name Theodor Steinbüchel is even less visible on the academic radar of the Anglosphere although he was the most significant moral theologian of his generation in Germany. Carl Muth is similarly almost unknown in English-speaking circles. He was not a professional academic but a public intellectual whose editorship of the journal *Hochland* brought together a highly influential ecumenical network of writers and artists in the first half of the twentieth century. For German Catholics *Hochland* (1903–71) was the precursor to the *International Catholic Review: Communio*, founded in 1972 by Hans Urs von Balthasar, Henri de Lubac and Joseph Ratzinger, among others, and now published in some seventeen languages.

Many volumes could be written on each of these authors. The focus of this collection is on what each had to say to the idea of a Christian humanism. Each one defended the possibility of a 'humanism of the Incarnation' in a period of intense intellectual and spiritual despair. Not only had the carnage of the First World War caused many to lose their faith in the God of Christianity, it has also caused many to lose their interest in the ideas put forward by the philosophers of the *Aufklärung*. Paul Tillich's experience is paradigmatic: 'All that horrible, long night I walked along the rows of dying men, and much of my German classical education philosophy broke down that night – the belief that man could master cognitively the essence of his being, the belief in the identity of essence and existence.'[5] Writing in *Stimmen der Zeit* in 1924, Max Pribilla SJ observed:

> It is a confused, uprooted time in which we are placed. The harshest contrasts abruptly stand side by side: exuberant lust for pleasure and bitterest poverty, tenderest conscientiousness and animal treachery, warmest charity and coldest selfishness, crystal clear

---

5. Paul Tillich, *Time* 73 (11), 16 March 1959, p. 47. Quoted in Douglas John Hall, 'The Great War and the Theologians' in *The Twentieth Century: A Theological Overview*, Gregory Baum (ed.) (New York: Orbis, 1999), pp. 3–14 at 6.

mind and blurred mysticism, blindest belief in miracles and the flattest materialism. From all the phenomena of the present there is a profound dissatisfaction with the status quo and helplessness about what should follow … The cultural crisis creeps across Europe, but it has undoubtedly taken its sharpest form in Germany.[6]

More recently Holger Zaborowksi contributed an article to a special edition of the journal *Modern Theology* focused on German theology between the two world wars. He noted that after the First World War the 'narratives of the Enlightenment tradition, of progress, reason, science, and freedom, became deeply questionable' and 'new points of reference and of meaning became important'.[7] Specifically, 'Nietzsche, the radical critic of the Western tradition' replaced Hegel, who 'claimed to complete this very tradition', while 'Kierkegaard, the fideist, took over from Kant, the rationalist'; interest in St Paul spiked above interest in the liberal theology of the nineteenth century, and 'Augustine, the early existentialist' began to outshine 'Aquinas, the systematic thinker'.[8]

Moreover, it was not uncommon for European intellectuals to trace the primary intellectual cause of the carnage of the First World War to the father of German Idealism, Immanuel Kant. Obviously, there were other factors at play like Bismarck's 'Blood and Iron' thesis and other markers of nineteenth-century nationalism, as well as random factors like the assassination of an Austrian archduke, the reign of a Kaiser who had a troubled relationship with his English mother and the desire of some, especially those in Freemasonic lodges, to exploit the conflagration as a means to destroy the Habsburg Empire. Nonetheless the culture of Prussia was deeply influenced by German Idealism, and

---

6. Max Pribilla, 'Kulturwende und Katholizismus', *Stimmen der Zeit* 107 (1924), pp. 259–78 at 259. Cited by Joachim Schmiedl, 'Der katholische Aufbruch der Zwischenkreigszeit und die Stimmen der Zeit' in Michel Grunewald et al. *Le Milieu Intellectuel Cathololique en Allemagne, Sa Presse et ses Réseaux (1871–1963)/ Das Katholische Intellektuellen-Milieu in Deutschland, seine Presse und seine Netzwerke (1871–1963)* (Bern: Peter Lang, 2006), pp. 231–55 at 233.

7. Holger Zaborowski, 'Contradiction, Liturgy, and Freedom: Romano Guardini's Search for Meaning after the Cataclysm of World War I', *Modern Theology* 35 (1) (January 2019), pp. 43–54 at 44.

8. Ibid., p. 44.

was certainly an important component of the intellectual antecedents of the First World War.⁹

This claim that Kant was the intellectual preceptor of these events was made as early as 1914 by the Russian philosopher Vladimir Ern (1882–1917), author of *La Critique kantienne du concept de vérité* (1912) in his famous 'From Kant to Krupp' lecture.¹⁰ Ern declared that 'the arms of Krupp are full of the most profound philosophical content', and that 'the internal transcription of the German spirit in Kant's philosophy naturally and fatally coincides with the external transcription of that same German spirit in the arms of Krupp'.¹¹ In the following passage Ern offered a defence of these theses with a genealogy that identified the ideas of Kant and of his successors as one of the many causes of the First World War:

> The crux of Kantian thought, finding its most extreme and dispassionate expression in the first edition of the *Critique of Pure Reason*, reduces to two principles: to the absolute phenomenality of all external experience and to the absolute phenomenality of all internal experience. Two of the most radical propositions flow from these two principles, established in the transcendental *Ethics* and the transcendental *Analytics*: 1) no *noumenon*, i.e. nothing ontological, can be encountered in our external experience, and 2) nothing noumenal, i.e. relating to the world of the truly Real, can be given and realized in our internal experience. And since there are no other paths of cognition besides external and internal experience, the *Critique of Pure Reason* has become the global historical herald of the purist form of *absolute immanentism*. Of course, in Kant lived the remains of Platonic transcendentalism, and these remains are: the idea of intelligible freedom and the concept of 'things-in-themselves'. But these Platonic reminiscences of Kant absolutely do not tally with his basic principles.¹²

9. See, for example, Charles William Super, *German Idealism and Prussian Militarism* (Worcestershire: Neale, 1916), reprinted by Sagwan Press in 2015 and Andreas Vrahimis, 'Legacies of German Idealism: From the Great War to the Analytic/Continental Divide', *Parrhesia* 24 (2015), pp. 83–106.

10. Vladimir Ern, 'Od Kanta do Kruppa', quoted by A. Mrówczyński-Van Allen in *Between the Icon and the Idol* (Oregon: Cascade, 2014), p. 130.

11. Ibid.

12. Vladimir Ern, 'From Kant to Krupp', in *Mech i krest. Stat'i o sovremennykh sobytiiakh* [*The Sword and the Cross. Essays on Contemporary Events*] (Moscow,

Ern went on to argue that 'the basic principles of Kantian phenomenalism were the unassailable axis of all further movement of German thought' from Fichte to Hegel, and then onto the neo-Kantians. He concluded, 'The cry of Nietzsche: "*der alte Gott ist tot*", is an obvious anachronism. The old God is dead, and he was guillotined in the labyrinth of Transcendental Analytics.'[13]

While Ern focused on the influence of Kant, the German sociologist Alfred von Martin, focused upon Hegel, Nietzsche and Spengler. In his *Geistige Wegbereiter des Deutschen Zusammenbruchs: Hegel – Nietzsche – Spengler*, published in 1948, Martin skipped from Luther to Hegel without going through Kant. He argued that a major effect of the Reformation was that the human person, having been 'theologically degraded to nothing before God', was handed over to the authorities. Hegel then identifies God with history and the Prussian state. The Romantic movement, including Nietzsche's contribution, becomes a uniquely German substitute religion, and with this the political becomes exaggerated. Nietzsche's superman – as 'lord of the earth' – replaces God after God himself has been declared dead. By the time Spengler arrives, 'the will to power, the world's last explanatory principle, remains the only yardstick left'.[14]

With less passion, but nonetheless concurring with the main lines of Ern and Martin's arguments, Leszek Kołakowski (1927–2009) concluded that the 'recurrent German philosophical desire' is one which 'consists in the attempt to discover God without God, to find secular and transcendental foundation for moral and epistemological security apart from God'.[15] In his *Love Alone Is Credible*, Balthasar summarized much of the above-style analysis with the statement, 'Luther deposes Aristotelian reason in order to make room for faith, but this rejected reason acquires a Cartesian structure and Kant tries to tame it by bringing it under human control. Being thus limited, reason

---

1915), pp. 20–34. From a speech given to the Religious Philosophical Society, 6 October 1914. English translation available at https://ceulearning.ceu.edu/pluginfile.php/274077/mod_resource/content/1/Ern%201915.pdf.

13. Ibid.

14. Alfred von Martin, *Geistige Wegbereiter des Deutschen Zusammenbruchs: Hegel – Nietzsche – Spengler* (Recklinghausen: Bittler, 1948), pp. 27–31.

15. Leszek Kołakowski, 'Reprodukcja kulturalna I zapominanie', in *Czy diabel moze byc zbawiony i 27 innych kazan* (Kraków: Znak, 2006). Quoted in A. Mrówczyński-Van Allen in *Between the Icon and the Idol*, p. 130.

no longer has anything to with religion and it becomes what Karl Barth called an "idol factory".[16]

In a more recent work, *The Kingdom of Man: Genesis and Failure of the Modern Project*, Remi Brague, Professor Emeritus of the Romano Guardini Chair of Philosophy at the Ludwig-Maximilians-Universität in Munich, also tackled the subject of the social impact of German Idealism. Brague drew a distinction between the humanists of the fifteenth century and those of the nineteenth. The humanists of the fifteenth century were those who had studied the *literae humaniores* of the Ciceronian tradition.[17] Humanists of this kind had recourse to the wisdom of the ancients in order to reflect upon the nobility of the human spirit made manifest in the human person's relationship to the gods, to nature and to fate. In contrast, the humanists of the nineteenth century and those following in their tradition want to affirm the sovereignty of the human person against both God and nature and for some against fate as well. Brague calls the humanists of the nineteenth century and their contemporary heirs proponents of an 'exclusive humanism', because their form of humanism excludes both God and nature. He also identifies the interventions of Kant as a watershed in the rise of this exclusive humanism, especially Kant's treatment of nature in his *Critique of Judgment* (the so-called Third Critique). In Brague's account Kant reaches the conclusion that man has the physical possibility of subjecting the totality of nature to the supreme end he contains in himself. Schiller carries through the logic of this principle by 'reaffirming the neutral character of nature, its indifference to human activity, and hence the impossibility of taking it as a moral model; quite the contrary it must be dominated'.[18] Fichte goes one step further and argues that man only exists as a project. Finally, the positivists and pragmatists agree that the project is based on man's domination of nature which may require the renunciation of truth.[19]

All the authors surveyed in this work agree that attempts to find secular and transcendental foundation for moral and epistemological security apart from God – above all the attempt to find any meaning at all in human life apart from God – are destined to end in some form of

---

16. Hans Urs von Balthasar, *Love Alone Is Credible* (San Francisco: Ignatius, 2004), p. 16.

17. Remi Brague, *The Kingdom of Man: Genesis and Failure of the Modern Project* (South Bend, IN: University of Notre Dame Press, 2018), p. 121.

18. Ibid., p. 104.

19. Ibid., p. 106.

anti-humanism. Conversely, our sextet of authors affirms the intrinsic goodness of nature as given, even as a gift. They link human dignity to the project of deification, not to the project of the mastery of nature. They believe in truth, in goodness and in beauty as transcendental properties of being. They reject the proposition that truth is a dispensable luxury if it becomes a barrier to the technological mastery of nature or an undemocratic element in civic culture. In a discourse to commemorate the White Rose martyrs of Munich, Guardini described the university as 'one of the most noble worlds in existence, [precisely] because it has obligations only to the truth'.[20]

Some themes reappear like a musical motif in the publications of each of the authors. One of these is the influence of John Henry Newman (1801–1890), another is the spiritual disposition of Goethe's Faust, and yet others are the intellectual turmoil initiated by Kant and the charges upon which Nietzsche indicted Christianity. All the authors agree that the Kantian equation of freedom with autonomy was a most terrible intellectual error, and that Nietzsche's verdict that Christianity is a crime against life itself is a very serious criticism that demands a response. Nietzsche cannot be dismissed as a person with mental-health issues or a common garden-variety libertine. They also agree that two widespread problems in the years of the Weimar Republic and its Nazi successor were despair and depression. These conditions are viewed as the logical consequences of what Brague called an exclusive humanism. Haecker diagnosed the condition in the following passage:

> [Max] Scheler and countless others who have followed him are right in saying that men *en masse* were themselves never as problematic as they are today, but they forget to provide the reason for this, or they do not know it. Yet the reason is nothing other than the fact that man has himself become the last and only guarantee of that life which alone comprises his goal, the sole reason for his existence: the spiritual life, the living spirit. And he has no real trust in this final guarantee; he suspects its bankruptcy and its complete inability to pay in the end. Quite rightly! ... This situation of objective and subjective angst – which can only be drowned out or muted by fanaticism or suggestion, but can never really be taken away ... is the situation within which today the question is posed: What is man?[21]

20. Romano Guardini, *La Rosa Bianca* (Brescia: Morcelliana, 1994), p. 39.
21. Theodor Haecker, *Was ist der Mensch?* (Frankfurt am Mein: Ullstein Bücher, 1959), p. 111.

The theological vignettes collected here all centre on this question. Each author reviewed is trying to provide a response to the crisis of the nihilist cul-de-sac in which post-Enlightenment German humanism found itself. They each respond with some account of an alternative Christian humanism casting light upon the shadows of late modern culture. Theodor Haecker expressed the idea thus:

> This revelation of true being [the Incarnation] illumines the chilling paradox that the most obedient, the one who was obedient even to death on the cross, the Son of Man, is simultaneously in essence the second person of the Trinity, is simultaneously the absolute 'Lord'. It also illumines the delightful paradox that the *ancilla domini*, the handmaid of the Lord, is simultaneously – and for precisely that reason – the creaturely dominatrix of all creatures, the most free, the *regina coelorum*. It also illumines, of course, the general paradox, that each higher grade of human sanctity, that is, of obedience towards God, is also a higher grade of true freedom and domination. Where there is such holy domination and thus freedom, there is no chaos in the sense of befuddlement and perversion. The chaos of this age is a consequence of a false freedom that leads to anarchy and to the despotism which is its accompanying correlative and consequence.[22]

Each of the six scholars linked the crisis of post-Enlightenment German humanism to the crisis of European identity. They all wrote essays on Europe's place in world history and reflected upon the possible ways forward when the totalitarian utopian visions had exhausted themselves. The Christian humanism presented in the essays of this Munich circle of Catholic scholars is thus the literary treasure of this rather dark period in European history. It is well overdue for reception into the world of anglophone Catholic theology. It was the seedbed that produced quite a number of the virtuoso performers of the second half of the twentieth century, including, no less, Ratzinger and Balthasar. It offered hope to a despairing generation and its culture.

This body of scholarship is also relevant, not merely because of what it produced in the world of Catholic letters but because of the strength of contemporary atheism that demands an analysis and response. At the St Xavier Symposium held in Chicago in the aftermath of the Second

22. Ibid., p. 48.

Vatican Council, Henri de Lubac had this to say about contemporary atheism:

> Just as the New Testament revealed the hidden meaning of the Old Testament, but by discarding it as old and as belonging to the dead past, so contemporary humanism does with its understanding of Christian theism. It believes that it understands it, does it justice, and raises it up into a second life within itself which is more-true and is indeed the only truth. But by this fact it relegates Christian theism in its first sense to the cemetery of myths. Should the thing of the past strive to survive or revive, it would then become an evil influence. The embrace that understands therefore grips in order to stifle.
>
> Today such is the usual claim of atheism, the general form of its strategy, whether it be triumphant, despairing or placid; whether it inclines to collectivism or to anarchy; whether it derives from metaphysical renunciation, or from earthly ambition; or whether, in its totalitarian imperialism, it speaks in the name of sociology or psychoanalysis. So in order not to be 'understood' in this sense, only one way is open: to do some understanding. Therefore the Christian must understand atheism.[23]

The authors surveyed in this book are worthy of our reflection precisely because they did understand atheism, or important facets of it, since they had to live through some of its severest cultural manifestations. Communism in all its forms and factions is decidedly atheistic. Fascism was more inclined to a new paganism. In its German manifestation Fascism drew heavily upon Nordic mythology, but also included both atheistic and residual pseudo-Christian elements, as well as an interest in the occult and astrology. One of the most prescient of de Lubac's comments is that contemporary forms of atheism are particularly lethal because they do not entirely reject Christianity, they continue to relate to it parasitically. Just as J. K. Rowling's fictional dark lord Voldemort is depicted as someone who needs to inhabit the body of another in order to exercise power, de Lubac's insight is that contemporary atheism is similarly parasitic. It does not entirely discard Christianity or otherwise operate outside of it, but rather seeks to 'do it justice', by raising it up into 'a second life within itself which is more-true and is indeed the only truth'. In other words, it 'mutates' authentic Christianity. This process

---

23. Henri de Lubac, 'Nature and Grace' in *The Word in History: The St. Xavier Symposium*, T. Patrick Burke (ed.) (London: Collins, 1968), p. 29.

takes place both within the formal structures of Christian institutions and within the structures of ostensibly 'secular' institutions, such as the modern, state-sponsored university. Accordingly, de Lubac advised that a Christian must:

> Detect behind its deceptive hermeneutic the real sources from which it [atheism] springs ... [He] must suspect any mediocre and superficial 'comprehension' based on [a] desire of conciliation, since that will leave him defeated before he begins. He should be especially alert to reject the compromise formulas easily accepted unconsciously or half-consciously, that this atheistic hermeneutic puts out as bait, since through them he may slip into apostasy.[24]

Therefore, an objective of these chapters is to help those born so recently that the Weimar Republic and the twelve years of Nazi tyranny that followed it are almost ancient history, a window into the neo-atheistic attempts to raise Christianity into a 'life within itself', to transvalue its values and thereby present the world with a mutant form of Christianity. The severance of faith from reason, reason from love, love from fidelity, fidelity from virtue, virtue from nature, nature from goodness, goodness from beauty and beauty from truth are all hallmarks of the quintessentially modern projects whose shadows were illuminated by the six authors located in Munich in the early to mid-twentieth century.

Overarching all these dimensions of the human soul that ought to operate in harmony is the relationship between history and ontology. In his *Principles of Catholic Theology* (1987), Joseph Ratzinger made the claim that *the* deepest crisis in Catholic theology in the twentieth century hinged on the issue of how to understand the mediation of history in the realm of ontology. The idea that there is any relationship at all between history and ontology was strongly resisted by leaders of the neo-scholastic movement. No doubt neo-scholastic circles feared that any concessions on this point would lead to an outbreak of historicism. Nonetheless, in his *The Paradoxical Structure of Existence*, Frederick D. Wilhelmsen noted that the 'stumbling block [for the neo-scholastics] is the Aristotelian contention that science is of the necessary, not of the accidental'.[25] For Aristotle, history is a mere accident and therefore

---

24. Ibid.
25. Frederick D. Wilhelmsen, *The Paradoxical Structure of Existence* (New York: Preserving Christian Publications, 1991), p. 179.

not as important as substance. The Aristotelian influence within the Thomist tradition unfortunately led to a kind of Thomist indifference to history while the Romantic interest in history only served to confirm the suspicions of Thomists that history was a threat to ontology and thereby to moral absolutes. Wilhelmsen suggested that the issue needed further elucidation, and he offered the argument that a place to find a better understanding is in the first part of St Thomas Aquinas' *Summa Theologiae*, question three, article four. In a discussion on the relation that predicables bear on human nature, Aquinas concluded that it was impossible to include existence within the class of accidents: *quia nulla res sufficit quod sit sibi causa essendi, si habeat esse causatum* ('for nothing can be the sufficient cause of its own existence, if its existence is caused'; *Summ Theol*, first part, Q. 3, Art. 4). Wilhelmsen noted that neither Cajetan (1469–1534) nor John of St Thomas (1589–1644), two of the leading baroque-era Thomist commentators, seriously addressed this passage, but Domingo Bañez (1578–1604) used it to launch into an extensive study of the meaning and primacy of existence in being.[26] Bañez argued that if existence is an accident, so too is substance, because substance ultimately is simply a way of existing. Following the lead of Bañez, Wilhelmsen concluded that 'to call St. Thomas' *esse* a predicable accident is not only an abuse of language; it is also a radical failure to understand the revolution the Angelic Doctor worked within the history of metaphysics'.[27] For Wilhelmsen, 'a Christian metaphysics is purely and simply an intellectual discipline bearing on being in the exercise of its act of existing. This act is neither substantial nor accidental but transcends each pole of the Greek distinction by englobing them both'.[28] This approach was eventually taken up by those described as 'existential Thomists' in the mid-twentieth century, foremost of whom was Etienne Gilson.

Thus, early-twentieth-century Catholic theology and philosophy found itself in a situation where it either had absolutely nothing to say, or was even capable of saying, to the many Romantic movement concerns like history and culture and the uniqueness of each human person, or, if it wished to engage with these issues it needed to develop a more sophisticated account of the relationship between history and ontology. The development of a Christian existentialism was an

26. Ibid., p. 182.
27. Ibid., p. 183.
28. Ibid., p. 185.

urgent desideratum! This explains the interest in Kierkegaard and Newman: neither were scholastics, both braved the historical, cultural and subjective aspects of human existence. It also explains Guardini's interest in proposing an entire Christian *Weltanschauung*, rather than merely specializing in some particular branch of theology, like dogmatics or morals; it explains the emphasis within Steinbüchel's projects on *Menschenbilder* (different visions or images of humanity in different historical contexts). It also helps to understand what Przywara was doing with his hefty tomes examining the *Humanitas* theme from the perspective of hundreds of different scholars and then writing other books and articles on the *Analogia Entis*, a topic at the heart of metaphysics. It makes sense of Söhngen's enthusiasm for Newman and his interest in revisiting many topics in fundamental theology, and finally it explains why Muth wanted Catholic literature to be more realistic, more grounded in the realities of human existence, and why Haecker was so frustrated with German Idealism's failure to engage 'the real world'. For each of these scholars, the subjective and the historical were significant elements of Christian life, but in pursuing these interests they did not wish to jettison the metaphysical. Nor were they Hegelians, either of the Left or Right. They wanted Catholic intellectual life to engage with Romantic themes, and because of this interest they often found themselves at loggerheads with the neo-scholastics of their era. Nonetheless they agreed with the neo-scholastics in wanting to avoid a crude historicism.

The theological chaos that arose after the Second Vatican Council was due, at least in part, to the fact that the generation of 1968 was not nearly as cautious and respectful of the immutable elements within the Catholic tradition as the two preceding twentieth-century generations had been. These two generations had endured two world wars, an economic depression and the rise of ideologies that justified the mass murder of races and classes of people. In the midst of the terror and the darkness that led many to despair of the entire Western intellectual heritage, the six Catholic scholars profiled in the following pages stood firm in their belief in a Christian *Humanitas* built upon the perennial truths of Christian revelation, which is no less than the *memoria ecclesiae*, the memory of the Church.

Sadly, significant numbers of the generation of 1968 did not follow in the trajectory they set. They were, in the words of de Lubac, 'overcome by a desire for conciliation that left them defeated before they had begun'. They swallowed the bait of compromise formulas mediated by atheistic hermeneutical frameworks, and many slipped willy-nilly into apostasy.

The chaos created by this generation of the 1970s through 1990s has driven many young millennials to conclude that they need to 'reboot' Catholic theology to 1959, at least as they imagine it: a scholasticism that refuses to have anything to do with the mediation of history and culture in the domain of ontology. The authors surveyed in this book offer an alternative way forward that does not jettison ontology and metaphysics, but is open to understanding the role of history in the formation of the person. Following the lead of St John Henry Newman, among others, they open up ways of relating history and ontology within an overarching framework of Catholic tradition.

In choosing to undertake what a scholar-friend called an exercise in 'intellectual excavation', it was necessary to make some foundational decisions about the 'excavation sites'. Four extra 'sites' might have been included, namely the publications of the philosophers Peter Wust, Josef Pieper, Dietrich von Hildebrand and Alfred Delp SJ. Lest the project become unmanageably large it was decided to leave the terrain of this primarily philosophical quartet to be mined at a later date. Further, Wust and Pieper did not have such strong Munich connections as the other six authors. Although they were both *Hochland* contributors, they were never professors at the University of Munich or an editor of a Munich-based journal. Hildebrand did have a strong connection with the University of Munich but spent much of his life in the United States, for which reason many of his publications are already available in English. Thanks to Ignatius Press, Josef Pieper's most significant works have also been translated.

Alfred Delp SJ was an important philosopher of the era who wrote articles on metaphysics and began a critical engagement with the existentialism of Martin Heidegger. He was based in Munich and worked on the *Stimmen der Zeit* journal. He was banned from entry to the University of Munich on political grounds. Unlike Hildebrand, however, he was not so fortunate in escaping the Nazi violence. He died a martyrs' death on 2 February 1945. The street where Hitler's mistress Eva Braun once lived, Wasserburgerstrasse in Munich-Bogenhausen, has been renamed Delpstrasse, and the cause for Delp's beatification was opened in 1990.

This quartet deserve to be acknowledged as German Catholic scholars who, in spiritual union and solidarity with the other six names here 'excavated', cast light upon the theological virtue of hope in dark times. Pieper, himself influenced by Przywara, wrote extensively on the theological virtue of hope; Wust's final lecture to his students in 1940 took the form of an exhortation on the power of prayer, and

Hildebrand's intellectual opposition to fascism was so strong his name was on a Nazi hit list. He had to flee from three countries: first Germany, then Austria, then Nazi-occupied France. Along with Wust, Hildebrand was one of the most significant Catholic personalist philosophers of the twentieth century. Delp, as already stated, died a martyr.

This book is written in memory of Fr Paul Stenhouse MSC (1935–2019), who was a Missionary of the Sacred Heart and the editor of the journal *Annals Australasia* for some five decades. He was a character not unlike Munich's Carl Muth, remembered for his urbanity and renowned for his facility with languages modern, classical and Semitic (Hebrew, Aramaic, Samaritan and Arabic), his friendship with scholars, political leaders and journalists, his pastoral care of refugees from brutal regimes, his practical support for Aid to the Church in Need and his intelligence-gathering skills for the Vatican. He was likened to the fictional character Indiana Jones, a person who travels to parts of the world no government would deem 'safe', speaks the obscure language of the locals, uncovers plots by evil people and sorts out the problems of the good. Unlike Jones, he also offered Mass, heard confessions and witnessed and blessed marriages. He would have been right at home with Muth and his circle of *Hochland* contributors.

Chapter 1

CARL MUTH

(1867–1944)

Hochland was borne by the personality of Muth.[1]

Carl Borromäus Johann Baptist Muth was born in Worms on the Upper Rhine where some five centuries ago in 1521 the Diet of Worms issued the Edict of Worms declaring Martin Luther a heretic. Worms is also associated with the *Nibelungenlied* whose characters include historical figures from the fifth and sixth centuries when Worms was the capital of the Kingdom of the Burgundians. Muth was a child during Bismarck's *Kulturkampf* – the program of asserting Prussian government dominance over switch-points of Catholic cultural influence – and he died in November 1944 when Hitler's regime would soon be defeated. In the era of Muth's birth, Catholic parents distanced themselves from the Protestant majority of the Reich by giving their children unmistakably Catholic names. In his case he was named after a cardinal responsible for the reforms of the Council of Trent and St John the Baptist, otherwise known by his biblical title, 'the voice crying in the wilderness'. Both names were to prove apt for Muth. He grew up to be both a reformer of Catholic intellectual life and one of the voices against the Nazi regime.

At the age of 14, one year after the death of his mother Katharina, he entered the boarding school of the mission house of the Society of the Divine Word (SVD) located in Steyl on the Meuse River in the Netherlands. He remained there for three years before moving to Algiers to study with another missionary Order known as the White Fathers. This Order was founded in 1868 by the French Cardinal Charles Lavigerie, Archbishop of Carthage and Algiers and Primate of Africa. Muth eventually decided against a missionary vocation and returned

1. Josef Schöningh, 'Carl Muth: Ein europäisches Vermächtnis', *Hochland* (1946–7), pp. 1–19 at p. 8.

to Germany. He was to retain an appreciation of the French Catholic spirituality he had come to know in Algiers for the rest of his life.

After military service in Mainz (1890/1) he began to study economics, constitutional law, philosophy, history and literature in Berlin (1891/2), but then changed course to art history studies in Paris (1892/3) and Rome (1893) where he built relationships within the literary circles of these great cities. A year later he married Anna Thaler from Hessen with whom he had five children (Reinhard, Lulu, Wolfgang, Othmar and Paul). Reinhard was to die in the final months of the First World War, one of the nine million military victims of this conflagration.

From 1894 to 1896 Muth worked in Strasbourg for the newspaper *Der Elsässer*, and from 1896 to 1902 he edited the Catholic magazine *Alte und Neue Welt* that was based in Einsiedeln, the Swiss town renowned for its tenth-century Benedictine Abbey of St Meinrad, and more recently as the location of Hans Urs von Balthasar's Johannes Verlag.

In 1898 Muth published a *Streitschrift* (polemical article) on the subject of Catholic fiction under the pseudonym Veremundus in which he was highly critical of the ghetto culture of German literary Catholicism, one of the side effects of the *Kulturkampf*. Having spent some time in France where 'believing Catholics moved with great freedom in the intellectual elite of the country, taking part in the big discussions as equal partners who felt superior', Muth wanted the same situation to prevail in Germany.[2] His solution was to found the journal *Hochland* with Paul Huber-Kempten, the director of Kösel-Verlag, a Catholic publishing company based in Munich.[3]

Hochland operated from 1903 to 1941 when it was shut down by the National Socialists on the bureaucratic ground of paper rationing. In reality, however, it was closed because it published articles the Nazis did not like. *Hochland* was 'an ark of Christian and humanist thought during a period of total apostasy'.[4] Some of the articles took an esoteric

---

2. Ibid., p. 2.

3. In some publications the Greek 'K' is used rather than the Latin 'C' so one can find references to Karl Muth and Carl Muth. Of the two options the Latin C tends to dominate, but both spellings of the name can be found. The Latin option will be used throughout this chapter.

4. Gilbert Merlio, 'Carl Muth et la revue *Hochland*: Entre catholicisme culturel et catholicisme politique', in *Le Milieu Intellectuel Catholique en Allemagne, sa Presse et ses Réseaux (1871–1963)/Das Katholische Intellektuellen-Milieu in*

form. Konrad Ackermann is reported as saying, 'We write against Napoleon and everyone knows that it is Hitler who is targeted.'[5]

Hochland reopened in 1946 and continued until 1971. From 1902 to 1932 and from 1935 to 1939 Muth was *Hochland*'s editor and based in Munich. During the final years of his life, from October 1941 to February 1943, he befriended Hans Scholl, one of the martyrs of the White Rose resistance movement and gave him a job putting his library in order. Speaking of the relationship of the White Rose students with Muth, Paul Shrimpton wrote:

> Their encounter with Muth opened a window onto another world, as he introduced them to scholars and writers who were vehemently opposed to National Socialism, and it also effected a remarkable religious awakening in Hans, Sophie and their friends. But Muth was not just an entrée to a circle of dissidents; he had a talent for teaching and dealing with young people. The support Muth had given to hearts and minds in the face of Nazi ideology was not stifled by the suppression of *Hochland* in 1941; he simply diverted his energies to the Scholls and their friends. He conversed with them, lent them books, tutored them in theology, and introduced them to other writers and thinkers. In turn, this younger generation helped Muth not to lose hope that the German people would regain its conscience; for him they represented a 'secret Germany' who could uphold and pass on the values he cherished and had made his life's work.[6]

In an essay of tribute to Muth published in a revived *Hochland* in 1946, Josef Schöningh, the new post-war editor, remarked that Muth 'surrounded every talent he encountered with demanding care, more for their own sake than for the sake of *Hochland*'.[7] He then cited Hans

---

Deutschland, seine Presse und seine Netzwerke (1871-1963), Michel Grunewald and Uwe Puschner (eds) (Bern: Peter Lang, 2006), pp. 191–211 at p. 204.

5. Quoted by Gilbert Merlio, 'Carl *Muth* et la revue *Hochland*: Entre catholicisme culturel et catholicisme politique' in *Le milieu intellectual catholique en Allemagne, sa presse et ses réseaux (1871–1963)*, Michel Grunewald and Uwe Puscher (eds) (Bern: Peter Lang, 2006), pp. 191–210 at p. 202.

6. Paul Shrimpton, 'At the Heart of the White Rose Movement: Cultural and Religious Influences on the Munich Students', in *Treasures of the Taylorian*, A. Lloyd (ed.) (Oxford: Taylor Institute, 2019), pp. 23–33 at p. 29.

7. Schöningh, 'Carl Muth: Ein europäisches Vermächtnis', p. 18.

Scholl as an example: 'In the Summer of 1942, when [Scholl] was cataloguing Muth's library, he had long conversations almost every day with the sage and was confirmed in his Christian-German protest against the rule of the monsters.'[8]

In a work on the student dissidents, titled *A Noble Treason: The Story of Sophie Scholl and the White Rose Revolt*, Richard Hanser offered the following sketch of Muth:

> Carl Muth lived on the outskirts of Munich in a little house surrounded by a modest garden and bulging with books, some of them written by him. He was a Catholic thinker of a high order, and the absorption of his life was to reveal and foster the relationships between the aesthetic and the spiritual. He saw the two as interlocked and inseparable. One of his most admired and widely discussed essays was called 'Religion, Art and Poetry'. His ideas were often daring and unorthodox, and it was said that he hovered between sainthood and excommunication.[9]

In a memorial essay published in 1953, Werner Bergengruen, a Baltic German novelist and poet and Catholic convert, recounted the story of Muth's providential escape from the Gestapo following the arrest of the Scholl siblings:

> After Hans and Sophie Scholl were arrested, two Gestapo officers appeared at Muth's house late in the evening. He was asked whether he would admit that he knew Hans Scholl and saw him often. Muth answered in the affirmative. Then you are one of the intellectual authors? In response, Muth yelled at him: 'They'll have to prove that to me!' With this declaration, Muth had usurped control of the situation. When the officials, who by the way had become polite after Muth's outburst of anger, paced over his desk, it occurred to him, simmering hot after his declaration, that the manuscript of Theodor Haecker's 'Day and Night Books' was in a compartment on this desk! In the next instant it could be in the hands of the Gestapo. Haecker and Muth would both be trapped. In this moment of need Muth turned to St. Thomas More, the martyr of the upright Christian

---

8. Ibid.

9. Richard Hanser, *A Noble Treason: The Story of Sophie Scholl and the White Rose Revolt* (San Francisco: Ignatius, 2012), p. 122.

conscience. ... The Gestapo officers passed over the subject, Haecker's manuscript remained untouched.[10]

Hochland (literally highland) can be a reference to the Bavarian alps, but it also carries the connotation of the highest place, and it was this idea that featured in the journal's motto: *Hohen Geistes Land – Sinn dem Höchsten zugewandt* (meaning to turn the realm of the spirit/mind toward the highest things). The name was initially proposed by the Alsatian writer Friedrich Lienhard (1865–1929) for another journal (*Die Heimat*), but when it was not taken up by the editors of *Die Heimat*, it was adopted by Muth. Professor Dr Alois Dempf (1891–1982), a medievalist and cultural historian, also had an integrating influence on the *Hochland* project, particularly in terms of the general concept of the journal.[11] *Hochland* was noted for being non-confessional and equally critical of liberalism and fascism. Its authors condemned modern individualism together with 'shallow democratism' as a 'faith of the mob' (*Pöbelglaube*).[12] *Hochland* also stood out from other journals in so far as it published articles across the whole spectrum of humanities subjects, not exclusively theology and philosophy papers but also essays on art, literature, history, politics and music. It was thus one of the earliest attempts to offer reflections on cultural life through the lens of theology and philosophy and other humanities' disciplines. Unlike the orientation of Leonine scholasticism then dominant in the Roman academies, and unlike the universities influenced by German Idealism, especially by the ideas of Kant and Wilhelm von Humboldt with their strict observance of sharp divisions between the disciplines, *Hochland* was open to the

10. Werner Bergengruen, 'Erinnerungen an Carl Muth', *Hochland* 46 (1953), p. 79.
11. Wulfried C. Muth, *Carl Muth und das Mittelalterbild des Hochland* (München: Neue Schriftenreihe des Stadtarchivs, 1974), p. V.
12. Carl Muth, 'Der Ruf nach Eliten', *Hochland* 27 (1929), p. 86.
'*Der tiefste Grund geistiger Verflachung aber liegt in dem durch einen oberflächlichen Demokratismus genährten Wahnglauben, daß es der innere Sinn der neuen Ordnung sei, das Glück aller zu begründen und möglichst vielen das Leben leicht und bequem zu machen. Man möchte am liebsten umsonst leben, wie es denn auch von jeher ein Pöbelglaube galube, daß das Leben uns Glück schulde.*'
Cited in the DPhil. dissertation of Simon Ungar, 'Consensus in Conflict the Making of a Common Intellectual Culture in Germany, c. 1920–1950', submitted to the University of Oxford in 2018 at p. 68.

integration of disciplines and to the concept of a *Weltanschauung* or world view composed of multidisciplinary elements. Muth regarded what he called 'a bird's eye view' as 'essential to the maintenance of the spiritual order'.[13] He described the German universities in the early twentieth century, where the shadows of Kant and Humbolt loomed, as 'diversities' characterized by 'partial stucco work everywhere' with no 'grooves' to draw their work into a synthesis.[14] Moreover, *Hochland* not only featured articles. The articles were interspersed with sketches and watercolours and other paintings, as well as with the occasional musical score. As a typical example, volume 2 of 1927 offered eight different subsections: (i) Books, Novels and Poetry, (ii) Religion, History, Philosophy and Education, (iii) Literature, Theatre, Art and Music, (iv) Biographies, (v) Natural Science, Medicine, Physical and Cultural Geography, (vi) Economics and the Administration of Justice, (vii) Art Supplements and (viii) Book and Theatre Reviews.

Given this strongly humanistic orientation, the translator Alexander Dru noted the similarities in outlook between Muth and leaders of the French Catholic literary renaissance of the same period – people like Maurice Blondel, Henri Brémond, Paul Claudel and Charles Péguy. Claudel famously complained about Catholics suffering from the poverty of a starved imagination. *Hochland* gave a voice to those with imagination. Dru wrote, 'Muth had the courage, the authority and flair that makes an editor, which enabled him to weld the contributors into a whole without sacrificing their individuality, and to pick out and foster an undeveloped talent.'[15] Jakob Knab, the author of several works on the White Rose movement, described Muth as a 'master of clarifying critique'. As an example, he referred to Muth's description of the poetry of Stefan George as an 'artfully forged monstrance, intricately decorated with precious stones, in which the sacred is missing'.[16]

13. Carl Muth et al. 'Das Gesicht der Zeitschrift Hochland (1930): Ein Rundfunkgespräch am Berliner Sender zwischen dem Herausgeber Professor Karl Muth, Dr. Friedrich Fuchs von der Hochland–Redaktion und Dr. Otfried Eberz', in *Carl Muth und Das Hochland (1903-1941)*, Thomas Pittrof (Hg) (Freiburg i. Br: Rombach Verlag, 2018), pp. 236–51 at p. 236.
14. Ibid.
15. Alexander Dru, *The Contribution of German Catholicism* (New York: Hawthorn Books, 1963), p. 119.
16. Jakob Knab, 'Carl Muth – Mentor des Widerstands', *Die Tagespost*, 15 December 2017.

Friedrich Fuchs, who for a short time (1932–5) edited *Hochland*, began a festschrift article to mark Muth's 60th birthday by noting that the writer Joseph von Eichendorff (1788–1857) warned Catholic Germany not to starve itself intellectually, 'like a fortress besieged by the *Zeitgeist* behind the bulwark of formulas'.[17] He also noted that Karl von Dalberg (1744–1817), the Prince Primate of the Federation of the Rhine, had been influenced by the spirit of the Weimar intellectuals, that his writing was inspired by a vision of a Herderesque humanitarian religion and that the time-honoured bishopric of Salzburg sent its theologians to study under Kant in Königsberg. In other words, in the wake of eighteenth-century German philosophy, one section of the Catholic community was inclined to barricade itself into a ghetto, while another section, led by people like the Prince Primate of the Federation of the Rhine, had been busy surrendering itself to the precepts of German Idealism. Neither of these options appealed to Muth who was born a decade after the death of Eichendorff. Muth was critical of both the mere humanitarian religion of the German Enlightenment and the intellectual narrowness of many nineteenth-century Catholic attempts to fight against this. In a more recent collection of essays titled 'Carl Muth und das *Hochland* (1903–1941)', Maria Cristina Giacomin described Muth as offering 'an alternative to the ecclesiastical-clerical understanding of Catholic literature':

> Categories such as autonomy, consciousness of form, history, realism, individuality and subjectivity (Muth spoke of religious experience) were clearly upgraded in his literary aesthetic concept. However, he did not want to surrender this attempt to emancipate literature from the Church's sovereignty of interpretation to a directionless and unattached modern age. Muth set poetry limits in terms of its content and form. A work of art had to represent the beautiful ... Muth did indeed tie poetry to religion, namely to the 'objective' religion, by expressly emphasizing that 'the most favorable position for a truly poetic and artistic world view' was Catholicism. For him, Catholicism was 'comprehensive' in the primordial sense,

---

17. Friedrich Fuchs, 'Die deutschen Katholiken und die deutsche Kultur im 19. Jahrhundert: Zur geistesgeschichtlichen Einordnung von Karl Muth's Werk', in *Wiederbegegnung von Kirche und Kultur in Deutschland*, Max Ettlinger, Philipp Funk und Friedrich Fuchs (eds) (München: Verlag Josef Kösel & Friedrich Pustet, 1927), pp. 9–59 at p. 9.

not to be confused with narrow-minded casuistry, a view that pre-programmed the conflict with the Jesuits.¹⁸

While today, in the second decade of the twenty-first century, the Society of Jesus is renowned for its 'gnoseological concupiescence', to use Karl Rahner's expression, in the late nineteenth century, the intellectual profile of the Society was quite different. Muth was often accused of 'modernism' by those with a Jesuit education. The Jesuits viewed literature primarily as a vehicle for denominational apologetics. Muth's perspective was broader and included an interest in the subjective side of the experience of faith. Muth never denied the importance of the objective side; he merely thought that a literary Catholicism needed to encompass both dimensions. In his essay 'Modernität' (On Modernity) published in a collection of essays titled *Die Wiedergeburt der Dichtung aus dem religiösen Erlebnis* (*The Rebirth of Poetry from Religious Experience*) Muth began by noting that 'if the opponents of the progressive literary movement among German Catholics want to summarize their official disposition, confession and feelings of uneasiness towards it in one word, they say with great predilection that it is "modern".¹⁹ He added that 'the nonsense driven by the word "modern" from a certain part of the world of Catholic letters is truly shameful'.²⁰ He declared that 'Catholic truth is the most modern truth'.²¹ He believed that literature and Catholicism would eventually be reconciled because a purely positivist cultural foundation leaves people without hope, but he did not think that one could offer the Catholic world view to artists as a kind of quick-fix solution. He noted that 'like all isms, Catholicism is initially only an abstraction' – 'it gains a persuasive power, influence and importance only to the extent that it works convincingly and creatively in the life of its confessors'.²² He

18. Maria Cristina Glacomin, 'Ein "goldener Mittelweg" zwischen Kirche und moderner Welt? Carl Muth und das Hochland 1903–1914 Mit einem Exkurs zur Gründungsgeschichte des *Hochland*', in *Carl Muth und das Hochland (1903–1941)*, Thomas Pittrof (ed.) (Freiburg i. Br: Rombach Verlag, 2018), pp. 35–71 at p. 37.
19. Carl Muth, *Die Wiedergeburt der Dichtung aus dem religiösen Erlebnis* (München: Jos-Kösel'sche Buchhandlung in Kempten, 1909) p. 92.
20. Ibid.
21. Ibid.
22. Ibid., p. 101.

therefore thought that it was the task of Catholics to provide 'practical proof of the vitality of this teaching'.[23] This was a better way forward than a constant battery attack on 'modernity'. He wanted Catholicism to be presented positively as an attractive alternative to the anti-humanism of a demythologized and thus disenchanted world. He pointed to the fact that the 'greatest anti-modern is called Nietzsche!'[24] He noted that Nietzsche hated modernity because he thought it was weak and sick and because he saw it as Christian. Muth tried to explain that if what so many people dislike about modernity is what they perceive to be its decadent Christian elements, then something has to be done about the decadence before proposing Christianity and indeed Catholicism as the way forward. As he expressed the position, '[Nietzsche] said: "Weak and sick because Christian."' We say, at the most, 'Weak and sick because not consistently and consciously Christian.'[25] Muth was prepared to concede that Nietzsche had a point, and he thought that this point had to be acknowledged. As he rhetorically asked:

> Do you want to antagonize an artist filled with optimism for the future when he struggles against such pessimism? Do you think that this could make him more fertile, more effective, more understanding, more loving? Many modern people long for a positive religious view of the world, but they also want their honesty, their sense of truth and everything that is strong and good in the present time to be honored.[26]

Rudolf Lill described Muth's achievement as 'the liberation of Catholic *belles lettres* from an apologetical and backward-looking parochialism'.[27] Similarly, Elena Raponi concluded, 'The magazine founded by Muth can well be considered an expression of that intellectual and moral awakening that animated the German Catholic culture at the end of the nineteenth and early twentieth centuries, marginalized until then

---

23. Ibid.
24. Ibid.
25. Ibid.
26. Ibid.
27. Rudolf Lill, 'German Catholicism between *Kulturkampf* and World War I', in *History of the Church: The Church in the Industrial Age*, Hubert Jedin and John Patrick Dolan (eds) (New York: Seabury Press, 1981), pp. 494–507 at 501.

by the prevailing positivist scientism and by a tired materialism.'[28] Friedrich Fuchs wrote that people 'who discovered or rediscovered their supernatural home in the church found their cultural home, needed for the sake of spiritual nourishment and effectiveness, in the *Hochland* journal'.[29] For their part, 'they in turn directed streams of cultural power into German Catholicism as did the great converts at the beginning of the nineteenth century'.[30]

Although Muth was frustrated by the tendency of some Catholics at the turn of the last century to reject everything they found disagreeable with the adjective 'modern', he was nonetheless intellectually engaged with the cultural history of the western world and the identification of the hallmarks of different epochs and their turning points. Wulfried Muth (his nephew through his half-brother Jakob Friedrich Muth) noted that his uncle Carl regarded the cultures of the Western Mediterranean in the medieval period as the most congruent with the teachings of Jesus Christ, and he therefore saw the Reformation as a tragic disruption of these cultures. The 'transition period to the Reformation touched and interested him so deeply' he thought it needed to be studied in order to better understand its causes.[31] In particular he was interested in the changes to the understanding of the Petrine Office that accompanied the papacy of Gregory VII (1073–85) and the changes to the understanding of the Holy Roman Empire throughout the late medieval period. He was also interested in the great spiritual movements, including the struggle between revelation-believing movements and counteracting revelation-hostile enlightenment and science movements. Another of his interests was the rise of nominalism from Roscelin of Compiègne (*c*.1050–*c*.1125) through to William of Ockham (c. 1285/7–c. 1347) and nominalism's influence on the Protestant movements.[32] If one ties each of these interests to an academic discipline, they cover the territory of ecclesiology, political theory, theology and philosophy. One could therefore describe Muth's project as one of illuminating modernity by investigating the transitions from the medieval to modern period

28. Elena Raponi, *Antonio Fogazzaro – Carl Muth, Carteggio (1903–1910)* (Vincenza: Accademia Olimpica, 2010), p. 15.
29. Friedrich Fuchs, 'Die deutschen Katholiken und die deutsche Kultur im 19. Jahrhundert: Zur geistesgeschichtlichen Einordnung von Karl Muth's Werk' in *Wiederbegegnung von Kirche und Kultur in Deutschland*, p. 34.
30. Ibid.
31. Muth, *Carl Muth und das Mittelalterbild des Hochland*, p. 1.
32. Ibid., p. 3.

on all four of these fronts. He was thus a genealogist of modernity before this concept became an academic fashion in the late twentieth century. In an essay published in *Hochland* to celebrate its twenty-fifth year in publication Muth argued against a nostalgic return to the Catholic culture of the middle ages as the only legitimately Catholic culture possible and also against the idea of a synthesis of Christianity and modern culture, since he recognized that significant elements of the culture of modernity were secularized Christian concepts. While they owed their pedigree to Christianity, they had undergone a process of secularization that made them unfit for any uncritical synthesis.[33] This problem of the secularization of Christian concepts was to feature prominently in late-twentieth-century scholarship on modernity, including the works of Joseph Ratzinger, Hans Urs von Balthasar, Louis Dupré, Alasdair MacIntyre and Charles Taylor.

In his collection of essays titled *Schöpfer und Magier* (*The Creator and the Magician*), posthumously published in 1953, Muth addressed the 'what is man?' problematic that runs through the publications of so many German scholars of the interwar years. He declared that 'if man of our day is threatened with the loss of an art that would be greater than the loss of poetry, music and all other arts, it is the loss of the art of mastering life':[34]

> When a time like ours hardly knows what a person is, when it lacks the elementary knowledge of what life means, when its people lack self-knowledge because they no longer have the will to do so, and if their experience ... can no longer shape itself into a unity, then how could artists still be possible and how should art have any meaning at all! It is not for nothing that the anthropological problem stands in the foreground of our philosophical thought today, and the question of what man is will occupy our best minds for a long time.[35]

In contrast to the early-twentieth-century 'man' who could no longer shape his experience into a unity, Muth presented Goethe as someone who did at least *try* to shape his life into a unity. He described Goethe as

---

33. Carl Muth, 'Bilanz: Eine Umschau aus Anlass des 25. Jahrgangs', *Hochland* XXV (1) (Oktober 1927–April 1928), 1–23 at p. 7.
34. Carl Muth, *Schöpfer und Magier: Drei Essays* (München: Kösel-Verlag, 1953), p. 65.
35. Ibid., p. 66.

the person who in recent times and 'within the natural sphere' was 'the human being par excellence'.[36] Specifically, in Goethe the 'dual nature of man, his contradictions, his godly and animal nature' was 'alive and well'.[37] Goethe 'knew that human beings can put their very highest powers at the service of the lowest, in order to be even more animal than the animal', but he also knew about grace – 'grace was not a dead concept to him and the notion of a love that participates from above was its most concrete description'.[38] Muth also observed that with regard to marriage, 'Goethe was closer to the views and demands of the Catholic Church than to those of his fellow Protestants ... He called the concept of the sanctity of marriage a cultural achievement of Christianity of such inestimable value that it must not be given up "at any cost"'.[39]

In another passage from the same essay, one finds an exposition of Muth's understanding of the human person as an artist:

> Modern man, drifting around in a whirlwind of bustle, in a restless back and forth of buying and consuming, of saving and of spending, is usually no longer able to give an account of the individual in the abundance of the impressions that assail him. One sensation devours the other, and the impressions that we, for example, receive from a work of art, are usually only kept in our minds as a knowledge of it, but not as a living force in our work. Only where people live more intensively than extensively – and this is the case with all artistically creative people – that is, people who live intensely, do people have what we call an educational experience, that is, are influenced from the sphere of mental representations in such strength and duration that the human person under its influence feels as if driven to activity, and to creative devotion to the world thus experienced.[40]

Muth noted that since an aspect of modern life is endless activity and busyness, this social pathology has made some people receptive to what he called 'quietistic teachings' found in Christian mysticism and Indian contemplation. Muth regarded this flight to mysticism as too extreme a reaction. He claimed that 'restlessness cannot be controlled

---

36. Ibid.
37. Ibid.
38. Ibid.
39. Ibid., pp. 108–9.
40. Ibid., p. 68.

through rest, but only through a spiritualized way of being active.'[41] He insisted that only if people have such a mode of being, it is possible for the prayer found in the hymn *Veni Creator Spiritus* (Come, Holy Spirit, Creator blest, and in our souls take up Thy rest) to be fulfilled. Moreover, Muth argued that such a notion of a spiritualized way of being active 'corresponds perfectly to the Goethean concept of activity'.[42] He wrote:

> The calm without activity, a quietistic indulgence in peace and quiet, was so repugnant to Goethe that he declared that he himself did not know what to do with eternal bliss without the idea that there, too, we were to be given new tasks and difficulties to solve. All activity must only be a means, it must always be conditioned by a higher end that lies in man himself. All unconditional activity leads to bankruptcy; it humiliates man under the dictatorship of outside things, which is the worst that can happen to a man who should never let himself be determined by the world. Goethe regards it as the greatest gain if we determine the circumstances as much as possible and let them determine as little as possible. The latter, however, is only possible where the activity becomes 'a worthy act', where serene meaning and activity live together. Goethe accuses modern times of overestimating themselves because of the large amount of material they hold, while the main advantage of man is precisely how he knows how to handle and control the material. 'What does it help me?', it says in *Wilhelm Meister*, 'to manufacture good iron when my own interior is full of slag'? And what good is a country estate if I am at odds with myself?[43]

In the following passage Muth affirmed Goethe as the alternative 'modern' German cultural icon to Kant or Hegel:

> Pure, so to speak, contentless thinking was impossible for him [Goethe]. He even preferred to proceed from what was sensually viewed. One can almost call him a sensual thinker. He hated everything abstract, and he could only offer a superficial respect to the philosophical heads of his time. Kant was no exception to this. Goethe actually says of Hegel that he spoiled the thinking of the Germans. He regards the German philosophers of his time as strange people who looked as if they had not been outdoors for thirty

41. Ibid., pp. 77.
42. Ibid., pp. 77–8.
43. Ibid.

years; instead of observing the world, they preoccupied themselves with chewing on their own ideas and found in them an inexhaustible source of original, great, useful thoughts. However nothing emerges from these thoughts but mist. Long enough he had committed the folly of being angry about it; in his old days he had no choice but to laugh at it.[44]

In this essay on Goethe, one detects the beginning of themes that become amplified in the publications of Romano Guardini who was highly critical of 'the form of the machine' becoming the form of modern man and his culture. The juxtaposition of Kant and Goethe as two alternative 'intellectual heroes' offering two different agenda for the world of German letters is also typical of the theology and genealogy of modernity found in the works of Balthasar.

A significant question about any German writer of the interwar years is what was his or her positions on the political issues of the era? Clemens Bauer has described Muth's political orientations as 'social democracy with a conservative twist' akin to the ideas of August Pieper.[45] Pieper (1866–1942) was a theologian and author of several publications concerning social and political issues. Muth's tendency was to judge 'regime forms and political systems essentially according to what they achieved for social justice, the social balance of interests and social welfare'.[46] In an essay published in 1922, Muth described 'conservative' as meaning 'reflection on the creative forces of the past, on our very own historical ideals' and the conviction that 'growth is only possible in organic connection with the old', though it does not mean 'holding as sacrosanct everything that is traditional'.[47] Muth also declared that 'the future of democracy will be Christian or it will not be at all'.[48] Democracy would need to be undergirded by a Christian cultural foundation, otherwise it could degenerate to rule by a mob. As

---

44. Ibid., p. 89.

45. Clemens Bauer, 'Carl Muths und des *Hochland* Weg aus dem Kaiserreich in die Weimarer Republik', *Hochland* (1966/7), pp. 234–47 at p. 245.

46. Ibid., p. 247.

47. Carl Muth, 'Ein Rück - und Ausblick zum 20. Jahrgang', *Hochland* XX (1) (Oktober 1922–März 1923), pp. 1–15. Cited in Bauer, 'Carl Muths und des *Hochland* Weg aus dem Kaiserreich in die Weimarer Republik', pp. 243–4.

48. Muth, 'Ein Rück - und Ausblick zum 20. Jahrgang', p. 13.

1. Carl Muth

Muth acutely observed, 'the modern state democracy is only a purely rationalist form of rule calculated and applied to the emergency of a completely atomized social body, capable of exploiting the people by flattering their instincts'.[49] In today's academic landscape, his brand of conservatism would be described as more MacIntyrean than Burkean. MacIntyre is not a defender of long-standing traditions just because they are long-standing traditions. For MacIntyre, there needs to be something about the internal rationality of traditions to make them worthy of contemporary appropriation. Muth was of a similar mindset. He recognized that traditions need to serve some higher good than the good of the tradition itself.

In an essay published in *Hochland* in May of 1919, Muth offered a critical though also in part sympathetic reading of socialism. Although he criticized many of socialism's flawed foundations, such as the idea that 'original sin' might be cured by a change in social conditions, he nonetheless regarded the position of the working classes as something of legitimate concern to the Church. He concluded the essay by affirming some of the insights of the Spanish statesman, Donoso Cortés. Describing Cortés's engagement with 'the dissimilar civil brothers, liberalism and socialism' as a 'brilliant confrontation', he concurred with Cortés's observation that although socialists do not want to be considered to be the heirs of Catholicism, but rather its antithesis, they are merely trying to achieve a universal brotherhood without Christ, without grace and thus are really just 'misshapen' Catholics. Moreover, Muth noted that Catholicism is not a thesis, but a synthesis, and the socialists, in spite of their efforts to break away, were still caught within its spiritual atmosphere.[50] Their fundamental problem was that 'the social-democratic movement proceeds from the premise that man emerges well from the hands of nature and only society makes him brutish; thus he does not need a saviour in the religious sense, but only the redemption of those ailments of his environment'.[51] Muth described this as 'that error of Idealism which begins to grow into the worst utopia of the century, in which all other utopias of revolutionary socialism have their roots'.[52] Muth thus affirmed socialism's interest in improving

49. Ibid.
50. Carl Muth, 'Die neuen "Barbaren" und das Christentum', *Hochland* (May 1919), pp. 385–596 at p. 596.
51. Ibid., p. 590. Cited in Josef Schöningh, 'Carl Muth: Ein europäisches Vermächtnis', *Hochland* (1946–7), pp. 1–19 at p. 14.
52. Ibid., p. 590.

the conditions of the working classes but thought that the theory was operating with a flawed anthropology.

In the essay 'Carl Muth et la revue *Hochland*', Gilbert Merlio noted that the political positions of *Hochland*'s contributors were not perfectly homogeneous. However, he suggested that they were on the whole in accordance with Catholic tradition going back to political Romanticism, offering 'an "organic", hierarchical and corporatist conception of public affairs'.[53] At the same time they rejected the concept of a nationalist state solely focused on the powerful – 'its corporatism must avoid the atomization of and exploitation of the individual in mass society'.[54] Merlio concluded that 'Christian conservatism, returning to certain values and structures of the Middle Ages, blends here with Christian socialism which wants to be an alternative both to liberal capitalism and to collectivist proletarian socialism'.[55] This would seem to be a good description of the general line of Muth's political theory.

Muth lost his eldest son Reinhard on 22 March 1918 and his wife Anna was to die in 1920. These deaths, along with that of his mother when he was barely a teenager, and the martyrdoms of the Scholl siblings gave Carl Muth more than his fair share of Good Friday experiences. Spiritually weaker men would have despaired. His courage in the face of the deepest darkness the modern world has seen, and his creative flair for building a Catholic culture that could inspire several generations wanting to escape Bismarck's ghetto prepared the way for the post-war 'virtuoso' generation. In the summer of 1946, the French poet Paul Claudel wrote a letter to Josef Schöningh saying, 'I salute the revival of *Hochland*. I know all that German Catholicism owed it in the past and I send it my best wishes for the future. I am not an enemy of Germany and I desire with all my heart that it will prove itself worthy of the great tasks which God holds out before it.'[56]

---

53. Gilbert Merlio, 'Carl *Muth* et la revue *Hochland*: Entre catholicisme culturel et catholicisme politique', in *Le milieu intellectual catholique en Allemagne, sa presse et ses réseaux (1871-1963)*, Michel Grunewald and Uwe Puscher (eds) (Bern: Peter Lang, 2006), pp. 191–210 at p. 197.
54. Ibid., p. 197.
55. Ibid.
56. Schöningh, 'Carl Muth: Ein europäisches Vermächtnis', p. 19.

Chapter 2

THEODOR HAECKER
(1879–1945)

Aachen stands for more than Weimar and Potsdam in the destiny of the German people. There the roots go down into a real, not a fictitious, soil.[1]

Theodor Haecker was described by Joseph Ratzinger as one of those writers who most directly inspired members of his generation of Bavarian seminarians.[2] He was a friend of Carl Muth and the Scholl siblings and a regular contributor to *Hochland*. It was through their friendship with Haecker that Hans and Sophie Scholl became acquainted with Newman's ideas on conscience. According to Josef Schöningh, in his old age Muth had been strongly supported by his friendship with the taciturn Haecker:

> They had both gone through heaven and hell, they had both experienced the immeasurable abundance of their religion and the distressing inadequacy of some of its representatives, and they were both united in a passionate hostility to the political development of Germany and Europe at that time. They both died when the external catastrophe of Germany occurred under blazing fire and stinking smoke, which they had both long foreseen with horrid clarity.[3]

1. Theodor Haecker, *Virgil: Father of the West* (London: Sheed & Ward, 1934), p. 108.
2. Joseph Ratzinger, *Milestones: Memoirs 1927–1977* (San Francisco: Ignatius, 1998), pp. 42–3.
3. Josef Schöningh, 'Carl Muth: Ein europäisches Vermächtnis', *Hochland* (1946–7), pp. 1–19 at 10.

In the final months of his life in 1945, Haecker had to deal with the news that his youngest son Reinhard had been reported missing on the Eastern front. There is something particularly poignant about the fact that Carl Muth lost his eldest son named Reinhard in the final months of the First World War, while Haecker lost his youngest son, also named Reinhard, in the final months of the Second World War.

Alexander Dru, Haecker's English translator, offered this biographical snapshot:

> Theodor Haecker was born in 1879 in the Swabian village of Eberbach in Württemberg, and though he lived all his life in Munich he never, as he says in the *Journal*, lost the sense of having a home. Indeed, he took an almost naïve pride in being a Swabian, and what will probably seem to many a romantic delight in the history and character of his province, in its Staufen Emperors and its early greatness, and not least in belonging to the people from whom so many of the poets and philosophers of Germany had come.[4]

Like Muth, Haecker was not a professional academic but a public intellectual who earned a living working for a publishing house. When living in Berlin as a young man he did nonetheless study cultural history, world history, the history of philosophy, French literature, Old Norse literature, classical philology (Plato, Virgil, Sophocles and Suetonius) and Greek cultural history.

Haecker first made a name for himself as a satirical writer and then later as a translator of the works of Søren Kierkegaard and John Henry Newman and the poet Francis Thompson.[5] Between the years 1914 and 1923 he was a regular contributor to Ludwig von Ficker's journal *Der Brenner* which was a semi-monthly publication of essays on art and culture. Its name was a play on two themes: first, the Brenner Pass located near Innsbruck where the magazine was published, and second, the Austrian satirist Karl Kraus's publication, *Die Fackel* (the torch). The German noun 'Der Brenner' means the burner. Hence *Der Brenner* was the burner and *Die Fackel* the torch. In his essay 'Theodor

---

4. Alexander Dru, 'Introduction to Theodor Haecker', *Journal in the Night (1939–1945)* (New York: Pantheon Books, 1950), p. xi.

5. For a list of Haecker's translations of Kierkegaard see Jon Stewart (ed.), *Kierkegaard's Influence on Theology Tome I* (Farnham: Ashgate, 2012), fn. 105 at p. 293.

Haecker: The Mobilisation of a Total Writer', Markus Kleinert concluded that Haecker's contributions to *Der Brenner* 'exercised an enormous influence on everyone who stood in direct or indirect connection with *Der Brenner* – and to this category belong such significant and different representatives of intellectual history as Ludwig Wittgenstein (1889–1951), Martin Heidegger (1889–1976), Theodor Adorno (1903–1969), and Martin Buber (1878–1965)'.[6] During these years, which were predominately Haecker's pre-conversion years, he wrote biting satire in a manner similar to Kraus. However, after his conversion to the Catholic faith in 1920 – which followed his translation of Newman's *Grammar of Assent* – the articles he submitted to Muth's *Hochland* were far less satirical, the first appearing in 1923, the last in 1941, the year that *Hochland* was banned by the Nazis.

Eugen Blessing, author of *Theodor Haecker: Gestalt und Werk*, described Haecker's Christian Humanism in the following passage:

> It is his conviction in the exploration of the matter that the human and the Christian, nature and super-nature, are not two incommensurable worlds, since Christ lives in both. Philosophy and theology are not two completely separate disciplines ... so that apart from the particular in the two areas of philosophy and theology there is also a peculiar common domain of Christian philosophy and of Christian philosophical anthropology. While this Christian philosophical anthropology presupposes the eternal, it is not itself theology. It does not deal with the incarnation of God nor with the creation of man, but with the orientation of man and the world towards its evangelization by God.[7]

It was a mark of the non-scholastic German Catholic scholarship of this era that it worked in a terrain between the fields of theology and philosophy. Perhaps this was no more strongly the case than in the work of Romano Guardini whose professorial Chair at Berlin was named neither for Philosophy nor for Theology, but as a Chair in the Philosophy of Religion and the Catholic *Weltanschauung*. The same

---

6. Markus Kleinert, 'Theodor Haecker: The Mobilization of a Total Writer', in *Kierkiegaard's Influence on Literature, Criticism and Art*, Jon Stewart (ed.) (Farnham: Ashgate, 2013), pp. 91–114 at p. 96.

7. Eugene Blessing, *Theodor Haecker: Gestalt und Werk* (Nürnberg: Glock und Lutz, 1959), p. 125.

predominating tendency is observable in French Catholic thought of the time, as in Maurice Blondel's critique of 'extrinsicism' (sharp separations between nature and grace, faith and reason, the secular and the sacred), in which he significantly anticipates Henri de Lubac's full frontal attack on 'two-tiered thinking' (operating within a framework that separates the natural from the supernatural) in the late 1940s.

Not only was Haecker a friend of Carl Muth and a contributor to *Hochland*, but he was also close to the White Rose martyrs Hans and Sophie Scholl; it was through their friendship with Haecker that they became acquainted with Newman's ideas on conscience. In 1933 Haecker was arrested on suspicion of promoting anti-Nazi ideas but released after only one day in custody, on the interventions of Carl Muth and of Cardinal Faulhaber, the Archbishop of Munich from 1917 to 1952. Thereafter, until the time of his death some twelve years later in April 1945, Haecker lived in a situation of internal exile. In a letter to Richard Seewald, another Catholic convert in the *Hochland* circle, Haecker wrote:

> I am looking forward to work again, but on the other hand I am also afraid to see and hear public life. It is very sad and actually a tragedy to have to live in his [Hitler's] fatherland *in partibus infidelium*. The behavior of the German bourgeoisie is a burlesque or a farce. It is ripe for destruction and Hitlerism is a stage. The political noun is '*Gleichschaltung*' [totalitarian uniformity]. Everything that I have said in truth and life about the fall of man from the analogy of the living (the plant) to that of the dead (the machine), does not find its final fulfillment in this grisly application of the term '*Gleichschaltung*' to the institutions of man only, but on heart and mind and even on the word of God himself, on the revelation, on the church.[8]

Against the concept of '*Gleichschaltung*', which carries a nuance of levelling down and making all the same, Haecker countered with the phrase '*wir sind Hierarchisten*' – we are hierarchists! This phrase decorates his pages like a literary confetti. In his *Über den Abendländischen*

---

8. Theodor Haecker, letter to Richard Seewald written on the 29 April 1933, cited in Hanssler and Siefken, pp .107–8. The author's translation is from the German original cited in Helena M Tomko, 'The Reluctant Satirist: Theodor Haecker and the Dizzying Swindle of Nazism', *Oxford German Studies* 46 (1) (2017), pp. 42–7 at p. 43.

Menschen (*On Western Man*), posthumously published in 1947, the phrase *wir sind Hierarchisten* is followed by the statement, 'Only here is the actual and final answer given to the question: What is the human?' This answer, that humans are hierarchists, is 'the answer in which all other subordinates find their end, their goal and their fulfillment'.[9] Haecker also observed that 'by virtue of its nature, the human mind can to a certain extent determine the nature of matter, of the plant and of the animal, but not of its own nature: this is first determined by God Himself in His revelation'.[10] In other words anthropological truth comes from *above*; the meaning of the human can only be understood by reference to the divine because 'the last answer to the question: What is man? is given in the spiritual sphere by God himself, and revealed to man'.[11] It is only in this 'highest sphere' that 'an absolute, definitive, infallible answer' is given. All answers in the lower spheres are only opinions: *mundum tradidit disputationi eorum*.[12] Only the higher can explain the lower.

Haecker's *Wir sind Hierarchists* principle is consistent with a Catholic preference for power and authority descending from above rather than power and authority arising from the *Volk* below. In entry number 45 of his *Journal* for the year 1939, Haecker wrote, 'Christ also died for "barbarians", but he did not become man as a barbarian, nor did he live among them, or choose his disciples among them.'[13] In other words, no special epistemological status is to be accorded the opinions of the 'Volk', the 'People', the 'Proletariat' or any other social subgroup, as if they occupied a privileged status as a sacred minority. Truth comes from above, through the revelation of the prophets and the Incarnation, as anticipated in part by the greatest of the Greeks and Romans. To affirm the barbarian, the savage, the unskilled labourer or uneducated person on the grounds of some supposed epistemic purity, such as Rousseau thought, and some on the Marxist wing of the Romantic tradition, requires a prior rejection of the patrimony of the Greeks, Romans, Hebrews and the early fathers of the Christian world. Once this patrimony has been eliminated, the subject has no

---

9. Theodor Haecker, *Über den Abendländischen Menschen* (Kolmar im Elsass: Alsatia Verlag, 1947), p. 22.
10. Ibid.
11. Ibid., p. 26.
12. Ibid.
13. Haecker, *Journal in the Night*, entry 45, 1939, p. 10.

standard beyond the self by which to make judgments. This argument was underscored by Haecker in the following paragraph taken from his *Was ist der Mensch?*:

> The origin of the chaos of this age is a human, subjective reason – an unsettled reason – and a sick heart, a false or weakened perception and a perverted or weak will and certainly, ultimately, a deficiency of love ... The chaos of this age begins with a misjudgement of that which constitutes true freedom ... To be free is to be lord. Yet man is undoubtedly only lord within an *ordo* and through it ... the freedom of man has an intellectual substrate, namely recognition of the truth or, more accurately, of true order. The true order of things, however, is a holy order, a hierarchy.[14]

In *Was ist der Mensch?* Haecker also rebuked the nominalist emphasis on the individual for fostering a 'vacuous levelling of higher being'. To him, the goal and salvation of man is not to be found in a fixation on the *principium individuationis* which is based in matter, but on allowing oneself to be drawn up to higher orders.[15] Like Vladimir Ern and later Leszek Kołakowski, Haecker thought that German intellectuals were particularly attracted to the project of finding rational certainty *without God*, that is, they betrayed an aversion to being 'drawn up to higher orders', wanting instead to confer upon themselves God-like attributes. He observed:

> We Germans in particular still wish to be like God Himself in terms of creativity ... the god who comes to be *through us men*, is the customary theology of our prevailing literature and philosophy. It is in fact we Germans, who so often let grotesque words fall from our lips, who articulate what Faust so risibly mistranslated: in the beginning was the Act, or what Fichte wrote: 'There is a drive within me towards absolutely independent auturgy. Nothing is more insufferable to me than that I should be only by another, for another and through another: *I want to be and become something for and through myself*.[16]

14. Theodor Haecker, *Was ist der Mensch?* (Frankfurt am Mein: Ullstein Bücher, 1959), pp. 46–7.
15. Ibid., p. 20
16. Ibid., p. 49.

According to Haecker the egocentrism of such an exclusive humanism gives rise to secondary social phenomena such as a 'mindless, manic attitude', the 'state of an almost purely physical angst' and 'the fear of suffocating from a lack of oxygen within the next moment'.[17] These are all traits he identifies as the epiphenomena of an underlying intellectual pathology. Romano Guardini made similar observations when identifying the hallmarks of what he called 'Mass Man'.

Haecker's insistence on the priority of 'thinking from above' is also in accord with Guardini's principle that *logos* must precede *ethos*. Truth is ontically prior to *praxis* because *praxis* embodies some rationale that gives it meaning. The ethos of any institution is built upon practices, while the practices themselves carry a logic, a rationality, which can be either good or bad, but it will not be theologically neutral. Practices can be more or less open to the work of grace. Thus, Haecker declared, 'The salvation of philosophy rests upon the primacy of thought over act, of theory over *praxis*; that in the beginning was the word, the *Logos* and not the Faustian act. God as self-reflecting Trinity *precedes* by an insuperable abyss His entire creation, which is indeed the act of acts, the work of all works'.[18] Consistent with his insistence on the priority of *logos* over *ethos*, Haecker concluded that 'the scandal caused by a false doctrine is often greater than the scandal given by a deceitful life. As a general rule people recognise more easily and see more clearly that a man's life is deceitful, than that a doctrine is false.'[19]

The recognition of the social power of ideas and a respect for the role of doctrine are another two Catholic watermarks to be found on the pages of Haecker's publications. Although Haecker was strongly attracted to the thought of Kierkegaard because the Danish philosopher was not embarrassed to draw attention to the subjective dimension of the human person and to the role of affectivity in human cognition, or what in theological parlance is called the relationship between love and reason, Haecker was disappointed that Kierkegaard never followed the logic of his intuitions to the same end as Newman. Kierkegaard failed to show any 'burning intellectual desire for the unalloyed perfection and purity of the true doctrine so impressively demonstrated in the letters of the apostles, the early fathers, the history of the Church and of saints', which 'gave Newman no rest' until

---

17. Ibid., p. 110.
18. Haecker, *Was ist der Mensch?*, p. 56.
19. Haecker, *Journal in the Night*, entry 436, 1940, p. 119.

he was reconciled with the Catholic Church.[20] In Haecker's opinion the primary cause of Kierkegaard's omission was his 'predominantly ethical tendency and constitution which caused him to make the vulgar and unworthy observation that there should be less talk about right teaching and more about right behaviour'.[21] Since for Haecker truth descends from God, and is found in revelation, God himself is the teacher, and his teaching is determinative of good and bad behaviour. Haecker praised Newman for getting this right and for further understanding the importance of not merely knowing the truth, or having the right ideas, but actually *loving* God, so that truth and love work in tandem. A Christianity that emphasizes truth but mutes love can be reduced to a mere intellectual system, while a Christianity that emphasizes love but mutes truth can dwindle into mere moralism. Haecker thought that Newman got the faith–reason and love–reason relationships right, while Kierkegaard only got as far as flagging the importance of the affective dimension of human nature without linking it up to the work of sound doctrine.

Nonetheless Haecker did credit Kierkegaard with understanding that 'complete subjectivity implied complete objectivity'. Kierkegaard simply did not follow this insight as doggedly far as Newman.[22] In the following passage, Haecker vented his frustrations with those who fail to appreciate the priority of *logos* over *ethos*:

> People who miss seeing this point remind me of the spectator who, on seeing an accomplished dancer whose every movement is rhythmical flow and poise, tells me that the dancer does not need strong bones or a solid skeleton, since these are no longer apparent, and that such a fact should be obvious at a glance to any unbiased observer. Is there any trace in the life of a perfect saint, or in his ardent expressions of love, of the rigid mould of the dogmatist? I honestly consider this shows a maddening deficiency of observation and thought. It is true that it is unnecessary for the dancer to know that her bones and skeletal structure form an intrinsic part of her movements and her art, but the anatomist and physiologist surely must know it. It

---

20. Theodor Haecker, *Kierkegaard the Cripple*, C. Van O. Bruyn (trans.) (London: Harvill Press, 1948), p. 20.

21. Ibid.

22. Theodor Haecker, *Søren Kierkegaard*, Alexander Dru (trans.) (Oxford: Oxford University Press, 1937), p. 28.

is also true that there are wholly unlearned yet perfect saints who know nothing explicit about dogma, but the theologian must know it. There is one Church whose branches and talents and offices are devoted to theology, which is concerned with spotlessly pure and true teaching. This purity and truth of teaching can certainly not be achieved and maintained on the principle *Credo quia absurdum* favoured by Kierkegaard, because this produces bad and not good theology, demonstrated by the popular and cheaply polemic meaning which it has acquired.[23]

Haecker recognized the importance of paradox in the thought of Kierkegaard, and he affirmed this concept but not Kierkegaard's tendency to equate the paradoxical with the absurd. Haecker's position on the inherently reasonable nature of a paradox was much more in accord with the thinking of Henri de Lubac.[24] In tune with de Lubac, Haecker noted that rationalism does not like the language of paradox and equates it with irrationality, but in doing so it excludes the 'super-rationality' of divinity and creation and simply has no 'feeling for mystery'.[25] He describes the fact that many of Christ's sayings as recorded in the Gospels are paradoxical as a 'form of honourable acknowledgement, on the part of human understanding, of the majesty of the divine mysteries and of the fact that His ways are not our ways'.[26] In other words, it is 'an expression of the otherwise indefinable relationship between finite man and the infinite Creator, between the being created from nothing and the incomprehensible Being of God'.[27] Haecker also noted that the fact that the human person is a being in time, or what he called 'a mysterious unity of time and eternity', constrains human thought towards the

23. Haecker, *Kierkegaard the Cripple*, p. 21.
24. Aaron Riches, in *Ecce homo* wrote: 'For de Lubac, the Christological paradox entails that the Church's doctrine will be constituted by "a comprehensive assembly of opposing aspects", and that these "opposing aspects" are raised to signify the full depth of the mystery of truth in direct relation to the degree that "they are mutually supported like flying buttresses (*arc-boutant*), each one braced against the other in the most extreme degrees of tension". The tensive image of the *arc-boutant* as the soul of orthodoxy, suggests the polyphony of the synthesis of theology at the service of the one objective truth.'
25. Haecker, *Kierkegaard the Cripple*, p. 22.
26. Ibid., p. 23.
27. Ibid.

paradoxical. He believed that Kierkegaard was right to acknowledge that much about Christianity is paradoxical, but it was a 'lamentable metaphysical error' to equate this fact with absurdity.

When dealing with the territory of metaphysics, Haecker was absolutely hostile to the whole tradition of German Idealism from Kant to Hegel and everyone in between and since. The pithiest outbursts of opposition appear in his *Journal* where he mentions Kant ten times and Hegel nine times. In entry 397 in 1940 he wrote:

> I am coming more and more to the conclusion that the history which derives from German Idealism – a professorial history – is simply humbug. In that thin, pale atmosphere, personalities and passions evaporate. And no one could tell from reading it, that Satan was the Prince of this world.[28]

Two entries later, Haecker added that a knowledge of the catechism and of criminal psychology was worth more in the era of Adolf Hitler than a knowledge of German Idealism.

Conversely, some of Haecker's strongest words of praise for Kierkegaard come in the form of an assessment that Kierkegaard was a very effective opponent of German Idealism, especially in its Hegelian modulations:

> Kierkegaard grew up in the third generation of Goethe and the second generation of Hegel, and came of age in an atmosphere laden to excess with their ideas. It was for him to fight, not in the widespread middle class, nor in the official class, but as genius versus genius; which was most necessary, since every sphere requires its own saviour, to defend the supernatural against the natural, the transcendence of God against the immanence of the rational philosophers, the personal God against pantheism, to urge the absolute singleness of the God-Man, the reality of sin and salvation, and the love of God as opposed to that which men call love, the Holiness of God as against the impurity and sentimentality of the 'beautiful soul' of Rousseau. This part of his mission Kierkegaard fulfilled as a servant of God in the service of Christianity.[29]

---

28. Haecker, *Journal in the Night*, entry 397, 1940, p. 109.
29. Heacker, *Søren Kierkegaard*, p. 58.

Besides his praise of Kierkegaard for not getting lost in the blind alleys of Idealism, Haecker's most sustained denunciation of German Idealism by far is found in the following passage from his book on Virgil:

> Ever since the German Faust violated the truth in its theological, philosophical and philological aspects by substituting the phrase 'In the beginning was the Act', for 'in the beginning was the Word', the German genius has fallen into confusion without end. In comparison with the immense consequences of this spiritual crime, this personification of an absurdity, the whole mischief of Nietzsche fades into insignificance as but one symptom of the malignant influence of this word, this act, nay, this crime upon which generations have been nourished in ridiculous and pitiful pride. It has extinguished the light of intelligence, making of it what all the modern sophists make of it, a perversion that interferes with the free operation of the Act *which was in the beginning*. It is a fallacy that denies the foundations of humanity as we received them from Greece and Rome, of that Adventist's humanity which has its beginning and its end in the *Logos*. Language is a faithful betrayer of thought. As it is easy for the Germans, with their word 'Schicksal' [destiny, fate], to misconceive the intellectual foundations of being, so it is difficult for the Latins even in their darkest moments to lose sight of it, so deeply embedded does it lie in their language.[30]

The above paragraph appeared in 1935. It echoed the ideas of George Moenius (1890–1953) who was the editor of Munich's *Allgemeine Rundschau* from 1929 to 1933. In his preface to a book titled *Verteidigung des Abendlandes* (1930), Moenius wrote that 'in the Roman-Germanic antithesis, everything centres upon an antipathy between subjectivism and objectivism which comes to fruition in the most multifaceted varieties. The German turns the hierarchy of values around. The inner life and *Ethos* dominate'.[31] Moving in the opposite direction of appreciation, Moenius had been impressed by Haecker's earlier article on Virgil published in *Der Brenner* in December 1932 in which Haecker declared, '*Wir leben im Imperium Romanum*' – we live in the Roman Imperium. Moenius made the *Wir leben im Imperium*

---

30. Theodor Haecker, *Virgil: Father of the West* (London: Sheed & Ward, 1934), pp. 83–4.

31. Georg Moenius in Henri Massis and George Moenius, *Verteidigung des Abendlandes* (Berlin: J. Hegner Verlag, 1930), pp. 29–30.

Romanum idea the theme of the first issue of the *Allgemeine Rundschau* in 1933.[32] According to Haecker the culture and identity of Western man rests on two foundations. First, on the Greco-Roman *humanitas*, in particular 'the unique providential discovery of the natural *Logos* in the hour of the heathen Advent, in the hour of Virgil', and second, on Christian revelation and the wisdom of the Hebrew prophets. Nordic mythology with its obsession with fate or destiny, *Schicksal* in German, is nowhere in this picture.

Haecker's understanding of the first of these foundations is set out in his book *Vergil: Vater des Abendlandes* published in 1931. Ernst A. Schmidt summarized the leading ideas in Haecker's book, along with a 1930/1 lecture simply titled 'Vergil' by the poet and essayist Rudolf Borchardt and an essay on 'Vergil's Historiosophie' by the Russian philologist Wjatscheslaw Iwanow, that also appeared in 1931, in the following list of principles:

(a) Virgil's *Aeneid* is seen as the beginning of the Middle Ages and the *magna carta* of the *Sacrum Imperium*, the medieval idea of *Kaisertum*;
(b) Virgil is an *anima naturaliter Christiana*;
(c) The poem is characterized by melancholy and tears;
(d) The *Aeneid* espouses a new image of man (*Menschenbild*);
(e) Human life gets meaning from a mission and a calling (Mission, *Sendung, Berufung*) that involves obedience to the voices of fate and destiny;
(f) Men are to steer their life's course by the stars of loyalty, faith, piety, and sacrifice, renunciation and self-abnegation (*Entsagung*).[33]

Schmidt also noted that 'these voices of the German *literati* were taken up in England by T. S. Eliot and C. S. Lewis and that the British in general were equally open to expressing admiration for the Romans along with the Greeks.[34] In Germany however, an appropriation of

---

32. Gregory Munro, 'The Holy Roman Empire in German Roman Catholic Thought (1929–1933)', *Journal of Religious History* 17 (4) (December 1993), pp. 439–65 at p. 463.

33. Ernst A. Schmidt, 'The German Recovery of Vergil in the Early Years of the 20th Century (1900–1938), *Vergilius* 54 (2008), pp. 124–49 at 142–3.

34. Ibid., p. 143.

the Roman's cultural treasure was not so much a pan German affair as a phenomenon associated with scholars and writers within the Catholic *Länder*. Conversely, E. M. Butler's *The Tyranny of Greece over Germany* famously addressed what might be called the 'Hellenophilia' of Germany's great Protestant writers.[35]

Haecker's expression the 'heathen Advent' refers to the Augustan age immediately preceding (and accompanying) the birth of Christ. Virgil, the greatest literary representative of this age, died a mere nineteen years before the Christian era began. Haecker described Virgil as the 'only pagan who takes rank with the Jewish and Christian prophets', while the *Aeneid* is 'the only book, apart from holy Scriptures, to contain sayings that are valid beyond the particular hour and circumstance of their day, prophecies that re-echo from the doors of eternity, whence they first draw their breath: *His ego nec metas rerum, nec tempora pono: imperium sine fine dedi*'.[36] The adjectives Haecker used to describe Aeneas, the hero of Virgil's epic poem, are pious, paternal and magnanimous. He wrote that 'to be pious meant to be "son", and lovingly to fulfil the duties of the filial relationship'.[37] This of course anticipates the importance of the filial relationship between God the Father and God the Son in Trinitarian theology and between God and the human person in theological anthropology. In the following passage, Haecker tied these two foundations of Western man together:

> In the last hour before the fullness of time he [Virgil] fulfilled the measure of what was good in the ancient paganism, as others fulfilled the measure of its evil. This he did on the very threshold of the Advent, after which it was granted to man, a mere creature, to exceed his own limitations, and that without doing violence to his status as a creature. Thereafter it was given to man to be limitless, though in one direction only, namely in the love of God, which is the supernatural excess. The loftiest ideal and reality of the ancient world was the hero, the ultimate motive of whose being was his own glory, achieved, whether in life or in death, through two things – fate, and the heroic deed accomplished through freedom of the will. After the Incarnation the loftiest ideal and reality is the saint, the

---

35. E. M. Butler, *The Tyranny of Greece over Germany* (Boston: Beacon Press, 1935).
36. Haecker, *Virgil: Father of the West*, pp. 77–8.
37. Ibid., p. 62.

ultimate motive of whose being is the glory of God, also achieved, whether in life or in death, through two things – first grace, which implies Providence, the greater name for Fate, more full of light; and secondly, a boundless love of God, which also implies a heroic quality of mind and heroic action achieved through the mystery of freedom. The essential nature of the two ideals remains the same: each is achieved through the agency of one divine and one human factor; but between them lies the Incarnation and the Revelation.[38]

In his book on Virgil, Haecker also made a few comments on linguistic philosophy which help explain what he meant by the German attraction to 'Schicksal' (fate or destiny) and the alleged Latin inoculation against this fascination. Haecker suggested that languages have what he called their 'heart tones'. These are words that are used over and again in a particular language revealing some underlying fixation on the concept conveyed by the word within the culture that the language is embedded. Anyone who has that language as a mother tongue readily understands the meaning of the 'heart-tones', whereas for outsiders it is difficult to get a deep grasp of the concept in all of its nuances and complexity. Today in linguistic philosophy, this kind of theory goes by the name of the expressivist theory of language, associated with the 'Sapir Whorf hypothesis' (that culture precedes language) to be contrasted with the instrumental theory of language. According to the expressivist theory, one must first be immersed within a culture to understand a language. Culture is prior to language rather than language being prior to culture. The best way to illustrate this idea is to consider words that carry different connotations in different cultures that share a common language. For example, the words 'farm', 'ranch', and 'estate' carry different nuances if used in Australian, American and British cultural contexts. In each case, an anglophone person can get the gist of what is meant by the concept, but an appreciation of its particular nuances will depend on one's cultural background. Haecker is making a similar kind of point about the pet philosophical concepts that different languages often carry. He associates the word *logos* with those of a Greek cultural background, *res* with those under strong Roman influence, *raison* with the French, *sense* with the British and *Schicksal* and *das Wesen* with the Germans. He suggests that those for whom *logos* is important are more resistant to the Hegelian virus than those for whom *Schicksal* is a concept

38. Ibid., pp. 13–14.

deeply embedded within their literary and philosophical culture. The Latins write operas about forbidden love coming unstuck within an inflexible moral order, inflexible because of the logic within nature itself, the Germans, however, write operas about fate and destiny. (Even if one thinks of Giuseppe Verdi's *La Forza del destino* as an exception that undermines the argument, one finds that the libretto for this Italian opera was influenced by Friedrich Schiller's *Wallensteins Lager*.)

If Haecker is right about the influence of these philosophical 'heart-tones', and in particular, if he is right that they signify certain strongly embedded philosophical presuppositions within given linguistic cultures, it raises a raft of interesting genealogical possibilities about the differing receptions of Christianity in the various German provinces (in German *Länder*), and in Italy and France. These kinds of issues were of interest to the generation of German Romantics who followed the period of the French Revolution for whom the differences between French and Germanic cultures were often judged to be due to a French affinity for the philosophy of the Romans and a German affinity for the philosophy of the Greeks. German cultural historians also highlight the differences between the cultures of the *Länder* in the south and south-west of Germany, including the Rhineland – those within the *Limes Germanicus*, the fortified frontiers of the ancient Roman provinces of *Germania Inferior, Germania Superior* and *Raetia* – and those in the north and north-east. There is also the comical German expression *Weißwurstäquator* (white sausage equator) referring to the cultural boundary between southern (white sausage eating Germany) and the non-white sausage eaters of the northern *Länder*. The fact that the *Länder* beyond the *Limes Germanicus* and *Weißwurstäquator* are predominately Lutheran rather than Catholic is a commonplace observation leading some historians to argue that the north and north-eastern *Länder* carry an anti-Roman disposition deep within their cultural DNA. Haecker sided with the analysis of Catholic writers such as Georg Moenius for whom this cultural dichotomy is central to any understanding of German history. Implicit in Haecker's references to the German fixation on fate and destiny in contrast to the Latin emphasis upon reason is that those *Länder* to the north of the *Limes Germanicus* retained elements of German paganism resistant to Christian analogues and alternatives to fate such as grace, providence and free will.[39]

39. For a more extensive analysis of the cultural differences between the Catholic and Lutheran *Länder*, see Gregory Munro, 'The Holy Roman Empire

A final thread in Haecker's quarrel with German Idealism is the claim that the violence of the Nazi regime played out the resentment of men who lacked the intellectual aptitude to immerse themselves in the complexities of German philosophy as taught in the schools and academies. More broadly he saw it as a 'poisonous *ressentiment* for the drudgery and sweat and the inferiority complex which a too high ideal of education brought upon them'.[40] This 'too high an ideal' included German Idealist philosophy, but was more generally a classical education composed of large doses of foreign languages, philosophy, poetry, history and music. Haecker believed that German youth who lacked the aptitude for this kind of education used their membership in Nazi organizations to take revenge upon those who in the pre-Nazi social order were their social superiors. Under the Nazi ascendency, a knowledge of philosophy, a facility with languages, a high classical education counted as nothing, while a willingness to take part in brutality could enhance one's chances of upward social mobility. In his *Journal* entry 480 of 1940, Haecker laments that the 'men who lay down categorically what is to be the German way of life' are a combination of people 'itching for revenge because they did not satisfy the requirements of a certain educational ideal (false in itself, or falsely applied), because they could not understand the *participium absolutum* or indirect speech', along with the crude and the brutal and the ones with criminal tendencies.[41]

Haecker did concede something to Nietzsche's critique of Christianity insofar as he accepted that a major indictment of Christianity is that for all of its high-mindedness, or hierarchical thinking, it does not seem to elevate or refine the humanity of many of its adherents. Nonetheless Haecker argued that even if only a small number of Christians in any generation are saints, the fact that there really *are* saints, even if few in number, is an argument for Christianity. Haecker's treatment of the Christian saint is reminiscent of the Jewish idea of the *Lamed Vav* – the notion that at any given time in history there must be thirty-six just men in the world to justify a continuation of the covenant. In *Was ist der Mensch?* Haecker declared:

in German Roman Catholic Thought (1929-1933)', *Journal of Religious History* 17 (4) (December 1993), pp. 439-65.
 40. Haecker, *Journal in the Night*, entry 420, 1940, p. 114.
 41. Ibid., entry 480, 1940, p. 138.

The canon, the actual *Summa* of the existentiality of the European peoples is not an ethic, neither that of the Stoics, nor that of Kant's categorical imperative – a terribly provincial concern – indeed, not even the Ten Commandments of themselves, but rather the Sermon on the Mount in which, however, all these are fulfilled and obtain blissful clarity ... all *ressentiment* of the oppressed and insulted and enraged which is no longer kept silent within the womb of the European peoples themselves, but is rather vociferously expressed, lives upon this hiatus, this *abyss* between the Sermon on the Mount and the *real* lives of the European peoples, which would have long since devoured it had there not lived in every generation a few known and unknown saints who have fulfilled and continue to fulfil the unshakable standard by which the Christian peoples are measured.[42]

This passage is evocative of Nietzsche's comment that if Christians want him to believe in their God, they should at least try to look as though they have been redeemed. It is also echoed in the statement of Joseph Ratzinger that 'the true apologetics for the Christian message, the most persuasive proof of its truth, offsetting everything that may appear negative, are the saints, on the one hand, and the beauty that the faith has generated, on the other'.[43] For Haecker, John Henry Newman was such a saint and a man who defended beauty.

The transcendental of beauty was often muted in scholastic theology where the accent was on the transcendental of truth. Beauty, however, was a central preoccupation of the nineteenth-century Romantic movements as they manifested themselves across the continent of Europe and even in England and predominately Calvinist Scotland, so deeply influenced by the iconoclasm of the Cromwellian era. One thinks, for example, of the novels of Sir Walter Scott and the poetry, paintings and art criticism of the members of the Pre-Raphaelite Brotherhood. While John Henry Newman is the most outstanding example of an English theologian who shared the Romantic interest in beauty, German Catholic scholars of the nineteenth century were similarly keen to address the importance of this much neglected transcendental. This interest reached its zenith in the twentieth century in the theology of Hans Urs von Balthasar from the German-speaking city of Lucerne. Balthasar's fifteen volume

---

42. Haecker, *Was ist der Mensch?* pp. 77–8.
43. Joseph Ratzinger, *On the Way to Jesus Christ* (San Francisco: Ignatius, 2005), p. 38.

magnum opus, which laid out an approach to theology based on the transcendental properties of truth, beauty and goodness, devoted a full seven volumes, that is, almost half the volumes, to the transcendental of beauty. These volumes, published between 1961 and 1985, rest on the argument that the transcendental properties of being should exist in a *perichoretic* (interweaving) relationship. According to Balthasar a major problem with the culture of modernity is precisely that these transcendental properties are now rarely found *together*. In both our arts and our social practices what should be the intrinsic relationships between these transcendental properties have been severed. This is one of the reasons why the Catholic culture of many once strongly Catholic countries has imploded. While this particular cultural pathology analysis is commonly associated with Balthasar, it is worth noting that Haecker had already reached the same conclusion as early as his 1931 book on Virgil, where he wrote, 'If Beauty really vanishes from the life of man then the Good and the True must likewise slowly perish, and vice versa, for these three are one.'[44]

A common Catholic criticism of the Romantic movements of the nineteenth century is that their pursuit of the 'beautiful soul' (*die schöne Seele*) often took the form of exalting the beautiful at the expense of the true and the good, or replacing a Christian conception of the trio with neopagan alternatives. In *Über den Abendländischen Menschen*, Haecker underscored the theological principle that there is only one end to human nature, the eternal beatitude of the just, and he emphasized that all the cultural sophistications of a neopagan social elite pursuing beauty for beauty's sake, but without reference to the true and the good, would be of no value at all at the moment of divine judgement:

> No doubt Neanderthal man did not look like the Apollo of Belvedere, but he too was a spiritual person whose salvation was at stake. Many a Neanderthal who, in so far as he was capable – before the Incarnation – fulfilled God's unmediated command, will on the last day of history, and thus at the general judgment, arise *transfigured* in contrast to a highly cultured and civilized enemy of God.[45]

If severed from truth and goodness, the seeking of beauty can become idolatrous. Human genius first needs consecration, needs to be set

---

44. Haecker, *Virgil: Father of the West*, p. 103.
45. Haecker, *Über den Abendländischen Menschen*, pp. 37–8.

within its rightful place within the hierarchical order. As Haecker wrote in his essay 'Betrachtungen Über Vergil Vater des Abendlandes', when St Augustine lay dying and his city was being besieged by Vandals, he was not dreaming of the Romanesque domes, Gothic cathedrals or Renaissance and Baroque palaces that were to come but of his heavenly homeland, the *Pax Domini*, the final peace.[46]

While most of Haecker's publications appeared in the period between the two world wars and then posthumously in the late 1940s and therefore addressed the issues of these times, significantly his indictment of German Idealism on several charges of providing the intellectual subsoil from which neo-barbarian ideologies might sprout and grow, also anticipated the assault on ontology which became a hallmark of western scholarship in the late twentieth century. When the 'modern' project appeared to the generation of 1968 to have failed, they replaced it with various neo-nominalist postmodern projects. Although he never used the expression 'postmodern philosophy', Haecker was concerned about developments in the philosophical field which so amplified the role of history in the realm of ontology as to dissolve it effectively. Haecker observed that 'no one studying the various kinds of plants and animals, even though specially concerned to discover the differences between these various kinds, would be likely for one moment to forget, much less to deny, that there is such a thing as Plant and Animal, each with eternally unchanging characteristics'.[47] However, he concluded, 'There are many to-day who appear to believe in a radical change in the essential nature of man through the centuries.'[48] This is a pathological symptom of a modern or postmodern culture arising from a severance of two or more things that ought to exist together in a relationship.

The history and ontology relationship was one of the subjects addressed in Haecker's *Der Christ und die Geschichte* published in 1935. Reading it today, one would immediately observe that Haecker was strongly influenced by the Gospel of St John. Haecker returned time and again to the Johannine Prologue – In the Beginning was the Word! The paragraph below taken from *Der Christ und die Geschichte* is typical:

---

46. Theodor Haecker, 'Betrachtungen Über Vergil Vater des Abendlandes' in *Theodor Haecker: Essays aus den Jahren 1917-1944 Werke 1* (Munich: Kösel-Verlag, 1958), pp. 433–4.
47. Haecker, *Virgil: Father of the West*, p. 3.
48. Ibid., pp. 3–4.

> This world was created through the *Logos*. Revelation is unequivocal and is in no way open to multiple interpretations. *Omnia per ipsum facta sunt* (John); *per quem fecit et saecula* (Paul); *unus Dominus Jesus Christus, per quem omnia, et nos per ipsum* (Paul); *quoniam in ipso condita sunt universa in coelis, et in terra, visibilia et invisibilia* (Paul). The Word takes precedence, it precedes act in good and in evil, eternally and in time. Creation is in the *Logos* and through the *Logos*. The confession of our faith (*per quem omnia facta sunt*) is as clear here as it can be. The experience of this temporal life constitutes being according to revelation, but in a weak analogy. Matter, flora, fauna and the human being are created through the *Logos*.[49]

It is clear then, that Haecker was well aware of the danger of nominalism, of that denial of universals which leads to an attack on ontology. His belief that creation is rent through with rationality, with a reason or logic and hierarchical order, that there is in contemporary parlance 'a human ecology', precisely because all of creation is the work of the *Logos*, is very strong. Yet he was also aware that the history–ontology relationship could just as easily be undermined by exalting rationality and denying history. *Der Christ und die Geschichte* therefore offered a defence of the reasonableness of historical revelation against Lessing's so-called 'ugly great ditch' – the ditch being the idea that historical truths cannot mediate metaphysical truths. In the following passages, Haecker took a quintessentially Catholic position in wanting to affirm both history and metaphysics:

> For the Christian, there is no absolute law of enmity between philosophy and history, but between certain philosophical systems and history, of genuine history. The knowledge of the real meaning of the historical is compatible only with a philosophy and metaphysics. There are philosophies that make it impossible from the outset to make a real account of history, because they render it meaningless, destroy the mark, rob it of all reality, turn it into a dream of humanity or even of the deity itself. This includes all purely idealistic philosophies, which see the process of the world in the development of pure ideas only, and must consider everything historical a completely incomprehensible delay.[50]

---

49. Theodor Haecker, *Der Christ und Die Geschichte* (Leipzig: Jakob Hegner, 1935), p. 79.
50. Ibid., p. 36.

Theology has metaphysics for the naturalistic presupposition, so to speak, a presupposed nature. She could not move at all without her. She would be dumb, she would have no language; but on the other hand, she is theology first through faith, that is, first through a supernatural revelation, through the revelation whose 'who' is to be, [I am who am] and to be a tri-personal God. However this revelation is not only in history, it is itself history, not a history under the many others, but is *the* history.[51]

In the third chapter of *Der Christ und die Geschichte*, Haecker argued that there are three powers that have an effect on history – (i) the Holy Trinity, (ii) the 'fallen angel' or 'Prince of this world' (*der Fürst dieser Welt*) and (iii) man himself. Here again Haecker does not miss an opportunity to take a swipe at the German Idealists saying that 'apart from Hegel, who is a chapter in himself', the Idealists 'tipped history into the tension between freedom and necessity', creating 'a "summa" of abstraction' that resulted in 'frightfully dull books and a *taedium vitae* that only transcendental Idealists can endure or cannot feel at all'.[52] For Haecker, the really interesting issue is the question of whether history is a matter of God's will, or the devil's will, or the will of man.[53] In one of his typically satirical moments he concludes that the chronicler, who began the history of his small community with the creation of the world and Adam and Eve and the Fall, had more sense of the inseparable connections of the whole and all its parts than numerous tremendously learned and knowledgeable historians, such as the French who declared 1789 to be Year Zero.[54] According to Haecker the causes of the French Revolution were primarily economic issues, not matters of cosmic significance like the original catastrophe in the Garden of Eden. He concluded that 'the Christian is of the opinion that his conception of history comes closest to the being of history without eliding anything'.[55] This makes the Christian view of history superior to the 'one-sided religions and philosophies', some of which 'rob God of his honour, such as any Manicheanism that places evil upon the same metaphysical rung of being as the good', while some 'deny the

51. Ibid., pp. 20–1.
52. Ibid., p. 90.
53. Ibid., p. 91.
54. Ibid., p. 92.
55. Ibid.

power of the evil that came into the world through the fallen angel, and simply merge everything into physical evil or want, that error of aesthetic and rationalistic religions and of Leibnizesque theodicy', or 'deny the dignity of the human person, which is based on the freedom of his person and in his having been made in the image of God, which also includes a power to establish and create, so to make history himself'.[56] For the Christian, history is primarily universal history. Haecker noted that physicists have long given up the concept of a 'closed system'. He declared that the concept of a closed system is itself a fiction, because everything is related to everything else.[57] Nonetheless, Haecker acknowledged that there is a particular history, inserted within the universal, and thus 'while Christians can be somewhat clear about the meaning of universal history, namely as the return of the creature to God', they can also be at the same time 'in a frightening darkness about the partial meaning of the history of individual peoples who still linger in the process'.[58] Human beings are actors who do not know the outcome of the particular historical dramas in which they play – they are both actors and spectators at the same time.

Whereas Haecker's two books that explicitly concern the human person kept away from statements that were deep inside the territory of theology, the book *Schöpfer und Schöpfung* (*The Creator and Creation*) attempted to build a bridge between trinitarian theology and human psychology. The central theme of this work is that 'everything depends on the Trinity'.[59] Haecker described the resolution of the early Christological heresies in the Trinitarian theology of the Councils of Nicaea and Chalcedon as 'the most powerful event in the history of the human mind', and he further described Trinitarian theology as nothing less than 'the greatest power possessed by Christians in the struggle of the world-views, and in every respect, even politically'.[60] He added that 'if mankind would be given a man of the same sanctity of feeling and burning love of God, connected with the same natural power of the intellect, with the same undeniable, unerring, light-beaming force of will' as Thomas Aquinas, this person could lift Thomas's victorious principle of the *analogia entis* to the even greater heights of the

---

56. Ibid., pp. 92–3.
57. Ibid., p. 94.
58. Ibid., p. 95.
59. Haecker, *Schöpfer und Schöpfung*, p. 118.
60. Ibid.

Analogia trinitatis.[61] In a statement that today sounds prescient given the Second Vatican Council's emphasis on exploring the economic Trinity, Haecker declared that the task of the next decade and even the next few centuries is to investigate the *Analogia trinitatis*, the relationship between the human person and each of the Persons of the Trinity.[62] This task finally arrives at the magisterial level during the early years of the Pontificate of St John Paul II with his suite of Trinitarian encyclicals – *Redemptor Hominis* (1979), *Dives in Misericordia* (1980) and *Dominum et Vivificantem* (1986) – each one focused on the relationship between the human person and one of the Persons of the Trinity – the Son, the Father, and the Spirit respectively. It is also found in the works of Marc Ouellet, in Klaus Hemmerle's theses on Trinitarian ontology, in the theology of Chiara Lubich and others in the Focolare circles, in the theology of Santa Croce's Giulio Maspero, in the phenomenology of Jean-Luc Marion, Michel Henri, Emmanuel Falque, Kevin Hart and Robert Sokolowski and in the works of scholars in the circle of the British Radical Orthodoxy movement. Haecker would no doubt strongly approve of this trend in late twentieth century and contemporary theology and phenomenology.

One point that Haecker reiterated in several places is that the concept of the Trinity is not found in any philosophy or religious tradition outside of Christianity. Not even the Greeks or Virgil reasoned their way to a tri-personal God. Rather, the word Trinity 'is a tremendous invasion of the Word of God into human language, it is not a natural linguistic creation, it did not come from the poets, the natural linguists. It comes from the *ens realissimum* itself'.[63]

In *Schöpfer und Schöpfung* Haecker also noted that Thomistic philosophy described the human person in terms of the operations of intellect and will, but St Augustine spoke of intellect, memory and will. Haecker preferred a triadic analysis, but instead of following Augustine he offered his own triad built around the soul's functions of feeling, thinking and willing. Feeling, he noted, despite its often loud outbursts, is more hidden than thinking and willing, and its sources are more inaccessible, so it is not so easy to untangle its operations as clearly as Aquinas dealt with the interaction of the will and the intellect. Haecker nonetheless argued that all three functions – feeling, thinking

61. Ibid.
62. Ibid., p. 131.
63. Ibid., p. 156.

and willing – should work within an 'ordo' and that the problem is that all three have become relatively independent of each other, thus breaking the coherent internal order. He declared that 'Faust's "Feeling Is Everything" is certainly a false proposition, but it is no worse than the ideal sentence of Idealism, "thinking is everything", and again not more wrong than the view of Schopenhauer and other, more dangerous voluntarists: "willing is everything".'[64]

Haecker is quite moved by the historical fact that the Church fathers came up with Trinitarian dogmas long before contemporary psychologists started to think about the human person as a being who feels, thinks and wills and needs to integrate these three functions. In several places he remarked that when heresies rose over belief in the Trinity, and the human mind had to struggle with arguments, psychology did not play the slightest part in this struggle: 'The dogmas of the Trinity have been defined with the help of purely theological arguments based on revelation, and indeed with the help of the Holy Spirit ... they have been defined by people who had not the slightest knowledge that the human being himself is trinitarian in feeling, thinking, and willing.'[65] Conversely, today, we distinguish 'between a sentient man, an intellectual man, a volitional man, without being fully aware that we are being trinitarian and not monistic, not dualistic, not pluralistic, but in a strict sense trinitarian.'[66]

Haecker also found vestiges of the Trinity in the following three triads which can be arranged in a hierarchical order. At the base of his pyramid is the triad to be found in nature: plant, animal and human person. Above this there is the triad within the human person: body, soul and spirit, and above this triad, within the soul itself, there is the triad: feeling, thinking, willing. Haecker suggested that the devil operates by attacking the operations of the soul, perverting the will and obscuring the intellect and confusing the realm of feeling. He also asserted that the phenomenon of tragic human choices is a hereditary fault – a reference to original sin – that has not yet been solved sacramentally. Conversely, he noted that 'in the Trinity there is no shadow of the tragic. Here is the essence of love itself.'[67] He further argued that the contemporary struggle of world views and religions cannot be resolved solely in the

---

64. Ibid., p. 135.
65. Ibid., p. 137.
66. Ibid., p. 156.
67. Ibid., p. 170.

realm of arguments. Christians, he declared, 'must fight on sacramental ground'.[68]

The struggle of world views and religions has led to a crisis of European identity, since the European identity was forged in the synthesis of Greco-Roman, Hebraic and Christian conceptions of the dignity of the person. Remove those foundations from European culture and Europe has a crisis of identity. Haecker addressed this topic in a reflection on the *Imperium Romanum*. Like many historians he was of the view that the *Imperium Romanum* is a kind of subterranean connective tissue uniting the various countries of Europe culturally. He did, however, present the case with a great deal more passion than most cultural historians and no doubt the subtext is that the *Imperium Romanum* is actually more legitimate than the bogus claims to greatness of the so-called Third Reich. Here he wrote:

> For, whether we like it or not, whether we know it or not, we are all still members of that *Imperium Romanum*, which finally and after terrible errors accepted Christianity *sua sponte*, of its own free-will – a Christianity which it could not abandon now without abandoning itself and humanism too. The *Imperium Romanum*, which Virgil knew in all its natural grandeur and revealed in the splendour of beauty, is no hazy ideal; nor is it merely a true ideal, but a reality, deep though that reality may at times lie buried. The thing 'Rome' is not an idea alone, though a true one, but actuality, *res*, a thing of flesh and blood. Wherever there is the will and urge to empire, the measure of its wisdom or its excess, of its blessing or its curse, is to be determined by the standards of the enduring reality of the *Imperium Romanum*.[69]

In the following passage Haecker went on to argue that a revival of this empire could only occur in two ways: first by the suppression of all nations bar one, something he regarded as a monstrous idea – clearly he was gesturing towards the Third Reich project here – and the second as a spiritual commonwealth embodying all that was good in classical Greece and Rome as well as the Christian theological virtues of faith, hope and love. Here he seemed to be gesturing towards a renewal of the Holy Roman Empire:

---

68. Ibid.
69. Haecker, *Virgil: Father of the West*, p. 78.

A revival of this empire, which has never quite perished, could only be effected in one of two ways. It might be brought about through some renewal of the *Pax Romana*, whereby the Western world might be denationalised and levelled; this would be possible only if one nation were by force to gain overwhelming ascendancy over all the rest, and it would be the greatest crime against both humanity and Christianity. For today no nation enjoys such pre-eminence above the rest as did the Romans in their day – and even they with their *Pax Romana* did not accomplish any particularly lovely thing. Moreover the value of the 'nation' has been magnified by Christianity, inasmuch as the 'individual', the 'person' has acquired infinite value. It is not required of us that we should denationalise, and thereby renounce, our individuality, our uniqueness. Levelling in the spiritual realm is antichristian. Before 'the embannered throne of God' are ranged the angels of each nation – and who will level angels?

The second way which, through mutual understanding, conciliation and respect, would preserve all that is valuable in each nation, thereby uniting all in one higher commonwealth – which could only be a spiritual one – is infinitely the better. But this spiritual commonwealth must omit nothing essential in what has gone before, neither pagan Rome, which is also Adventist, but must be in the nature of a fulfilment and transcendence to a new age, and in the spiritual form of faith, hope and love.[70]

The rhetorical question 'who will level angels?' is a reference to the ideas of Pseudo-Dionysius as presented in his *De Coelesti Hierarchia*. Dionysius identified nine choirs of angels subdivided into triads. The first – seraphim, cherubim and thrones – are in direct contact with God. The seraphim serve at the throne of God. Whereas seraphim are characterized by an excess of love, cherubim are characterized by the excellence of their knowledge. The thrones, as their name suggests, are the carriers of the throne of God. The second triad consists of the dominions, virtues and powers. The dominions are angels of leadership who regulate the duties of the other angels and make known God's commands. They are the business managers of the heavenly court. The virtues have control over nature and are therefore in charge of miracles. The powers are warrior angels who fight evil spirits. Finally, there is the triad of principalities, archangels and angels. The principalities are

---

70. Ibid., pp. 78–9.

in charge of whole nations and groups of peoples and the guardian angels are in charge of individuals. Haecker's reference to the 'angels of each nation' is therefore a reference to the principalities.[71] The idea that each of the nations has its assigned principality is an affirmation of nationhood but not of nationalism. If each country has its own principalities then it follows that it should not be dominated by another super-power state with such domination defended by a nationalistic ideology. One of the great historic achievements of Christianity was precisely that it overcome the Roman idolatry of the state. Fascism represented at attempt to return Germany and the nations it invaded to the pre-Constantinian era. Haecker recognized that the Third Reich represented a neopagan form of state idolatry. The pseudo-religious nature of the Nazi ideology was evident not only in its political 'rites' and mass 'liturgies' but also its zeal to change the way that people think. In his *Journal* entry number 328 of 1940, he wrote:

> Overnight, National Socialism has succeeded in reducing the Norwegians, who have been free men for a thousand years, to a form of servitude that has never existed in the world. The nations which were led into captivity by the Egyptians, the Assyrians, the Babylonians were certainly not compelled to assert they were free. And that is precisely what the subjugated nations of today are compelled to do.[72]

In other words, the Nazi occupation of foreign countries had taken on a new dimension from all previous forms of conquest. The added dimension was the imposition of an ideology. The Nazis demanded something over and above territory, the adulation of the conquering state itself and the adoption of its civil 'religion'. Haecker concluded that 'the deification of the state amounts to the bestialization of man'.[73] He called the new state religion the '*hitlerian Herrgottreligion*', though he

---

71. For academic works on angelology see Serge-Thomas Bonino, *Angels and Demons: A Catholic Introduction*, trans. Michael J Miller (Washington, DC: Catholic University of America Press, 2016); and Jean Daniélou, *The Angels and Their Mission According to the Fathers of the Church*, trans. David Heimann (South Bend: University of Notre Dame Press, 1957).

72. Haecker, *Journal in the Night*, entry 328, 1940, p. 89.

73. Theodor Haecker, 'Notizen: Die Bestie', *Der Brenner* (Juni 1923), pp. 9–19 at p. 9.

thought it completely phoney as a religion. In his *Journal* entry 432 of 1940 he wrote that 'religions, even false religions, come from the East; they do not arise in the neighbourhood of Braunau'.[74]

While much of Haecker's work took the form of ridiculing the Nazi ideology as stupid and brutish, completely beneath the dignity of any reasonable person, and also ridiculing the hubristic nature of German Idealism, he did sometimes juxtapose these with an account of the comparative sweetness and genuine urbanity of the Roman *Humanitas* and its fulfilment in Christian revelation. His Virgil book is the prime example of this. One approach to the 'What is man?' question, that of the German Idealist, is unrealistic, a mere fantasy, another, the National Socialist, is vulgar and violent. In comparison, the Virgilian and Christian have none of the arrogance of the German Idealist and none of the bestiality of the National Socialist. Their hallmark is a childlike purity built upon piety. In the book on Virgil he remarked:

> The last and closest secret of a man, the ultimate foundations of his strength, his most intimate and personal motive, lies far back in the things and memories of childhood. The decisive factor for a man and his work is the extent to which he has been able to carry over into his adult years, or through grace to recover, the child that is in him. How strange and hostile is the face of a man in whom the child, the boy, is totally extinguished![75]

This theme of carrying over the spiritual strengths and dispositions of childhood or recovering them through grace is not uncommon among members of the generation who survived the First World War. There are shades of this in A. A. Milne, C. S. Lewis and J. R. R. Tolkien and parallel treatments in the works of Georges Bernanos, author of *The Diary of a Country Priest* and *The Dialogues of the Carmelites*. In his *Lettre aux Anglais*, Bernanos wrote, 'Experience has shown me too late that human beings can be explained, not by their vices, but, on the contrary, by whatever they have kept that is intact, pure, by that which remains in them of their childhood, regardless of how deeply we may have to look for it.'[76] It may be that Haecker knew of this judgment of Bernanos or

---

74. Haecker, *Journal in the Night*, entry 432, 1940, p. 118.

75. Haecker, *Virgil: Father of the West*, pp. 18–19.

76. Georges Bernanos, *Lettre aux Anglais* (Paris: Gallimard, 1942), p. 92, cited by Hans Urs von Balthasar in *Bernanos: An Ecclesial Existence* (San Francisco: Ignatius, 1996), p. 32.

that he independently came to the same or a similar conclusion, or that both men were influenced by St Thérèse of Lisieux's theology of spiritual childhood, often described as the most potent antidote to the spiritual pathologies of Friedrich Nietzsche and also to what Bathasar called 'the hard core of Pharisaism which persists in the midst of Christianity: that will-to-power disguised in the mantle of religion'.[77] The spirituality of St Thérèse is based on a childlike trust in Divine Providence, and this is particularly difficult for those who have encountered the power of what Haecker called *Der Fürst der Welt*.

A contemporary of Haecker and fellow *Hochland* contributor, the Saarland philosopher Peter Wust (1884–1940), also wrote about losing the faith of one's childhood and the difficulty of recovering faith once one has abandoned it to live by reason alone. Wust addressed this theme in his *Naivität und Pietät* (1925). In his early professional life Wust had flirted with neo-Kantianism and almost lost his faith, but recovered from this spiritual condition. His philosophical reflections upon this loss and recovery formed the subject of *Naivität und Pietät*. Wust's idea of a 'second naiveté' (the recuperation of religious faith subsequent to the work of critical intelligence) was discussed by Gabriel Marcel in his *Being and Having: An Existential Diary*.[78] One amusing anecdote from this period is that upon receiving a copy of Wust's book *Ungewissheit und Wagnis* (*Uncertainty and Risk*), Blessed Clemens August Graf von Galen, otherwise known as the 'Lion of Münster', replied with a note to the effect that he appreciated Wust's generosity, but he had no idea of what to make of the book since for him Christianity was neither 'uncertain' nor a 'risk'. In other words, Galen had no need of a second naiveté since he had never lost his first.[79]

Positively, Wust noted the deep fraternal relationship between the 'man who kneels in church before the gracious image of the Mother of God, be he statesman, artist or thinker' and 'the intellectually less cultivated man who kneels beside him'. They share 'the same supernatural atmosphere' such that 'a union is effected between them, in the very substance of the soul, which no method of intellectual

---

77. Hans Urs von Balthasar, *Two Sisters in the Spirit: Thérèse of Lisieux and Elizabeth of the Trinity* (San Francisco: Ignatius, 1998), p. 233.

78. Gabriel Marcel, *Being and Having: An Existential Diary* (New York: Harper & Row, 1965), pp. 213–36.

79. Stefan Hartmann, 'Peter Wust: Ein offensive Bekennender', *Die Tagespost*, Montag 13 April 2020.

cultivation that modern pedagogics could devise, however ingenious, could produce'.⁸⁰ Piety, which is one of the seven gifts of the Holy Spirit, protects the soul from pride, and the Thérèsian spirituality of childlike trust in Divine Providence is built upon this particular gift. In contrast to both the German Idealists and Nietzsche, Wust wrote that 'we are only entrusted to ourselves as works of art from the studio of an eternal master. We are not our own masterpieces.'⁸¹ All of this is completely consistent with Haecker's affirmation of the piety of Virgil and other spiritual dispositions of childhood. As Werner Becker remarked in his essay on Haecker's path from Kierkegaard to Newman, 'the German "*Frömmigkeit*" [piety] needs to be supplemented by the Roman *pietas*'.⁸²

In conclusion and summary, Eugen Blessing, one of the most notable of Haecker's German biographers, described the core of Haecker's philosophy as 'a thinking from above, not from below, from the whole to the part, from being and not from becoming'.⁸³ Blessing also suggested that Haecker's *Was ist der Mensch?* together with his *Vergil: Vater des Abandlandes* and *Schöpfer und Schöpfung* laid the foundations of a *Summa* of Christian philosophy for Haecker.⁸⁴ They are his principal works of Catholic theology and philosophy. Blessing described the book on Virgil as 'the deepest, most beautiful and most perfect among them', *Schöpfer und Schöpfung* as the heartiest, and *Was ist der Mensch?* as the 'most victorious, radiant, almost prophetic and groundbreaking'.⁸⁵ Speaking of the central message of *Schöpfer und Schöpfung*, Blessing concluded that Haecker's point was that 'the yes of love is the leap from the darkness of entanglement into the transcendent light of incomprehensible Providence and thus, [pace Nietzsche et al.] there is no Christian tragedy'.⁸⁶

---

80. Peter Wust, *Crisis in the West* (London: Sheed and Ward, 1931), p. 64.

81. Peter Wust, *Naivität und Pietät* (Munster: Verlag Regensberg Münster, 1964), p. 222.

82. Werner Becker, 'Der Überschritt von Kierkegaard zu Newman in der Lebensentscheidung Theodors Haeckers', *Newman Studien: Erste Folge* (1948), pp. 251–71.

83. Eugen Blessing, 'Theodor Haecker – Philosopher', *Philosophy Today* 1 (3) (Fall, 1957), pp. 186–94 at 188.

84. Ibid., p. 190.

85. Eugen Blessing, *Theodor Haecker: Gestalt und Werk* (Nürnberg: Glock und Lutz, 1959), p. 89.

86. Ibid., p. 125.

2. Theodor Haecker 65

Consistent with Blessing's judgment about a *Summa* of Christian philosophy, Erich Przywara praised Haecker for offering a synthesis of speculative philosophy with existential philosophy and theology. For Haecker 'the primacy of truth (in speculative philosophy) and experienced knowledge … of the existence of God (as a mode of Existential Philosophy) ultimately point to the unity of truth in the *Logos Christus* as the 'existential truth in the absolute sense'.[87] This is another way of saying, as Blessing emphasized, that Haecker was interested in an explicitly Christian anthropology. In his *Humanitas*, Przywara also concluded that Haecker's '*Wir sind Hierarchisten*' maxim represented an affirmation of his own account of the *analogia entis*.[88]

From a literary perspective, Helena M. Tomko has described Haecker's *Virgil* as a 'landmark of Weimar Catholic cultural criticism' whose influence went well beyond Germany when it was translated into English (1934), French (1935), Italian (1935), Dutch (1942) and Spanish (1945).[89] From a theological perspective, she suggests that he offered 'a Trinitarian anthropology of inner exile: a sustained study of human personhood in relation to intellect, will and feeling and how these "inner" powers of the soul can succumb to political and cultural manipulation'.[90] His own inner exile, she concluded, was an inner retreat in metaphor only.[91]

Finally, the writer and literary critic Albert von Schirnding concurs with Tomko that this inner retreat was in metaphor only. He described Haecker's *Journal in the Night* as 'a symbol of the intellectual resistance between 1933 and 1945'. Schirnding also compared Haecker to a modern St George:

> In Haecker's anti-*Kulturkampf* perspective, [the *Kulturkampf* being Otto von Bismarck's cultural war against Catholic Germany in the

87. Erich Przywara, *Humanitas: Der Mensch gestern und Morgen* (Nürnberg: Glock und Lutz, 1952), p. 771.

88. Ibid.

89. Helena M Tomko, 'Word Creatures: Theodor Haecker and Walter Benjamin between Geschwätz and Pure Language in the late Weimar Republic', *New German Critique 133* 45 (1) (February 2018), pp. 23–47 at p. 28.

90. H. M. Tomko, 'On Dark Nights in Dark Times: Catholic Inner Exile Writing in Hitler's Germany', *Logos: A Journal of Catholic Culture* 22 (3) (Summer, 2019), pp. 42–69 at 53.

91. Ibid., p. 58.

years 1872–1878] two antipodal forms of the time pull together to the point of confusion: nationalism and liberalism. The fight of this Saint George goes back to the 19th century, the dragon from which both heads have sprung. In Berlin, where Haecker studied before moving to Munich in 1905, he entered the cave of the dragon, the breeding ground for this inheritance ... Haecker took over from Kierkegaard the contempt for the 'public' as the abstract power of modernity, the hatred for non-binding aestheticism and free-floating intelligence, for a diversity of opinion and a tolerance that arose from the exhaustion of the search for truth.[92]

The need for Christian chivalry, for a knightly opposition to the banality of evil and the prejudices of the mob, is also a central theme in the publications of another Theodor – Theodor Steinbüchel – the subject of the next chapter.

---

92. Albert von Schirnding, 'Schreiben in der Nacht: Theodor Haecker in einer Marbacher Kabinett-Ausstellung', *Donnerstag*, 8 Juni 1989.

Chapter 3

THEODOR STEINBÜCHEL
(1888-1949)

We are still in the middle of the process of mental accounting with the German Enlightenment.[1]

Theodor Martin Wilhelm Steinbüchel was born in Cologne in 1888 and grew up in the parish of the great cathedral. His education took place at the Marzellen Gymnasium, formerly the famous 'Tricoronatum' (College of the Three Crowns), so named after the magi (Kasper, Balthazar and Melchior) who worshipped the Christ child in Bethlehem and whose relics are part of the treasury of the Cologne cathedral. The school was founded in 1450 and is one of the oldest in Germany. This background makes Steinbüchel a Rhinelander, not a Bavarian, but he was to become professor of moral theology at the Ludwig-Maximilians-Universität in Munich.

His own tertiary education took place at the Universities of Strasbourg and Bonn. The University of Strasbourg is the alma mater of Prince Klemens von Metternich, Johann Wolfgang von Goethe, Robert Schumann the political theorist, Louis Pasteur the microbiologist, Max Weber the social historian and Georg Simmel the sociologist. The University of Bonn counts among its alumni Prince Albert, the Consort of Queen Victoria, Friedrich Nietzsche, Karl Marx, Heinrich Heine, Konrad Adenauer (chancellor of West Germany from 1949 to 1963) and the social theorist, Jürgen Habermas. Steinbüchel completed his doctorate in philosophy in Strasbourg in 1911 with a dissertation on the Thomistic understanding of purpose,

---

1. T. Steinbüchel, *Zerfall des Christlichen Ethos im XIX. Jahrhundert* (Frankfurt am Main: Verlag Josef Knect, 1951), p. 21.

and was then ordained a priest in 1913. Throughout the years of the First World War, he served as a chaplain in Düsseldorf. In 1920 he completed his theology doctorate under the supervision of Fritz Tillmann at the University of Bonn on the subject of socialism as a moral idea, and this was followed in 1922 by his *Habilitationsschrift* on the relation between economics and moral values. In 1924 he took up the position of lecturer for Catholic *Weltanschauung* at the Johann Wolfgang Goethe University in Frankfurt am Main, and two years later he was appointed professor of philosophy at the University of Gießen. From 1935 until 1939 he was the professor of moral theology at the Ludwig-Maximilians-Universität in Munich. This position came to an end when the National Socialists forced the closure of his faculty. From 1941 until his early death in 1949 he was professor of moral theology at the Eberhard Karls University in Tübingen, where he was also rector from 1946 to 1948.

When in Munich he supervised the doctoral dissertation of Alfred Läpple who went on to become young Joseph Ratzinger's prefect of studies when Ratzinger was a seminarian. In the book *Milestones: Memoirs 1927–1977* Ratzinger praised Steinbüchel's studies on the philosophical foundations of moral theology as well as his book *Der Umbruch des Denkens: Die Frage nach der christlichen Existenz, erläutert an Ferdinand Ebners Menschdeutung* (*The Upheaval of Thought: The Question of Christian Existence as Explained by Ferdinand Ebner's Interpretation of the Human Person*). Ferdinand Ebner (1882–1931) was an Austrian philosopher and promoter of a Catholic personalism who moved in the *Die Fackel* and *Der Brenner* literary circles. Like Haecker, Ebner was influenced by the proto-existentialism of Søren Kierkegaard. Steinbüchel is widely credited with opening Ratzinger's horizons to the importance of personalist philosophy. He was indeed at the forefront of this movement among German theologians.[2] While the concept of the person had long been in use in theological parlance, its application had tended to be restricted to discussions about the Persons of the

---

2. E. Gaál de, *The Theology of Pope Benedict XVI: The Christocentric Shift* (New York: Palgrave Macmillan, 2010), p. 25; A. Proniewski, 'Joseph Ratzinger's Philosophical Theology of the Person', *Rocznik Teologii Katolickiej* XVII (3) (2018), pp. 219–36; J. Vallery, 'The Salvation of the Cosmos: Benedict XVI's Eschatology and Its Relevance for the Current Ecological Crisis', doctoral dissertation, Duquesne University, 2017; B. T. Oftestad, *The Catholic Church and Liberal Democracy* (London: Routledge, 2018).

Trinity. With the emergence of the personalist movement in early-twentieth-century philosophy, the value of its concerns for theological anthropology came to be recognized.

As Rector of the University of Tübingen in 1947, then in the French zone of occupation, Steinbüchel gave an address to the students of the University that had the tone of a paternal fire-side chat. He spoke about the lack of 'real values' and noted that if there is no truth, there can be no untruth either, no lie, and without truth and untruth 'the human being loses all dignity and all authenticity'.[3] He also spoke about the 'de-personalisation of existence', the 'decline to the mass and the reversal of all values in and through it'.[4] This in turn meant that not only were dignity and authenticity lost but the possibility of self-transcendence as well. People allow themselves to be distracted 'imperceptibly to death'.[5] He concluded that it was the 'real connoisseurs of the human heart, Pascal and Nietzsche, Kierkegaard and Newman, who broke open the abyss of human individuality'.[6] They understood that man is lonely, alone with himself, and that no one is alike in the depths of their spirit.

Steinbüchel's most sustained engagement with Nietzsche's thinking is summed up in a monograph published in 1946 titled *Friedrich Nietzsche. Eine christliche Besinnung* (*A Christian Reflection on Nietzsche*). He developed the argument that Nietzsche was a highly powerful opponent of Christianity, not primarily because of his attacks on Christian morality but more significantly because of his attempt to offer an alternative theological anthropology. Nietzsche not only went to war against God, reason and Christian morality. He understood that in order to dismiss the old Christian understandings of human life, he had to overcome them with a new vision of a higher humanity. Steinbüchel therefore described Nietzsche as 'one of the few opponents of Christianity who does not fight it by an enlightened shaving', or paring away.[7] For him, Nietzsche was not 'Voltaire and his many smaller followers'; he did not attempt to create an Enlightened Christianity by shaving the Christian world view of its deepest mythological components.[8] He understood

---

3. Theodor Steinbüchel, *Der Mensch Heute* (Stuttgart: Verlag von Ernst Klett, 1947), p. 8.
4. Ibid.
5. Ibid.
6. Ibid., p. 10.
7. Theodor Steinbüchel, *Friedrich Nietzsche: Eine christliche Besinnung* (Stuttgart: Deutsche Verlags-Anstalt, 1946), p. 21.
8. Ibid.

that 'the intellect is rooted in much deeper layers of the soul than the mere desire to know', and 'this is why his criticism of Christianity stands at a much higher level than that of the eighteenth century and the flat materialism of his own time'.[9] From the very beginning, Nietzsche set *mythos* above *logos*.

Nietzsche is quite explicit about wishing to replace the kerygma of Christianity with the mythology of the Greek gods Dionysius and Apollo. In Nietzsche's works Christ stands opposed to these pagan gods. This, for Steinbüchel, is the real issue. It was all part of Nietzsche's overriding concern about what it is to be human. What he thinks about morality, the masses, the state, the will to power or the eternal return is, for Steinbüchel, a mere sideshow. Therefore, just as Nietzsche had argued that attacks on Christianity would fall wide of their mark until they focused on assaulting Christian morality, Steinbüchel advised Christians that their defence of Christianity against the Nietzschean arrows would be weak if they allowed themselves to become bogged down in a war over moral norms, seeking to defend this or that Christian moral principle against some alternative neopagan practice, when the fundamental ground on which they should choose to fight is that of theological anthropology. This is the foundation stone of Christian morality, for once it is overturned, the entire Christian culture with all its practices, moral, liturgical and otherwise, will collapse in a pile of rubble on every side. As Steinbüchel argued in his book *Mensch und Gott* on the mysticism of Meister Eckehart:

> 'People', says Meister Eckehart, 'shouldn't think too much about what they should do, they should consider what they are.' 'If you are fair, then your works are fair too. Do not think to base holiness on actions; holiness should be based on being.' That is the great principle of Catholic morality. Catholic ethics is never a matter of pure norms – a pure doctrine of oughts. Catholic ethics bases norm and ought in being. And where it no longer did, as in the nominalism of the late Middle Ages, there came the arbitrary god, who no longer knew how to be bound to his being and essence, nor to his creation and order … the god Luther with all Christian right discarded.[10]

---

9. Ibid.

10. Theodor Steinbüchel, *Mensch und Gott: In Frömmigkeit und Ethos der Deutschen Mystik* (Düsseldorf: Patmos-Verlag, 1952), p. 248.

3. Theodor Steinbüchel

In other words, Luther was right to go to war against the God of nominalism whose moral exhortations and prohibitions appeared arbitrary and tyrannical when detached from being itself.

Accordingly, Steinbüchel was of the view that the Christian contest with Nietzsche should be over the meaning of the *humanum*, over human nature and its being, not in the first instance a battle over morality. Morality, while important, is a secondary consideration flowing from and following upon the primary issue of what it is to be human.

Notwithstanding Nietzsche's rejection of Christianity and his proposal of an alternative neopagan anthropology, Steinbüchel argued that Nietzsche was justified in his dissatisfaction with the state of humanity in the nineteenth century. He gave credit to Nietzsche for being the great exponent of the anthropological crisis within Western culture:

> Nietzsche calls people back to the authenticity of their own self-existence. He was the first to recognise the danger of the denial of the self, a danger to the humanity of mankind that today has become acute. The escape from the self and the numbness of the self through the dispersion and the loss of the self in the crowd and its 'apparatus' stands in opposition to Nietzsche who is a serious advocate, not to be ignored, for the rescue of the human self and personhood from the crisis.[11]

Steinbüchel thereby affirmed the Nietzschean concern for what Guardini was to call 'mass man' – people who fail to use the faculties of their souls to make value judgements and to develop their characters, who play the passive role of producers and consumers, prostrate before the gods of the market and of state bureaucracies – today, we might add, prostrate before the purveyors of media driven pop culture and the cult of the celebrity with a multitude of Instagram followers. Nietzsche was appalled by the kind of social trends that trivialize life with cheap entertainments and mute the uniqueness of each and every human person, practices which fall into the category of what French sociologists call *divertissement*. The American sociological expression 'Disneyfication' carries a similar connotation. In both cases people are mesmerized by the modern analogue of the ancient bread and circuses and kept permanently

---

11. Steinbüchel, *Friedrich Nietzsche: Eine christliche Besinnung*, pp. 6–7.

distracted from the task of developing their humanity.[12] Steinbüchel believed that Nietzsche's criticism of 'mass man' was valid – such a person's humanity is indeed impoverished – but he strongly disagreed with Nietzsche that it is humanity's belief in the Christian God that has led to this impoverishment and depersonalization. This charge, expressed by Nietzsche in the phrase 'Christianity is a crime against life itself', is, Steinbüchel noted, 'probably the most serious charge ever hurled against Christianity.'[13] He observed:

> Christianity has always considered itself to be the champion and preserver of the depth and authenticity of human existence, because in the creation of the human being by the personal God and in his determination for personal life with him, Christianity represented the personhood of man as one of its most elementary announcements and demands. In the encounter between the accused and the accuser, the Christian with the antichrist, the question [therefore] arises as to whether the accusation is well grounded and justified. Is the transcendence of God a danger to the immanent becoming of the human person, or is the relation of the human person to the transcendent God the guarantee for the real and full development of the personality of the human self and being?[14]

Steinbüchel concluded that Nietzsche's assertion that 'God is dead' is much more than a proclamation of philosophical atheism. It is more acutely a clear commitment to man alone and to the realities and possibilities that lie in this world alone – 'Nietzsche throws humanity back to its essential finiteness and exclusive worldliness':

> Nietzsche sets his new image of the world and man against the Western world view shaped by Attic Greece and decisively by

---

12. The expression 'bread and circuses' comes from Juvenal: ... *iam pridem, ex quo suffragia nulli/uendimus, effudit curas; nam qui debat olim/imperium, fasces, legions, omnia, nunc se/continent atque duas tantum res anxius optat/ panem et circenses*. In English: 'Already long ago, from when we sold our vote to no man, the People have abdicated our duties; for the People who once upon a time handed out military command, high civil office, legions – everything, now restrains itself and anxiously hopes for just two things: bread and circuses.'

13. Steinbüchel, *Friedrich Nietzsche: Eine christliche Besinnung*, p. 7.

14. Ibid.

Christianity, which is therefore just as much a counter-image against that of the Greek Socrates as against the Christian concept of a meaningful world. For Nietzsche, the world is no longer a universe, a space full of meaning. Nietzsche wants to smash the world as this space, to destroy the wonder before this space, to reveal the logic underlying what the world had previously thought to be a meaningful existence, because he knows that ... an orderly world cannot do without belief in divine reason, however one may conceptually grasp it.[15]

Nonetheless, Steinbüchel argued that it was fair for Nietzsche to go to war against a certain interpretation of Christianity. This he described as a 'bourgeois Christianity'. His description of the person caught up in this version of Christianity sounds rather like what Joseph Ratzinger was later to more precisely call a 'bourgeois Pelagianism'. Here the use of the adjective *bourgeois* is not to be taken literally as a member of the middle class. Rather it is a sociological expression meaning to have certain sensibilities that are often associated with middle-class people, like a strong desire for comfort and security. Among European scholars of the first half of the twentieth century, there was the tendency to associate a strong interest in moral codes with bourgeois Christianity. Steinbüchel is quite typical in this regard, and he argues that it is precisely bourgeois Christianity that Nietzsche found abhorrent:

> According to Nietzsche, the only thing Christianity knows is that it should be moral. Like all decadent culture it dissolves religion into morality. It no longer knows the being of God's port of being, human existence from the primal bases and depths of life. Nietzsche sees in this presence only the falsified Christianity of bourgeois enlightenment with its conventional morality of decency and correctness and above all a decision-averse tolerance. And this supposedly Christian image of man corresponds to the Christian image of God. According to Nietzsche, this god is only the protector of civil peace and security for Christian consciousness ... The man of this bourgeois world wants security in life, and God should protect it – that is the all of Christianity.[16]

15. Ibid., pp. 13–14.
16. Ibid., p. 21.

Rhetorically, Steinbüchel asked, 'If this really is Christianity, its God, its world, and its human image, then it really has, as Nietzsche says, entered upon its "euthanasia". Nietzsche can quite rightly believe in the "deathbed of Christianity". But is this Christianity?'[17]

Steinbüchel replied to his own question with the statement that this is not genuine Christianity but merely genuine Christianity's dilution by modern secularization, or what he called its 'dissolution into profane categories following the declaration of the autonomy of human reason from revelation'.[18] He further argued that it is only from revelation that the revealing God can be heard by man:

> In New Testament terms, it is the translation of God-given *Pneuma* by the human spirit … In this mystery God intervenes not only in the sphere of ethical generation, but also in the being of man through his being given life by *Pneuma*, the Holy Spirit, in faith and in the new and different life that man receives through and in God's grace. The divine gift of grace changes the being of man through the new creation of participation in the eternal life of God himself. And only from the new being can the new attitude, the Christian ethos, arise and should it arise. The moralistic flattening and emptying out of Christianity, which Nietzsche knows and which really drives his criticism with full force, is not the true Christianity of real Christian belief.[19]

Moreover, Steinbüchel noted that the 'trivialized God' who exists simply to fulfil human desires is *not* the God of Christianity, while the demonic dimension that is so strong in the thought of Nietzsche can actually be found in authentic Christianity. Far from being an insipid psychotherapy for the weak, Christianity recognizes that at the heart of the world and within every human heart there is a cosmic battle between the demonic desire for power and the divine commandment to love. Without mentioning any particular scholars or poets Steinbüchel concluded that at the beginning of the nineteenth century, 'German Romanticism saw the demonic in the world much more deeply than Nietzsche, and took it much more seriously than the optimistic Enlightenment and its bureaucratic, de-demonised Christianity, which

---

17. Ibid., p. 22.
18. Ibid.
19. Ibid., pp. 22–3.

is why it was much closer to real Christianity than Nietzsche was at the end of the century'.[20]

Thus Steinbüchel's argument was that Nietzsche had mistaken a 'bureaucratic, de-demonised Christianity' for the real thing and that it is fair and reasonable that this particular mutant version of Christianity be on its deathbed. By 'de-demonised' he meant a Christianity that has had all the spiritual warfare leeched out of it. The dimension of the Christian opposition to the demonic had been removed. As C. S. Lewis explained in his famous *Screwtape Letters*, the devil finds it very useful to get people to believe that he does not actually exist. A 'de-demonised Christianity' is therefore a belief system that has some Christian elements but not the idea that human beings have been born into a cosmic battle. What the 'bureaucratic, de-demonised Christianity' with its god of psychological comfort and the affirmation of human decency misses is precisely the whole field of sacramentality and deification and spiritual contest against the powers of evil. To put the matter differently, what this sort of 'bureaucratic, de-demonised Christianity' occludes is an understanding that Christianity is about a participation of the human person in the life of the Trinity and the fruits of the Tree of Life rather than those of the Tree of Knowledge of Good and Evil. Far from being *bourgeois* this sacramental understanding of Christianity is what sociologists call 'erotic' and/or 'aristocratic', meaning here a passionate quest for the most excellent. There is a 'democratic' element in Catholic theological anthropology in that the call to sanctification is for all alike, but this, so far from creating a 'mass man' or a depersonalized being, or, to use Nietzsche's idiom, a member of the herd, is nothing less than an approach to the self or soul formation that makes a person a member of a royal priesthood, participating in the divine life itself. Steinbüchel expressed the idea in the following terms:

> Nietzsche had so little understood the depth of the Christian conception of God, and the depth of the Christian understanding of man! Sin and redemption are part of it, but beyond this point he hardly touched a Christian humanity. Nietzsche understood sin only in moral terms, and of course it was not too difficult to interpret guilt as merely a psychological burden for a weak person slavishly genuflecting to an illusory God. But, one may say, the meta-cosmic *depth* of sin, the world tragedy of the demonic uprising against the

20. Ibid., p. 23.

Lord of the world, and the world drama of the demons wrestling with the redeemed world, the lowering or self-emptying (*kenosis*) of the Son of God to the form of a servant, the satanic snatching at divinity and equalizing the creature with God, this mystery of the struggle against God with the exaltation to God on the part of the creature detaching itself from its creator and deifying itself – Nietzsche never saw it.[21]

Steinbüchel used the Latin expressions *mysterium caritatis* and *mysterium iniquitatis* (2 Thess. 2:7) – the secret or mystery of God's love working in the world and the secret or mystery of sin working against God's love – to describe the forces at play in the cosmic battle. The demonic realities arrayed on the one side were identified by St Paul in his *Letter to the Ephesians* 6.12. St Paul warned the Ephesians that they were *not wrestling against mere flesh and blood, but against principalities, against powers, against the rulers of the darkness of this world, against spiritual wickedness in high places*. Bourgeois Christianity may politely elide such passages as inconvenient, embarrassing or backward, obsolete thinking, but Steinbüchel clearly regarded this dimension of Christian faith as something both real and central to the Christian experience of life and he thought that Nietzsche had never really engaged with this dimension in Christian theology. He concluded:

> You have to bring up this depth of the Christian mystery as an event of salvation if you really want to counter the seriousness of Nietzsche's attack on Christianity, and not insist on the much easier criticism of Nietzsche's ethical misappropriations of Christianity. Anyone who, like Nietzsche, condemns the mythology of Christianity can only be answered with reference to the Mystery of Christianity.
>
> But then the level of moral evaluation can and must be undertaken. Then we shall certainly hear of the mystery of the man sanctified in the redemption, of his being redeemed to be new, of the person born again from God's *Pneuma* emerging in a moral act of freedom, carried and lived by the grace of redemption, the Christian *Ethos*, human accomplishment before God and for Him and for and in His strength.[22]

21. Ibid., p. 25.
22. Ibid., p. 26.

In the final analysis, Steinbüchel described the Christian confrontation with Nietzsche as 'God's call to the Christian himself, a wake-up call from within his conscience' to preserve through his Christian life, 'a deeper, higher and more genuine humanity'.[23]

In a 1947 monograph titled *Dostojewski: Sein Bild vom Menschen und vom Christen*, Steinbüchel not only offered an account of Dostoyevsky's theological anthropology but also devoted considerable space, especially in the first chapter, to a comparison of Nietzsche and Dostoyevsky. Nietzsche worshiped Dostoyevsky as the psychologist of the subterranean in man's consciousness, the only Christian from whom he 'had something to learn', yet Steinbüchel identified Dostoyevsky's *Menschenbild* as occupying an antipodal position from that of Nietzsche.[24] Even if Nietzsche was able to appropriate Dostoyevsky's insights into the darker side of the human soul for his own Dionysian *Menschenbild*, Steinbüchel thought Nietzsche read Dostoyevsky on a level of 'metaphysical myopia and religious blindness'.[25] Steinbüchel believed that Dostoyevsky had a far better understanding of the darker side of humanity than Nietzsche, that he could 'paint it more colorfully than Nietzsche' and that he saw it from a completely different perspective and discovered completely different possibilities in it.[26] Dostoyevsky depicted characters who can either capitulate to the devil or run to God, 'who can walk either way in their freedom: the way to their annihilation as a human being, and also the way to the realisation of their humanity, which is kindled and ignited by God'.[27] For Dostoyevsky, the realization of a true humanity requires the recognition of God-given limits. The Nietzschean exaltation of the human being to the superhuman is demonic, 'because *humanitas* only exists in relation to the really superhumanity of God'.[28] Dostoevsky therefore exalted precisely the type of person Nietzsche hated: the man who from a Christian perspective is poor and needy, steeped in sin and guilt but who finds redemption in and through God. Steinbüchel was of the view that 'the most peculiar and the most Christian thing

23. Ibid., p. 41.
24. Theodor Steinbüchel, *Dostojewski: Sein Bild vom Menschen und vom Christen* (Düsseldorf: Verlag L. Schwann, 1947), p. 27.
25. Ibid., p. 28.
26. Ibid., p. 29.
27. Ibid.
28. Ibid.

in Dostoevsky is that he gives the guilty man, whom he has portrayed in so many forms, hope for a deeper humanity, which is at the same time more than pure humanity: the hope for a new humanity because of God-redeemed and God-filled *Humanitas*'.[29] Steinbüchel concluded that Dostoevsky's humanism was neither the enlightened humanism of Germany's eighteenth century nor the demonic humanism of Nietzsche's nineteenth century, but the 'fallen-uplifted, the guilty-redeemed man of his eastern Christian belief'.[30] In summary:

> Dostoevsky's realism looks at real people, and people are real people when they are threatened by the demonic powers in themselves ... Man is the scene on which meta-cosmic powers wrestle with each other: God and the not-God. But man himself takes part in the victory of God and the Devil, in calling on his own freedom to make his own decision. Once again, there is a difference between the Christian Dostoevsky, and Nietzsche, the counter-Christian anthropologist, with whom the depth of Christianity's emphasis in secularized-Christian moralism, has been dropped ... Despite all his knowledge of the chaotic, or better, the chaos caused by the sin in man, Dostoyevsky did not represent an absolute anti-humanism, he still saw a god-like image in the fallen human creature. This anthropology connects him to the Catholic theology of the West.[31]

Steinbüchel's interest in Nietzsche and Dostoyevsky flowed over into an openness to currents of early-twentieth-century existentialism which he also interpreted as a reaction against bourgeois cultural sensibilities and mental attitudes and in particular, against the philosophy of German Idealism. He described existentialism as 'a reaction to the collapse of the Idealist way of life and philosophy', especially following the experiences of the First World War, and he endorsed Peter Wust's description of early-twentieth-century Europeans as a type of *insecuritas humana*. Steinbüchel identified Kierkegaard, Nietzsche, Marx and Dostoevsky as members of an unconscious alliance against Idealist philosophy, although in the case of Marx he regarded his position as ambivalent – in some ways strongly anti-Idealist, in other ways, still latently Idealist.

29. Ibid., pp. 30–1.
30. Ibid., pp. 31.
31. Ibid., pp. 32–3.

3. Theodor Steinbüchel

Steinbüchel also identified Kierkegaard and Nietzsche as the twin precursors to twentieth-century existentialism. They are like a pair of eagles, united around a similar cluster of concerns, but with their beaks pointing in totally different directions – one in the direction of human self-transcendence before God, the other in the direction of human self-exaltation after the death of God.

In his monograph *Existenzialismus und christliches Ethos*, published in 1948, Steinbüchel juxtaposed the Christian ethos formed out of conceptions of the self and the nature of historicity, with that of the ethos of the existentialist philosophers, principally from Kierkegaard and Nietzsche through to Martin Heidegger, Karl Jaspers, Jean-Paul Sartre and Albert Camus. In this work he wrote of existentialism facing two foundational questions: what is its stance towards Christianity and what is its stance towards Marxism? Noting the judgment of Albert Camus that in the 1940s French people were divided by their allegiance to three different prophets – Marx, Jean-Paul Sartre and Christ, in that order – Steinbüchel offered an analysis of the choices at play in this three-cornered cultural battle.

A direct engagement between existentialism and Marxism took place at the 1946 Philosopher's Congress in Geneva in the discussion between Karl Jaspers representing existentialism and György Lukács representing Marxism. Jaspers argued that the dualisms of 'I and society, state and humanity, progress and conservation … cannot be resolved dialectically' as Marx's conception of history, following that of Hegel's, holds.[32] Steinbüchel concurred with Jaspers that the balancing of these polarities ought not to take the form of the collapse of personal freedom into that of the collective: 'Before the personal God the freedom of the personal person stands, before the non-personal collective it sinks'.[33] Steinbüchel also considered Jean-Paul Sartre, 'despite his secularism and his atheism' was closer to the Christian ethos than to the Marxist precisely because of his commitment to human freedom.[34] In another work, *Europa als Verbundenheit im Geist*, Steinbüchel noted that while Christians agree with Marxists in rejecting the dehumanizing and depersonalizing elements of capitalist economic practices, Christian

---

32. Theodor Steinbüchel, *Existenzialismus und christliches Ethos* (Bonn: Verlag des Borromäus-Vereins, 1948), p. 41.
33. Ibid.
34. Ibid., p. 42.

personalism nonetheless 'fears the same de-personalisation on the part of Marxism as on the part of capitalism'.³⁵

In his reflections on the Christian ethos, Steinbüchel was critical of quietist interpretations of Christianity, especially the idea that Christianity favours withdrawal from the world. On the contrary he asserted that 'responsibility for the hour, attachment to the reality of the historical situation, the responsibility to work on the tasks that arise in the world and life is the ethos of both the modern and the old Christian interpretation of existence'.³⁶ He further argued that the Christian belief that 'God alone suffices' cannot lead to a devaluation of creation or to an escape from history because 'man by his creation is a thoroughly historical being, placed between God and death in a certain historical time by God', or, in other words, 'history is grounded in the fact that God created being' and 'the historicity of man is rooted in the fact of his being created and the Creator as his destiny given with it'.³⁷ Moreover, Steinbüchel asserted that 'the biblical religion is not a religion of nature but of history. History only exists because the world moves between God, the founder, and God, the goal of natural events', and 'in this movement man stands as the free being on whom God's claim is made in the historical hour'.³⁸ Since 'the path of the creature to God leads only through creation and the situations of history' it follows that any such 'flight of man from the claims of creation and the historical hour is a flight from God', as well as 'abandonment of his creative and historical being before God'.³⁹ Nonetheless, Steinbüchel also made the point that the Christian belief in God both 'binds man to history and at the same time frees him from it'.⁴⁰ Christianity frees man from history insofar as God's mercy and forgiveness of sin opens to us possibilities for overcoming the burdens of guilt and past failure.

In his final analysis Steinbüchel recognized a strong level of affinity between existentialism and what he called the Christian ethos. The two are connected by their common interest in the self or soul of the

---

35. Theodor Steinbüchel, *Europa als Verbundenheit im Geist* (Tübingen: Verlag von J. C. B. Mohr, 1946), p. 20.
36. Steinbüchel, *Existenzialismus und christliches Ethos*, p. 45.
37. Ibid.
38. Ibid.
39. Ibid.
40. Ibid.

individual and their common resistance to collectivism. He concluded, however, that existential philosophy is only capable of serving personal human existence if it does not fall victim to a 'bottomless nominalism'.[41] He thus warned against any wholesale occlusion of the realm of ontology or considerations of what is universal about human nature. Both universal human nature and the uniqueness of each and every member of the human species need to be held together as poles in tension. Any occlusion of the universal end of the pole leads to the disaster of a bottomless nominalism.

Steinbüchel was to die in 1949, only one year after the publication of *Existenzialismus und christliches Ethos*, but the project of developing a philosophical anthropology that would do justice to both universal human nature – an interest of Greek and Christian ontology – and the existentialist interest in history and culture and the uniqueness of each human person would be taken up by a young Pole named Karol Wojtyła at the Catholic University of Lublin (KUL) in the mid-1950s. So-called Lublin Thomism was the initial result. This approach, taken up in the framework of a Christocentric Trinitarian theology, became part of the wider theological anthropology project of the Wojtyła pontificate and its flagship theme of the nuptial mystery. Steinbüchel's focus on a personalist anthropology and on the task of building bridges between this philosophy and moral theology and his insistence on holding the ontological and historical dimensions of the human person together in any theological anthropology were also to become hallmarks of the theology of Joseph Ratzinger. It could be argued that Wojtyła and Ratzinger shared the same anthropological vision, although the former came to this vision by fusing elements of Thomism with elements of French philosophical personalism, while the latter came to it by fusing elements of Augustinian theology with elements of German philosophical personalism. While a doctoral level analysis may uncover shades of difference between them or different accent marks over different elements, the two scholar-pontiffs were nonetheless united in their efforts to develop a theological anthropology that was sufficiently multidimensional to include a place for both ontology and history, for universal human nature and the uniqueness of each person as an individual creature in a particular place in history, born into a particular family with his or her own unique networks of friends, and hence 'existential issues'.

41. Ibid., p. 49.

In his *Europa als Verbundenheit im Geist*, published a year after the end of the Second World War in 1946, Steinbüchel associated the existentialist movement in the first half of the twentieth century with a 'strong sense of crisis awareness' among scholars across the countries of Europe and the UK.[42] He made specific reference to the 'crisis theology' of Karl Barth, to Karl Jasper's concerns over the failure in transcendence, to Heidegger's notion of the human person as a being unto death, to the writings of the Belgian philosopher Alphonse de Waelhens (1911–1981), a leading European commentator on the thought of Heidegger and Husserl, to the voices of Miguel de Unamuno (1864–1936) and José Ortega y Gasset (1883–1955) from Spain. Unamuno, he noted, not only wrote *La agonía del cristianismo* (*The Agony of Christianity*, 1931) but also related the entire contemporary culture to this agony, while Ortega y Gasset analysed the nature of the crisis both phenomenologically and historically. Dutch cultural historian Johan Huizinga (1872–1945) offered an analysis similar to Ortega y Gasset, and England's Christopher Dawson (1889–1970) linked the process of secularization and the flattening of the human person by the machine to a 'tremor within western cultural unity'. In France, the poet Paul Valéry (1871–1945) and the philosopher Jacques Maritain (1882–1973) reached the same conclusion from different starting points, that western culture was in a state of profound crisis.[43]

Steinbüchel surveyed several 'crisis' assessments from scholars across Europe and the UK, and praised particular Catholic scholars for having offered solutions to the crisis. The first on his list was John Henry Newman whom he credited as a concrete thinker who had anticipated the crisis. The theology of Newman was directed to the 'concrete, believing man'. His was not a 'person-less kind of thinking', said Steinbüchel, but the thinking of a 'seeing, looking and acting person' – with a 'living conscience'.[44] He also praised the Frenchmen Henri Brémond (1865–1933) and Maurice Blondel (1861–1949), mentioning specifically Brémond's presentation of a *christiana humanitas* in the first volume of his *Histoire littéraire du sentiment religieux en France*. He noted that Brémond's interests 'went far beyond France, to England, to Thomas More and to John Henry Newman', and that his work 'spans educated Europe'.[45] Blondel is well known as the French lay philosopher who

---

42. Steinbüchel, *Europa als Verbundenheit im Geist*, p. 13.
43. Ibid., pp. 13–14.
44. Ibid., p. 26.
45. Ibid., pp. 22–3.

coined the expression 'extrinsicism' to describe certain deconstructions in neo-scholastic philosophy of what he thought were elements that needed to be related to one another rather than kept in different conceptual compartments. Blondel's philosophy strongly influenced the theologian Henri de Lubac. Steinbüchel praised Blondel as 'one of the rare true metaphysicians in Europe, the founder of an ontological and ethical personalism that affects us Germans particularly because of its references to our existential philosophy and our own ontology of the person'.[46] He nonetheless observed that 'Blondel is quite independent in relation to both of them, and his consciously *Christian* thinking also sets him apart from them in philosophical terms'.[47] In particular he regarded Blondel as having surpassed Hegel in attempting a unification of the general and the particular in anthropology since for Hegel 'the individual remained a mere emanation of the general being', a conclusion not tolerated by Blondel's theistic personalism. For Blondel, 'every human being remains a secret in depth because of his uniqueness and incomparability, despite the generality recognizable in his metaphysical nature'.[48]

Another of Steinbüchel's publications, *Zerfall des Christlichen Ethos im XIX. Jahrhundert*, published posthumously in 1951, traced the crisis back to the eighteenth century with the move towards the 'deeply unhistorical' rationalization and mechanization of all areas of life and its implementation by the aspirational urban bourgeoisie. The kind of religion promoted by the *philosophes* of the eighteenth century was one that sought to find a common moral code across all the religious traditions based upon a rationality disconnected from all traditions. Steinbüchel called the eighteenth century's religion within the boundaries of reason alone a 'new Pelagianism' and a kind of philanthropy. With it the mystery of the Cross vanished, and the idea prevailed instead that mystery, cult and ethos must be adapted to the people, with the result that the *regnum dei* became the *regnum hominis*.

Accompanying this 'new Pelagianism' was a new approach to revelation in which God reveals himself in human experience. Steinbüchel observed that a religion based on such a subjective account of revelation can no longer be the authoritative religion of traditional Christianity in which God's word stands above the human person. Such

46. Ibid., pp. 23-4.
47. Ibid., p. 24.
48. Ibid.

a subjective understanding makes religion 'very humanised and very impoverished, very devoid of its historical particularity and symbolic wealth'.[49] Nonetheless some account of the subjective reception of revelation was needed, without sinking into the waters of a deep subjectivism and relativism. The two figures of 'the deepest piety and philosophical-theological excellence' who best addressed these issues were, in Steinbüchel's judgment, Kierkegaard and Newman.[50]

By the nineteenth century, 'a rent had passed through time, a protest against all inheritance: against traditional education, against the traditional idea of man and God in the traditional religion, against the dignity and value of the nation'.[51] The 'three large circles of ideas' that had carried the Christian centuries were now in a defensive position.[52] The meaning of existence in general was denied by Schopenhauer, for whom the first sentence of his *The World as Will and Representation* (1818) was 'the world is my representation'. The view of the human person that had developed with reference to Christian revelation understood and articulated with some elements of Greek philosophy had been challenged by Nietzsche, and the concept of the national good and of identification with one's own folk history or what otherwise might be described as patriotism had been called into question by Marx. Thus, Christian metaphysics, theological anthropology and social theory with its debts to the Greeks, Romans and Hebrews was turned on its head. Schopenhauer, Nietzsche and Marx all 'write another freedom on their banner' and 'new gods emerge'.[53]

While *Zerfall des Christlichen Ethos im XIX. Jahrhundert* could be described as Steinbüchel's 'genealogy of modernity' book, another of his publications, *Vom Menschenbild des christlichen Mittelalters* (*On the Anthropology of the Christian Middle Ages*), offers an account of how things were in the pre-modern period before the synthetic tapestry of Jewish, Greek and Christian thought began to fray. This book was initially presented as a lecture to Tübingen students in November 1945 and then published posthumously in 1951. In a captivating manner Steinbüchel commands the attention of his students with the statement,

---

49. Theodor Steinbüchel, *Zerfall des Christlichen Ethos im XIX. Jahrhundert* (Frankfurt am Main: Verlag Josef Knect, 1951), p. 57.
50. Ibid., p. 58.
51. Ibid., p. 18.
52. Ibid.
53. Ibid., p. 32.

'Let us now hasten with large strides to medieval times in order to meet the people who were living in the most believable time of the Christian West, and to recognize their image of God, which always tells us in depth how a human being really understands his existence.'[54] In his foreword to the 1951 publication, Alfons Auer described the lecture as offering a 'rich abundance of concrete details and at the same time a clear overview of the great inner connections of medieval anthropology.'[55] At the beginning of the lecture Steinbüchel explained that his concept of a *Menschenbild* was that of 'a "meaning-image" as a synopsis of the human being and his meaning, of what he is and should be in the world.'[56] He also noted that since there is always in every period of history a gap between idea and reality, at no time does the reality agree with the ideal desired. This was no less true of the medieval period.

In a characterization of the medieval *Menschenbild*, Steinbüchel identified four different approaches to anthropology: (i) symbolic, which he thought was exemplified by the writing of St Hildegard von Bingen, the 'Sybil of the Rhine', who was declared a Doctor of the Church by Benedict XVI, (ii) scholastic, which he associated with the approach of St Thomas Aquinas, (iii) architectural-sculptural (as exemplified in Romanesque and Gothic architecture) and (iv) the knightly or chivalrous, exemplified in the poetry of Wolfram von Eschenbach.[57] Each of these four *Menschenbilden* shared an angle of perspective that it is only in their orientation towards God that men can reach the highest possibilities of their humanity. They also shared the disposition of *Pietät* (piety) understood as reverence for being and its orders, and especially reverence for God, the Creator.

Steinbüchel devoted the lion's share of his exposition to types (iii) and (iv). With respect to type (iii) he explained that medieval art grew out of the spirit of the liturgy, the worship of the community and its mystery. The God of the Romanesque era 'was a king concerned with his creation, the *pantocrator*, the world ruler, whose majesty shone forth from the Cross'. He was 'something very different' from Nietzsche's mistaken idea of the Christian God.[58] With the rise of the medieval

54. Theodor Steinbüchel, *Vom Menschenbild des christlichen Mittelalters* (Darmstadt: Wissenschaftliche Buchgesellschaft, 1951), p. 37.
55. Alfons Auer, foreword to *Vom Menschenbild des christlichen Mittelalters* (Darmstadt: Wissenschaftliche Buchgesellschaft, 1951), p. 6.
56. Steinbüchel, *Vom Menschenbild des christlichen Mittelalters*, p. 7.
57. Ibid., p. 36.
58. Ibid., p. 25.

towns, and hence of what Steinbüchel calls the 'urban-bourgeois culture', 'the era of strictly regulated feudalism and the Romanesque, yields to Gothic as the artistic expression of this new and last era of the Christian Middle Ages'.[59] Although Steinbüchel identified the symbolic *Menschenbild* of St Hildegard as a separate type of anthropology, he nonetheless regarded the symbolic as a constituent element of the scholastic and the architectural-sculptural. Here he noted that 'just as Gothic scholasticism cannot or does not want to deny its reference to symbolism, nor can Gothic art. The arches and towers of the Gothic cathedral point towards the sky, and all heavy structures seem spiritualized into an ethereal immateriality'.[60] Moreover:

> The Gothic building is transparent, full of light, which breaks through the high windows and spreads the colorful carpet of its colors on the holy ground, but in the center here too is the Divine mystery, indicated by the sanctuary lamp that swings in front of the *tabernaculum Dei cum hominibus*; here too the Gothic God of transcendence is in ineffable proximity to his creature.[61]

The fourth type of *Menschenbild*, the knightly or chivalrous, he traces back to the Old Saxon epic *Heliand* composed in the ninth century. The God depicted in *Heliand* was superior to all the old gods, a king reigning in heaven who sends his son to humanity and who, as the creator, blesses the most holy woman, the pure maid, with holy power. The Saxons were not evangelized by philosophical argumentation; instead, they received the Gospel by the replacement of the mythology of the old northern gods with a mythopoetic presentation of Christian revelation. During the Staufer era (the era of the Hohenstaufen dynasty that rose in the Duchy of Swabia in the eleventh century and ruled the Holy Roman Empire until that honour passed to the Houses of Luxemburg and Wittelsbach and ultimately the House of Hapsburg), the God of *Heliand* becomes a courtly God, served by his knights and ladies. Steinbüchel wrote:

> The [Holy Roman] empire is a service of the Grail, and the Grail is the symbol of the highest divine good in the hierarchical order.

59. Ibid., pp. 25–6.
60. Ibid., p. 26.
61. Ibid.

To serve the Grail is the chivalrous sense of the empire – that is the symbolic idea of the emperor. In this sense, imperial mysticism is neither a rational theological idea, nor a political idea of the empire, but the effective symbol of the highest vocation of a person, whom God himself – and God *specifically* – placed at the forefront of the *ordo* of his world, in and through which the agreement of worship and community service, this guiding principle in all the work of medieval people, was to find its realization.[62]

In this work on the medieval *Menschenbild*, Steinbüchel also noted the judgment of Alois Dempf that symbolic thinking about the world and man is a 'pre-scientific metaphysics'. Language, he argued, is the picture, not the concept. Scholasticism, in contrast, thinks conceptually. As a consequence:

> The knightly image of man stands out from the scholastic one. First of all: it does not define and systematize virtues as basic attitudes of man towards himself, towards others, the world and God. It condenses them into a poetic and vivid picture of the chivalrous man … In this image of man, something lives on from the Aristotelian *megalopsychia* (magnanimous man), the self-confident generosity that Thomas Aquinas also included in his table of virtues and values. But it is immersed in the Christian willingness to serve, which is paired with a sense of professional dignity in a strictly ordered community of soul and rank.[63]

Whereas scholastic science focused on the essential nature of the human being, not on the uniqueness of every life with its particular struggles and victories, its defeats and failures, its errors and confusion, its repentance and atonement, all of which can never be encapsulated in a formula, in Wolfram's *Parzival*, composed between 1200 and 1210, the reader is presented with a knightly man struggling with the very personal vicissitudes of life that fate, or maybe Providence, has handed him.[64] The relationship of the knight to his divine king is much more historically situated than the depiction of the divine–human relationship one finds in scholasticism. It does nonetheless presuppose a common

62. Ibid., p. 12.
63. Ibid., pp. 31–2.
64. Ibid., p. 33.

humanity with particular faculties of the soul such are the subject of analysis by the great scholastic authors. Sin is always sin, temptation is already temptation, good and evil are never culturally relative.

Steinbüchel's book *Mensch und Gott*, published a year later in 1952, can be read as a long footnote to *Vom Menschenbuild des christlichen Mittelaters*. This work is focused on the spirituality of Meister Eckehart (c. 1260–c. 1328), a member of the Dominican Order who found himself under investigation by the Inquisition, though he died before any verdict was reached. Attempts have subsequently been made to rehabilitate him, though the response from the Congregation of the Doctrine of the Faith has been that no rehabilitation is necessary since he was never actually condemned. Whatever of this issue, Steinbüchel read Eckehart as a proponent of the chivalrous type of *Menschenbild*: 'Announced in the midst of the emerging city culture of the late Middle Ages, Eckehart's ethos still bears witness to the knightly ethos of the medieval wedding.'[65] This is how the courtly monk Eckehart speaks: 'The good knight does not complain about his wounds when he sees the king, who was wounded with him, offering us a drink that he drank before us, offering us nothing that he had not endured himself beforehand and suffered himself.'[66] Steinbüchel concluded that Eckehart's spirituality is 'a noble ethos that knows how nobility obliges' and 'a final echo of the courtly ethos of the Hohenstaufen knightly culture.'[67]

Reading Steinbüchel in the second decade of the twenty-first century provides students with a cultural history of German Catholicism from the eighteenth to mid-twentieth century with a special focus on theological anthropology. It also offers students an insight into the different forms of medieval Catholic *Menschenbilder*. What is missing are pieces of the 'historical jigsaw' that might explain the demise of 'the courtly ethos of the Hohenstaufen knight culture', and its partial revival in a mutated neopagan form in Nazi Germany. The overarching conclusion of all of Steinbüchel's studies is that the judgement of Kierkegaard and Newman, that bourgeois Christianity with its bureaucratic morality is not genuine Christianity but rather a decadent or even diseased Christianity, is precisely the form of Christianity that was so effectively subjected to ridicule by Nietzsche and to critique by Feuerbach and Marx. This raises

---

65. Theodor Steinbüchel, *Mensch und Gott: In Frömmigkeit und Ethos der Deutschen Mystik* (Düsseldorf: Patmos-Verlag, 1952), p. 237.
66. Ibid., p. 238.
67. Ibid., p. 239.

a serious question about the need for a revival of the heroic and self-sacrificial and thus the chivalrous dimensions of medieval Christianity in our own times. Steinbuchel's works on Christian humanism could well serve as the basis for such a revival. This dimension of Christianity was appropriated by the Nazis who were certainly in favour of heroism and self-sacrifice, but they combined these elements with pagan, and indeed satanic, elements. A second conclusion is that mythopoetic thinking is at least as important as discursive reasoning in the work of evangelization. The perennial popularity of C. S. Lewis and J. R. R. Tolkien would seem to confirm this. Finally, one may conclude this survey of Steinbüchel's publications with the judgment that Christian humanism needs a strong personalist dimension as Ebner, Steinbüchel and then Wojtyła and Ratzinger and numerous others recognized, in the decades that followed the inhumanity of the First World War.

Chapter 4

GOTTLIEB SÖHNGEN
(1892–1971)

The supernatural and natural order do not lie next to each other, but the supernatural order encompasses and also penetrates the natural order.[1]

Clemens Gottlieb Söhngen (known as Gottlieb) was born in Cologne where he, like Steinbüchel, four years his senior, was educated at the Gymnasium that was formerly the Tricoronatum.[2] Emery de Gaál has described Söhngen as a 'lively, joyful, engaging, and extroverted' Rhinelander who was capable of conversing on a wide range of subjects, from the Church Fathers to John Henry Newman as well as the epistemology of Immanuel Kant and Anselm of Canterbury.[3] He was also highly knowledgeable about music and proud of his Rhenish accent and sense of humour.[4] His philosophy doctoral dissertation was written under the supervision of Clemens Baeumker (1852–1924), the historian of philosophy, and completed in 1914. Baeumker's research in literary history and the history of the Platonic, Aristotelian and

---

1. Gottlieb Söhngen, *Der Weg der abendländischen Theologie* (München: Verlag Anton Pustet, 1959), p. 55.
2. Söhngen was known as Gottlieb Söhngen, this name appeared on his publications, but in a biographical essay by Josef Graf, he places the name Clemens in first position before Gottlieb. See Josef Graf, 'Gottlieb Söhngen', in *Kölner Theologen: Von Rupert von Deutz bis Wilhelm Nyssen*, Sebastian Cüppers (ed.) (Köln: Marzellen Verlag, 2004), pp. 454–76 at p. 454.
3. Emery de Gaál, *The Theology of Benedict XVI: The Christocentric Shift* (New York: Palgrave MacMillan, 2010), p. 33.
4. Graf, 'Gottlieb Söhngen' in *Kölner Theologen: Von Rupert von Deutz bis Wilhelm Nyssen*, p. 455.

Neoplatonic roots of medieval philosophy familiarized him with ancient and medieval scholars and deepened his interest in the history of ideas.[5] In 1917 he was ordained a priest. From 1924 to 1930 he held the office of director of the Albert Magnus Academy in Cologne. In 1930 he then received his doctorate in theology on the scholastic axiom *ens et verum convertuntur* (the convertibility of being and truth) as the foundation of metaphysical and theological speculation. A year later, he completed his *Habilitationsschrift* at the Friedrich-Wilhelms-Universität in Bonn on the subject of participation in divine knowledge. There he taught as a private lecturer until 1937, where he was influenced by Arnold Rademacher (1873–1939), who was a Professor of Fundamental Theology. The *Habilitationsschrift* was completed under Rademacher's direction. In various speeches and publications Söhngen honoured Rademacher as his theological teacher.[6] He also described Rademacher as someone whose main concern, both as an academic and as a priest, was 'the unity of noble humanity with Christian holiness'.[7] In other words, Rademacher was interested in the compatibility of what Haecker had called Virgilian adventist humanism, or more succinctly, classical *Humanitas*, with Christian conceptions of sanctity. In a speech delivered at the University of Bonn in 1946, Söhngen began by noting that Rademacher had died just a few months before the outbreak of the Second World War, leaving a world 'that was no longer worthy of such a noble and Christian person' for the 'joy and peace to which the *humanitas* of our Savior had already prepared for him'.[8]

Between the years 1936 and 1942, Rademacher and Söhngen jointly edited a series of publications under the banner *Grenzfragen zwischen Theologie und Philosophie* (Border zone questions between theology and philosophy). As a fundamental theologian such border zones, as those between nature and grace, faith and reason, history and ontology, are of primary importance. The watermarks of Rademacher's interests and approach to fundamental theology appear in many of Söhngen's publications. Söhngen paid particular attention to the relationship

5. Ibid.
6. Gottlieb Söhngen, *Kardinal Newman: Sein Gottesgedanke und seine Denkergestalt* (Bonn: Verlag Götz Schwippert, 1946), p. 49.
7. Gottlieb Sohngen, *Humanität und Christentum* (Essen: Verlagsgesellshaft Augustin Wibbelt, 1946), p. 7.
8. Ibid.

between nature and grace, and so-called natural theology and revelation, and made significant interventions in the debates surrounding the *analogia entis* and *analogia fidei* relationships. In these matters he was decidedly *not* a neo-Thomist of the Leonine variety. He had no inclination to defend a complete separation of the orders of nature and grace, or of faith and reason, and in the works of Newman he found a way of bringing history and ontology together. In a biographical essay Josef Graf wrote:

> Despite his basic Aristotelian-Thomistic attitude, [Söhngen] had felt strong sympathy for the Augustinian tradition and the Augustinian scholastics since the beginning of his theological work. In the Catholic house of the natural knowledge of God there are many apartments: that of Augustine looks not a little different from that of Thomas, and these are different from those of Bonaventure and again, Anselm has arranged himself differently, and Pascal, Newman, Möhler and Scheeben each have their own apartments. Söhngen also wanted to have an office in the Augustinian apartment of this house.[9]

Graf also noted that Söhngen found the sharp separation of the natural and supernatural orders, typical of Leonine-era Thomism, to be alien to biblical and salvation-historical thinking.[10]

In 1947 Söhngen arrived in Munich to take up a Chair in Fundamental Theology and Philosophical Propadeutics, a position he held until 1958. It was by holding this position that he came to supervise the graduate research of a young Joseph Ratzinger. Given Söhngen's own interests in fundamental theology, it is not surprising then that when he supervised both of Joseph Ratzinger's theses, the doctorate and the *Habilitationsschrift*, the first was on the topic of Augustinian ecclesiology, and the second offered an analysis of the history and revelation topics in the theology of St Bonaventure. Famously, the latter was almost failed because of its initial explicit crticism of the Suárezian account of revelation then regnant in neo-scholasticism. Karl Rahner had described this Suárezian account as both the original and the

---

9. Josef Graf, 'Gottlieb Söhngen', in *Kölner Theologen: Von Rupert von Deutz bis Wilhelm Nyssen*, Sebastian Cüppers (ed.) (Köln: Marzellen Verlag, 2004), pp. 454–76 at p. 460.
10. Ibid., p. 461.

mortal sin of Jesuit theology. Ratzinger and Söhngen shared Rahner's sentiments on this issue, though not Michael Schmaus, the Professor of Dogmatic Theology at the University of Munich, who insisted on the removal of the anti-Suárezian sections of Ratzinger's *Habilitationsschrift* before it was passed. In the document *Dei Verbum*, the Dogmatic Constitution on Divine Revelation of the Second Vatican Council, the more historical account of revelation Ratzinger found in the work of St Bonaventure and others was vindicated.

In 1968 Pope Paul VI granted Söhngen the honorary title of Prelate of His Holiness or 'papal Prelate' which was some considerable achievement given that 1968 was the year in which he slashed the papal court's system of honorary positions and titles in his *motu proprio Pontificalis Domus* of 28 March. Söhngen acquired his honour exactly a week after the promulgation of the *motu*. He was to die some three years later in November 1971. At his Requiem Mass a young Professor Ratzinger, then at the University of Regensburg, commented:

> His greatness and his destiny lay in the breadth of his thinking. Anyone who asks such comprehensive questions will not be able to submit a closed, narrow synthesis. Söhngen knew that; he knew that the hour of theological *summae* had not yet returned. He knew that he had to be satisfied with fragments. But he always tried to look at the whole in a fragment, to think of the fragments as a whole and to design them as reflections of the whole. This also indicates his basic mental attitude: Söhngen was a radical and critical questioner. Even today one cannot ask more radical questions than he did. At the same time however he was a radical believer.[11]

A passage from Söhngen's preface to his book *Gesetz und Evangelium* (*The Law and the Gospel*) resonates strongly with Ratzinger's judgement. Söhngen wrote:

> Indeed, even in theology it is good to know several languages, such as the language of Thomas and the language of Augustine; and the

---

11. Joseph Ratzinger beim Requiem in Köln am 19 November 1971. Quoted in Markus Graulich, *Unterwegs zu einer Theologie des Kirchenrechts. Die Grundlegung des Rechts bei Gottlieb Söhngen (1892–1971) und die Konzepte der neueren Kirchenrechtswissenschaft*, zugl. Mainz, Univ., Habil.-Schr., 2004, Paderborn 2006, S. 22.

Reformation-evangelical language must not be incomprehensible to the Catholic theologian if he is concerned about such a topic. Where the reader and especially the professional expert disagrees, [I hope] he reflects back and does not dodge the questions that I at least dare to face myself. It annoys the mountaineer, if he is warned of the dangers of the mountains by the one who does not even dare to climb them and only looks at the peaks from below. However it is not advisable to get into the storms of the sea if one is not at all familiar with the sea. And further, the ship of theology has a purpose beyond lying in harbour.[12]

These words with their mixture of metaphors sound as though they have been written by someone slightly frustrated by people who are fearful of creative thought but nonetheless aware that one should not venture into territory beyond one's competence. In an article about Söhngen's influence on the intellectual formation of Joseph Ratzinger, Alfred Läpple remarked:

He usually never gave damning judgments on any author. He never refused a priori any contribution, from wherever it came. His method was to pick up and improve the good that could be found in any author and in every theological perspective, to weave the new things into the tradition and then go ahead, indicating the further development that could follow ... in Söhngen Ratzinger also saw a willingness to rediscover tradition understood as the theology of the Fathers and a willingness to do theology by going back to the great sources: from Plato to Newman, via Thomas, Bonaventure, Luther, and obviously Saint Augustine.[13]

The year before he took up his Chair at the University of Munich, Söhngen published a book on the theology of Cardinal Newman with a focus on his fundamental theology. The material within the book was presented in three parts on a Newman day organized by the two theological colleges in Bonn, the Collegium Albertinum and

12. Gottlieb Söhngen, preface to *Gesetz und Evangelium – ihre analoge Einheit theologisch philosophisch staatsbürgerlich* (Freiburg im Breisgau: Karl Alber Verlag, 1957).

13. Alfred Läpple, 'That New Beginning that Bloomed among the Ruins', *30 Days*, 1 February 2006.

the Collegium Leoninum, on the first Sunday of Advent in 1945. In his introductory remarks Söhngen honoured Newman as 'a thinker who inspired us Germans as if he were one of ours and as if he had written especially for us, without this taking anything away from his significance for the Christianity of England and the rest of the world'.[14] Söhngen then described Newman as 'an English thinker who avoids abstract and metaphysical concepts like ghosts', someone for whom 'the metaphysical order of essence and property almost completely recedes before the ethical order of its operation'.[15] Although Söhngen makes no reference to the then regnant neo-scholasticism, it is clear in passages like the following, that he sees Newman as offering an alternative approach to theology from that of the neo-scholastics of the nineteenth and early twentieth centuries:

> Newman does not see the world and the human person in the eyes of Aristotelian physics and metaphysics, and therefore does not ask what nature really possesses of man as such, of nature as such, that is to say of human nature as it is independently perceived or as it is abstracted from the historical-moral state in which man is in each case. Rather, Newman sees the world and man with biblical and Augustinian eyes, and thus never regards man, his nature or being, his abilities or powers differently than in concrete real contexts with the salvation-historical situation in which man here and now exists; and this salvation-historical situation is the state of fallen man, the status *naturae lapsae*.[16]

Any theologian reading those words in 1950, the same year as the promulgation of the encyclical *Humani Generis* by Pope Pius XII, would have been unlikely to miss the subtext. Newman does not begin with the supposition of a 'pure nature' but with the human person as he actually is, in the status *naturae lapsae*. For Newman, the human person is not composed of an Aristotelian nature with a Christian gloss. The human person can only be understood in the context of the salvation-historical situation, including the facts of the Fall and the Incarnation.

14. Gottlieb Söhngen, *Kardinal Newman: Sein Gottesgedanke und seine Denkergestalt*, p. 9.
15. Ibid., p. 32.
16. Ibid.

4. Gottlieb Söhngen

For those readers who may have been asleep, Söhngen reiterates the point in the following passage:

> So far we have noted in the spiritual image of Newman the Platonic-Augustinian traits. But we are also looking at Aristotelian traits. For the reason and purpose of his *Grammar of Assent*, Newman is not wrong in referring to Aristotle and his *Nicomachean ethics*, and indeed to what the great Greek methodologist does about the peculiarity of the practical, moral standard as opposed to theoretical knowledge. But how significant of Newman is such an appeal to Aristotle, a reference to ethics, not to the metaphysics of Aristotle, nor to a metaphysical piece of Aristotelian ethics! Newman remains here himself and not least an Englishmen, that is a theologian, the practical basic feature of English philosophy is written on his forehead.[17]

Söhngen also points out that consistent with Newman's focus on the ethical order is his practice of judging the historical forms of religion by the standard of their moral seriousness, by 'how strongly the sense of guilt manifests itself in them':

> Because of its 'dark and severe seriousness' Newman gives the religious 'need and tradition of barbarian times' the decided preference over the 'so-called religion of civilization and philosophy'; this educational religion of the one-sidedly educated and thus enlightened intellect is no longer a 'natural' but an 'artificial religion', in short, a great farce.[18]

Here Söhngen's observations on Newman's preference for the religious traditions of barbarian times are evocative of Haecker's defence of the moral superiority of the Neanderthal to the proponents of the religion of civilization and philosophy. While Söhngen identifies differences between Newman and the neo-scholastics on the nature and grace relationship, and the value of dialectics, he also identifies differences between Newman and the German Idealist tradition on the nature of ethical judgment. Speaking about Newman's idea of conscience, he wrote:

17. Ibid., p. 37.
18. Ibid., pp. 32-3.

The thesis I have said is that God, my Creator, is clearly in the personal voice of my conscience. For my conscience, 'does not rest in itself, but reaches in a vague way to something, beyond itself'. This, of course, applies only if the conscience becomes versed not merely as a 'moral feeling' or as 'rational judgment' but above all as the command of an authoritative admonisher. So conscience does not mean a purely ethical, but first and foremost a religious fact of the human spirit. To speak with Kant's words: The categorical imperative or unconditional duty lies for Newman, unlike for Kant, not in the purely ethical realm, but in the peculiarly religious realm.[19]

For Newman there is absolutely no possibility of a project like ethics within the bounds of reason alone, that is, a rationalist ethics. Newman's ethical understanding is fundamentally personalist, it is about the relationship between God and the human person, and the human conscience is something as personal as the voice of God within the human soul. In this context Söhngen observed that there are similarities between Newman's understanding of conscience and that of the poetess Annette von Droste-Hülshoff (1797–1848). The similarities are especially strong in her poem *Die ächzende Kreatur* (*The Aching Creature*), where she speaks of 'the sharp thorn of conscience'.[20] In a short monograph on Baroness Droste-Hülshoff to mark the anniversary of her death, Theodor Steinbüchel had also noted the similarity of Droste-Hülshoff's *Gewissensfrömmigkeit* (pious conscience) with Newman's idea of conscience, as well as the prescience of her insight that the meaning of existence is fulfilled in love, a theme which was to become a central element of the personalism of Ferdinand Ebner and Martin Buber in the twentieth century.[21]

Newman's personalism is based on a theological anthropology that gives pride of place to the human heart, understood in the biblical sense as the site of the integration of other faculties of the human soul, including the imagination and the memory, and not merely the *ratio* (discursive reason) favoured by the scholastics but the *intellectus* (intuition), so favoured by poets, as well. Söhngen also highlighted this particular hallmark of Newman's theology. It is another methodological

---

19. Ibid., pp. 20–1.
20. Ibid., p. 35.
21. Theodor Steinbüchel, *Annette von Droste-Hülshoff nach hundert Jahren* (Frankfurt am Main: Verlag Josef Knecht, 1950), pp. 14–15 and p. 42.

4. Gottlieb Söhngen

preference that separates his approach from that of the late-nineteenth-century scholastics who sought to defend the faith by constructing a logically coherent philosophical scaffolding and then topping it up with theological propositions borrowed from the history of dogmatic theology. Here Söhngen quoted Newman at length:

> On the title page of *Grammar of Assent* is found as a motto the saying of St. Ambrose: *Non in dialectica complacuit Deo salvum facere populum suum* – God did not accomplish the salvation of his people through dialectics. Already in the letters to the editor of *The Times* of February 1841 [Newman] says: 'The heart is commonly reached, not by reason, but by imagination, by immediate impressions, by the testimony of facts and events, by history, by description. People influence us, voices melt us, glances subjugate us, deeds ignite us. Many a person will live and die for a dogma; but no one wants to be the martyr for a conclusion. No one, I say, wants to die for his own calculations; he dies for realities … For most people, an argument makes the matter before them only more dubious and much less insistent. All in all, man is not a judgmental [that is, conclusion, proving] living entity, he is a seeing, feeling, looking, acting being … Life is not long enough for a religion of implications; we will never have made a start if we decide to start with a proof. (From *Grammar of Assent*).[22]

Söhngen concluded that, 'according to Newman, the art of syllogistic thinking is to starve every expression until it becomes the ghost of itself and is sufficiently tame and bandy to exist as a mere definition', and 'from this attitude of mind, Newman, in his *Grammar of Assent*, sets himself the task 'of drawing the method by which the spirit attains, not only to a conceptual, but to a pictorial or real consent in matters of religion, that is, to an agreement from a comprehension not only of what the words of the sentence mean, but of the object which is signified by them'.[23]

Söhngen therefore regarded Newman as having offered a different approach to fundamental theology from the late-nineteenth-century neo-scholastics. In this sense Newman is a precursor to people like Rademacher and to Söhngen himself.

---

22. Gottlieb Söhngen, *Kardinal Newman: Sein Gottesgedanke und seine Denkergestalt*, p. 38.
23. Ibid., p. 39.

In addition to offering an alternate fundamental theology, Söhngen also praised Newman for understanding what is now called the 'new atheism'. Newman, he said, was 'not satisfied with the cheap information of some apologists of Christianity, that there are no atheists out of conviction; at the bottom of their soul those who call themselves godless also worshiped some supernatural deity'.[24] On the contrary, 'Newman has guessed that the only serious antagonist of Christianity will be a serious atheism, that is, an atheism, so to speak, out of conscience, an atheism that does not deny God'.[25] In other words, Newman was onto the problem that a new kind of atheism was emerging that would not be content with a mere declaration of a lack of belief. The New Atheism is not indifferent to Christianity. It really cares about it intensely. It goes to war against it under the banner of a better, more noble humanity. Against the background of the influence of Nietzsche and others who followed in his trajectory in the early twentieth century, Söhngen concluded that 'the signs of the times suggest that atheism continues to grow into a destiny that beats at the gates of the West. Atheism has already become what Newman understands by a dogma, that is, a lived reality of which one is convinced and for which one is willing to die.'[26] Just as Steinbüchel ended his book on Nietzsche by describing the Nietzschean project as a 'wake-up call' to anyone wanting to defend a genuine Christianity from Nietzsche's genealogical analysis and pathology report, Söhngen reserved his highest praise for Newman for understanding the nature of the spiritual battle in which Christianity found itself in the last century:

> What is heralded in Newman's concept of God, and what renders Newman seminal as a religious thinker, is the de-bourgeoisation of a bourgeois Christianity [*die Entbürgerlichung eines verbürgerlichten Christentums*]; the unsettling of a settled, bourgeois Christianity and of a settled, Christian bourgeoisie. Only a Christian God disassociated from middle-class attitudes and a majority disassociated from the middle-class are able to genuinely complement one another. Yet how deeply enmeshed the Christian churches remain within a middle-class Christian milieu, even after all the revolutions that have occurred; a middle-class Christian milieu from which they wish to

---

24. Ibid., pp. 46–7.
25. Ibid.
26. Ibid.

depart just as little as the first Christians wished to depart from their Lord Jesus!'[27]

In other words, Söhngen credits Newman with understanding that a bourgeois Christianity with its interests in social security and upward social mobility would not be able to compete with what he called 'the atheism of the decadent masses'. Rhetorically, Söhngen asked, 'where can there be found the beginning of ecclesial movements which may be for the twentieth century what the mendicant orders were for the thirteenth?'[28]

Söhngen never answered his own question, but in his *Humanität und Christentum* published in 1946 he sketched an outline of the anthropological issues that any such new movements would need to address were they to engage with the existential crises of the time and offer something more than a warmed-up bourgeois Christianity. In his introduction he explained that *Humanitas* is a Western concept and that what the Roman orator-philosopher Cicero called *Humanitas* is precisely the same as what the poet-philosopher Plato called *paideia*, meaning the education of man to the intellectual nobility of a free and gentle humanity.[29] *Paideia*, he noted, can also be translated as culture. He also draws attention to the fact that in the Greek of the New Testament, Christian love is not called *Eros*, but *Agape*, and in the Latin bible it is *caritas* or *dilectio*. Thus, Christian *Caritas* or *Agape* 'keeps its distance' from the god of love. The word *Agape* is the container into which the new wine of Christian love is poured. Söhngen then observes that just as Platonic love and Christian love each have a different name, they are of different origins. Again, rhetorically, he asked, can Greek *Eros* and Christian *Agape* not still join hands like a youth and a virgin who both come from noble families and have received a noble education? Could it not be the case that in Christian *Agape* the divine revelation with divine wisdom and power has accomplished what human wisdom and power only incompletely knew and created in Greek *Eros*? An affirmative answer becomes Söhngen's central thesis and is made possible by the fact that the Platonic *Eros* is not an earthly love, but like *Agape* it is a heavenly love. Söhngen was quick to add the caveat that of course

27. Ibid., p. 51.
28. Ibid., p. 52.
29. Gottlieb Söhngen, *Humanität und Christentum* (Essen: Verlagsgesellshaft Augustin Wibbelt, 1946), p. 14.

it is not appropriate to speak of the Holy Spirit, the 'bond of love in God's lap between the Heavenly father and His only begotten Son', as *eros*. Nonetheless, Söhngen suggested that 'even if *Eros* does not dwell in the glory of the three times holy God, it does walk among the Gentiles as a virtuous spirit'.[30] This means that 'biblical and Platonic language sound together in counterpoint, as it were'.[31] Plato and St Paul may have meant something different when they spoke of the spirit, but for both of them the freedom of the spirit is linked to the development of what would later be called personality. Söhngen concluded that 'the Holy Spirit of a new love has not displaced the beautiful spirit of *Eros*; but Christian longing for eternal life borrows from *Eros* wings and delirious enthusiasm. The Greek goal of a humanity reaching for the highest and the most beautiful seems to arrive at the summit in such a way that *Agape* is mixed with Eros'.[32] *Agape* and *Eros*, *Caritas* and *Humanitas*, cannot avoid relating to one another. Their union has brought a *Humanitas Christiana* associated with the following illustrious names and projects: St Clement of Alexandria and his three books on the educator, St Augustine of Hippo with his synthesis of *Caritas* and *Eros*, Dante Alighieri with his appreciation of Virgil and love for Beatrice, Nicholas of Cusa, 'who allowed his Christian reform ideas to be fertilised by contemporary humanism' and last but not least St Thomas Aquinas, who 'built the Aristotelian concept of virtue and the Aristotelian table of virtues into Christian moral theory, so that medieval moral theory is now more like a triptych': on the middle panel the three theological virtues (faith, hope and love), on one side panel the Platonic cardinal virtues (wisdom, temperance, courage and justice) and on the other side panel, the Aristotelian virtues with their heart piece, the virtue of *Megalopsychia*.[33]

This honour board does not however come to an end in the thirteenth century. Söhngen went on to identify more modern creators of a *Humanitas Christiana* beginning with Philip Melanchthon 'with his plan for a complete edition of the purified Aristotle and with his educational ideal of the Christian nobility of the ancient world for the newly founded secondary school in Nürnberg' – followed by St Francis de Sales with his philanthropic '*Philothea*', Pascal and Fénelon with their

---

30. Ibid., p. 29.
31. Ibid.
32. Ibid.
33. Ibid., p. 37.

conceptions of *L'honnête homme*, Johann Michael Sailer's reflections on the 'religion of pure humanity' and St John Henry Newman's idea of a Christian Gentleman.[34] Söhngen also observed that the union of Greek *Humanitas* with Christian *Agape* is not limited to the works of theologians but is also evident in art and architecture and music. He was particularly proud of Rhenish art for 'bringing the ancient tradition of noble, controlled humanity to life preserved and instilled with Christian intimacy'.[35] Above all, however, he declared, 'The old church liturgy is that unique work of art in which the incomprehensible and overwhelming power of God's love for us in Jesus Christ fits into the beautiful balance of the ancient *logos* and the harmony of power and beauty'.[36] All of these creators of a *Humanitas Christiana* followed the advice of St Paul to test all things and hold fast to what is good. His message was 'everything good belongs to you, but you belong to Christ', and thus, '*Caritas* regards itself as the fulfilment of *Humanitas*'.[37]

Jumping ahead to the eighteenth century, or what Söhngen called the century of 'pure humanity', Söhngen introduced a third party to the relationship, the humanism of Kant and those who followed him. This humanism he described as 'the late-born sister of *Eros* who went through the Christian school'.[38] Kant's 'discovery trips' to the land of personality were made on the winged wheels of *Eros* and *Agape*. However, 'the cross becomes a real nuisance here' because its cruelty appears to be incongruent with any kind of humanism. Thus, the project arises 'to free the Christian message of God's fatherly love and the Christian commandment of our brotherly love from the historically accidental burden of the churches and their dogmas and to rediscover the Gospel in its universal, inner truth'.[39] In other words, 'instead of noble humanity under the law and spirit of the Christian faith, Christian love takes place within the limits of pure humanity'.[40] While dogmatic Christianity is 'the belief in the God-Man, that is, in the acceptance of human nature into a divine person through the descent of God to man', the religion of pure humanity is the belief in 'the acceptance of the Divine into human

34. Ibid., pp. 37-8.
35. Ibid., p. 38.
36. Ibid.
37. Ibid., pp. 38-9.
38. Ibid., p. 33.
39. Ibid., p. 40.
40. Ibid.

personality through the ascension of man to God'.⁴¹ The religion of pure humanity is thus the religion of *Eros* only. With *Agape*, man is 'raised up to God as a child of God by the fact that God really descends to man first', however, 'the divine that German Idealism confesses is the divine within human personality, the divine within pure humanity'.⁴² On this point there can be no reconciliation between the two versions of humanism. However, Söhngen also noted that in addition to the role of *Eros*, there is something new in the philosophies of the Enlightenment: 'it is the unprejudiced love of truth and the tolerant understanding of the inner truth, which is at the bottom of every belief, if it belongs to a true and sincere heart'.⁴³ The highest names on the honour board of proponents of a 'pure humanity' are Lessing and Kant, Schiller and Goethe, Mozart in *The Magic Flute* and Beethoven in *Fidelio* and the Choir of the Ninth Symphony and finally Schleiermacher, 'the great translator of Plato and the father of New Protestantism as a synthesis between German Idealism and Evangelical Christianity'.⁴⁴

Söhngen is not dismissive of this '*novum*' in the philosophies of pure humanity. He is happy to affirm the concept of 'brotherly love' as, for example, it appears in the fourth movement of Beethoven's ninth symphony. Both the Gospel of St John and the works of St Augustine concur that Christian brotherly love is something good and that it separates the true from the false Christians. Söhngen also affirmed pure humanism's affirmation of respect for the human conscience. He did, however, add two caveats to these affirmations. The first was that Christian brotherly love is inwardly and inextricably linked to Christian truth, and the second was that Christian love is greater than anything to be found in the 'temple of humanity'. Söhngen also adds that 'Christian love cares for the human concern of noble humanity without urgently seeking it' and that 'Christian love creates the condition without which no noble humanity can float'.⁴⁵

Having sketched the contours of these three different humanisms – the noble humanism of pre-Christian Greco-Roman culture, the *Humanitas Christiana* of Christian scholars from St Clement of Alexandria to St John Henry Newman and the 'pure humanism' of the eighteenth

---

41. Ibid., p. 42.
42. Ibid., p. 43.
43. Ibid., p. 44.
44. Ibid., p. 40.
45. Ibid., p. 46.

century – Söhngen concluded that the real stumbling block for the first and third vis-à-vis the second is the crucifixion. Good Friday theology is hard for either contemporary Greco-Roman classicists or the eighteenth- and nineteenth-century philosophers of the salons of Weimar and Berlin to appropriate. The crucifixion is such a problem that Söhngen identified a fourth humanism, what he called a *humanitas contra crucem*. Here the names on the (dis)honour board form a much shorter list. In Christian antiquity the stand-out examples were Celsus, the second century philosopher and author of *On the True Doctrine* and Julian the Apostate (331/332–363), the last non-Christian ruler of the Roman Empire, while in modern times the standard bearers are Friedrich Nietzsche and Stefan George. Söhngen thought that the mentality of Celsus and Julian was well captured in the following passage by St John Henry Newman:

> The accusation of the pagans of the ancient world was that instead of simply directing the mind to the beautiful and the pleasant, Christianity also brought to mind images of dark and painful content; that it put tears before joy and the cross before the crown, that it laid the foundation for a heroism of the masses, that it made the soul tremble by the news of purgatory and hell; that it insisted on a way of looking at God that it felt was low, cowardly and servile.[46]

Söhngen viewed the anti-Christian disposition of both Nietzsche and George as a modern variation on this ancient theme. He noted that 'it was not for nothing that Nietzsche, the Professor in Basel, the city with a humanistic tradition, came from classical philology' and that 'the new *Eros* of Zarathustra is not related to the Pauline and Johannine *Agape*, but to the clan of the Platonic Eros'.[47]

Söhngen identified St Paul and Martin Luther as the strongest opponents of those who would foster a *humanitas contra crucem*. Söhngen summarizes Luther's position with the principle, *Caritas* has nothing to receive from *Humanitas*; but *Humanitas* can only expect its salvation from *Caritas*. This means in turn that for Luther, the goal of noble humanity remains, but the power to realize it is not by *Eros*, a noble self-love, but only by *Agape*, that is to say, the love that is born from the cross and in which the ego is crucified. St Paul shares with

---

46. Ibid., p. 77.
47. Ibid., pp. 49 and 51.

Luther a disposition towards a *Dei humanitas in mysterio crucis* and here Söhngen suggests that the Pauline conception is composed of the following four elements:

1. Christian humanity is God's humanity, that means first and foremost humanity from God and His love. God's humanity appeared to us in His Son, who became man and our Saviour (Tit. 3. 4-6). So, it is in contradiction to pure humanity, that is, a humanity from man and his love.
2. Since humanity comes from God and from the depths of His love, it does not belong to this earth and its time but to heaven, the coming reign of the kingdom of God, and therefore it cannot be understood by the sages of this world, from the images and parables of pure humanity.
3. God's humanity is also mysterious because it is obscured by the absurdity of the cross. The cross, however, establishes the *humanitas Christi* as a divine creation. As a consequence, there is no longer the noble distance of the Greek from the barbarian, the lord from the slave, the wise and educated from the unlettered or artisan, because all people are called in Jesus Christ to the one new humanity (cf. Gal. 3.28).
4. From a Pauline perspective, *humanitas christiana* exists as an encounter between Christian love and noble humanity, but only as an encounter under the cross.[48]

This fourth element suggests that for Söhngen there is a significant difference between St Paul and Martin Luther, notwithstanding their common agreement that no *humanitas* is possible unless it is tied to the mystery of the cross. Söhngen presents St Paul as a proponent of a both/and position, typical of Catholic theology in general. There is space to incorporate the noble *humanitas* of the classical era providing the mystery of the cross is never occluded or otherwise marginalized.

The *Humanität und Christentum* publication began its life as an address to celebrate the sixtieth anniversary of the Kaiser Wilhelm Gymnasium in Cologne (the former Tricoronatum) and its strongly humanistic curriculum. In his conclusion Söhngen offered three further judgments all directed towards a defence of a humanistic education. First, he declared that Greco-Roman antiquity is the basis

---

48. Ibid., pp. 62–5.

of western history and its education, since the Greeks were founders of cultural life, the Romans the founders of public life, including western understandings of law and statecraft, and that the foundations of Catholic theology and liturgy were built in the confrontation of Christianity with Greco-Roman antiquity. Secondly, he declared that he believed in the superiority of Western education over that of other cultures. Christianity, he said, 'grew up in the Mediterranean' with its Greco-Roman history and culture. Although he did not mention Haecker's notion of a 'Heathen Advent', Söhngen clearly shared Haecker's attitude that the Incarnation occurred at a particularly propitious moment in history with the Greco-Roman culture serving as a *praeparatio evangelica*. Thirdly, he stated that Greco-Roman antiquity will continue to be the foundation of western education because it provides access to eternal truths that are of universal application. The common ground of Greek educational knowledge and Christian belief is enthusiasm for the eternal things in man. Söhngen summed up his analysis of the various humanisms on offer in the intellectual market place with a further three pithy statements: (1) Humanism has its great limit. (2) This limit is exposed by Christianity. (3) Christianity alone is capable of filling out the place where humanism fails, and thus of purifying humanism.[49]

While these three judgments were Söhngen's final defence to the jury as it were, he also acknowledged that he feared that the humanistic educational system was under attack from economic and ideological forces. A culture that gives priority to economics views education in an instrumental way. Education is equated with skills training, not soul or character formation, not the acquisition of cultural capital. Giving priority to economics is a social trait shared by capitalist and socialist economists. Humanism and socialism, he noted, are 'hostile brothers': 'humanism cannot deny its aristocratic origins and attitudes, just as little can socialism deny its democratic blood and stamp'.[50] Nonetheless, he exhorted his listeners to take consolation from the fact that those who propose a *Humanitas Christiana* are not without hope.[51]

In another essay on education, published in the 1951/2 volume of *Hochland*, Söhngen reflected on Immanuel Kant's three essays published under the title *Die Streit der Fakultäten* of 1798 (*The Conflict of the*

---

49. Ibid., p. 76.
50. Ibid., p. 74.
51. Ibid., p. 77.

Faculties), following the religious edict of the Prussian King Wilhelm II of 1788 and the royal rescript of 1794. The latter accused Kant of 'distorting and disparaging several principal and fundamental doctrines of Holy Scripture and Christianity'.[52] In his response Kant addressed the issue of the place of philosophy within the university hierarchy. The medieval hierarchy, exemplified by the University of Paris, recognized four faculties: philosophy, medicine, law and theology in this ascending order. According to Söhngen's reading this hierarchical relationship was not based on any anti-philosophical premise. Rather, philosophical study was deemed to be a necessary prerequisite for studies at a higher level, hence it was the lowest but first level of academic attainment. Kant, however, found the order of the faculties to be questionable and the end result in the system of the German universities was the demolition of the hierarchy and equalization of all the faculties. This process was not undertaken by Kant himself but followed on from his lead in the early nineteenth century, spearheaded by the University of Göttingen and the newly founded University of Berlin in 1810. Söhngen's paper is interesting from two perspectives. First it offers a summary history of the institution of the university and especially the influence of Kant upon the modern university, and secondly, it serves as a springboard for Söhngen's presentation of his own ideas on the relationship between philosophy and theology.

The first point that Söhngen makes is that there is a real tension between theology and canon law. There is, he says, a dogmatic and a legal view of the church, and they do form a unity, but not in such a way that we could exchange the two ways of thinking in a double counterpoint. The same he said applies to the relationship between dogmatic theology and the exegetical interpretation of the Bible. He referred to the example of Josef Geiselmann's study on the history of eucharistic theology which demonstrated that the dominance of a canon law perspective had led to a narrowing of the understanding of this branch of theology. He did not develop this topic further but focused more on the broader theology and philosophy relationship. He began this discussion by noting that in terms of methodology, theology is a borrowing science, theology adds scientific reason to the Christian faith. The possibility of such addition must, however, derive from the subject of the science of the faith. This science is super-rational (not irrational), and it is possible because of the

---

52. Gary Banham et al., *The Continuum Companion to Kant* (London: Continuum, 2012), p. 61.

4. Gottlieb Söhngen

analogia veritatis, the unity of all truth.[53] Kant's problem was that when he asked about the inner truth of Christianity, he saw it in the generally human content of Christianity, and this purely natural religion of the moral belief in reason became his understanding of Christianity. In short, Kant and his followers dissolved the peculiarly Christian into the generally human. As Söhngen saw the discipline of theology, however, the 'highest and most beautiful task of theology, an old and eternally new task' is to 'relate the Christian to the generally human without losing the peculiarly Christian'.[54] In the following paragraph, Söhngen summarized this approach to the issues raised by Kant in the 'Conflict of the Faculties' essays:

> If theology derives its methods purely as such from outside, from other sciences, it must not make us forget that theology has its own inner prerequisites, which are given in the peculiar object of theology. These prerequisites are of a religious and ecclesial-dogmatic nature. Theology is a science of faith, and as a science of faith and belief it works with scientific methods under conditions of faith. This is where the special position of theology in the circle of science comes to a head. And here lies the stumbling block for every way of thinking that remains decidedly worldly. Theology cannot and must not remove this stumbling block if it does not want to empty and invalidate the Christian message. The theologian should add science to faith; but he must not place faith in a natural knowledge or belief that takes the place of the revealed and proclaimed belief.[55]

Söhngen concluded his essay with the statement that 'if faith is the bedrock on which the theologian builds, and if science is the observatory that he builds on it, God's glory in His creation and man in God's love are the starry sky we look towards'.[56]

Söhngen was therefore strongly of the view that theology begins with a truth that has already been given to us. This truth is a gift of revelation. It is not created in the laboratory of the human mind. His

---

53. Gottlieb Söhngen, 'Die Theologie im Streit der Fakultäten, *Hochland* (1951/2), pp. 225–38 at 236.
54. Ibid., pp. 225–38 at 238.
55. Ibid., pp. 225–38 at 237.
56. Ibid., pp. 225–38 at 238.

understanding of the *analogia fidei* also rests on this foundation, as he expressed the idea in the following terms:

> The analogy of the faith is the *intellectus fidei e mysteriorum ipsorum nexu inter se et cum fine hominis ultimo*. The mysteries of the faith form a mysterious structure in which we can, and should, relate them to each other and thereby form a rich account of the individual mysteries in the midst of all their connections. More succinctly, the analogy of faith is the *ordo veritatum fidei*.[57]

More specifically, Söhngen argued that the analogy of faith signifies a unity within: (i) the unity of Scripture and the sense of Scripture, (ii) the unity of the words of Scripture and church proclamation, (iii) the unity and enigmatic coherence of the mysteries of the faith and (iv) the unity of nature and natural knowing with the obedience of grace and faith.[58]

In many of Söhngen's publications, one senses that he is trying to effect a synthesis between the conceptual clarity of the scholastics with the more typically patristic sense of awe before the mysteries of the faith and their recourse to a more poetic language. The following two paragraphs exemplify this tendency – the first sounds typically scholastic – the second more typically patristic:

> Let us think of each mystery as already in itself a nexus, each piece a great, comprehensive mystery, an analogous concept within itself and thus a unity of different attributes. From this idea we are further compelled to strive for an analogous understanding (one not simply metaphysically but theologically inspired) of both the 'inner possibility', or 'non-contradiction', of statements about the mystery, as well as the 'inner structure' and 'foundation', or the 'how and why' of the determination of its structure. We could describe the first side of the analogy of faith as the conceptual comprehension of the individual mysteries from the mysterious unity of their attributes…
>
> We must add, however, that if the pieces are parts of the mysterious and miraculous divine light, even if they lie behind the darkened veil of faith, then how much more will the whole be the light, and with its light illuminate the pieces! … The mystery itself is a mystery, and

---

57. Gottlieb Söhngen, 'The Analogy of Faith: Unity in the Science of Faith', trans. Keneth Oakes, *Pro Ecclesia* XXI (2) (2012), pp. 169–94 at p. 179.
58. Ibid., p. 170.

thus we can never grasp that nexus from outside using purely rational processes, but only from within, from faith and the understanding of faith, and only in this way we will be able to make it fruitful.[59]

As a consequence, Söhngen argues that:

> The *ordo veritatum fidei* – insofar as we do not 'construct' some gnostic system out of it according to the ideas of reason, but seek to 'reconstruct' it in the knowing of faith according to the standards and boundaries of the Word of God – is not immediately able to be grasped or understood from revelation and faith, but exists through the revealed mysteries of faith as revealed in them, or rather with them.[60]

Such a theological foundation stone or building block could not possibly be further from the idea that the teaching of the Scriptures needs to be analysed within the framework of contemporary social theory, an idea that gained momentum in the 1970s. Söhngen would probably describe such a theoretical starting position as quintessentially 'gnostic'.

In his work on the *analogia fidei*, Söhngen also argues that the *analogia fidei* is the 'most concrete' and 'most fruitful' when seen in the fullness of its relationships, specifically the *Trinitas et imago Dei* (relationship between the Trinity and the human person made in image of God), *Christus caput et membra* (the relationship between Christ as the head of the Church and the members of the Body of Christ) and *septem sacramenta et vita nova* (the relationship between the seven sacraments and the new life in Christ).[61]

Söhngen's interest in what in the first half of the twentieth century was called 'mystery theology' is a flow-on effect from the theology of Matthias Joseph Scheeben (1835–1888), another great Rhinelander, and the liturgical theology of the Benedictine monk Odo Casel (1886–1948). Scheeben's most important work was *The Mysteries of Christianity*. In it he wrote, 'The light derived from the consideration of each separate mystery spreads automatically far and wide over the inner relationship and the wonderful harmony pervading them all, and thus the individual pictures take their places in an orderly gallery, which

---

59. Ibid., p. 180.
60. Ibid.
61. Ibid, p. 181.

comprises everything magnificent and sublime that theology possesses far in excess of all the other sciences, including even philosophy'.[62] Following upon the work of Scheeben, Casel argued that the Christian faith is not primarily a collection of doctrines (such as one finds in Suárezian scholasticism) or a moral code (as Kant might view its primary relevance) but the worship of a sacred mystery. An example of the inner harmonic relationships Söhngen located within the orderly gallery of the *analogia fidei* may be found in the following paragraph:

> Baptism is the inner simulacrum of the death of Christ upon the cross and his internment in the grave as our rebirth to new life through the death of the old Adam; confirmation is the inner simulacrum of the sufferings of Christ as our consecration in the Holy Spirit for heroic witness; extreme unction is the inner simulacrum of Christ's combat unto death as our strengthening in the final combat; ordination is the inner simulacrum of the bloody sacrifice of Christ as the particular qualification for service in the new cultic sanctuary of the eternal High Priest that was inaugurated by the death of Christ; marriage is the inner simulacrum of the espousal of Christ in his death with the Church as the indissoluable bond between a man and wife in Christ and in his Church.[63]

The work in which Söhngen ties together his interest in mystery theology and the *analogia fidei* is his *Symbol und Wirklichkeit im Kultmysterium* (*Symbol and Reality in the Mystery of Worship*) published as the fourth volume in the *Grenzfragen zwischen Theologie und Philosophie* series in 1937 and dedicated to Arnold Rademacher. This is a very dense work requiring knowledge of both scholastic sacramental theology and the mystery theology of Scheeben and Casel, especially of Casel. Söhngen describes the core question of the volume as 'how, in word and sacrament, is grace – the mysterium of salvation – real or present within worship?' In other words, 'what sort of reality or presence is mysteriously contained within word and sacrament'?[64] In his answer Söhngen differentiates between a historically real and a symbolically

---

62. Matthias Joseph Sheeben, *The Mysteries of Christianity* (St. Louis: B. Herder Books, 1956), p. 21.

63. Gottlieb Söhngen, *Symbol und Wirklichkeit im Kultmysterium* (Bonn: Peter Hanstein Verlagsbuchhandlung, 1937), pp. 92–3.

64. Ibid., p. 32.

real appearance of the mystery, which he names with the pair of terms 'primeval mystery' and 'cult mystery' based on the terminology of Casel, the doyen of the Maria-Laach theological circle.[65] Söhngen also exhorts his readers to follow the trajectory of Casel by going 'back to the form of language in which Paul, the liturgy and the fathers speak of grace and the grace of the sacraments' and 'back to the way they neither express these realities in isolated concepts nor view them as compartmentalised within themselves, but rather as incorporated within the fullness of the nomenclature of salvation history and within the Church as the living presence of Christ through the spirit that gives life'.[66] As Josef Graf has explained the issue:

> The debate about mystery theology centered on the question of how this presence of the Christ mystery is to be understood in the liturgical cult of the church, especially in the sacraments. In contrast to the understanding of sacramental reality that predominates in neo-scholastic theology solely from the point of view of its grace effect, Söhngen and Casel emphasize that the mystery of Christ is really present in the cult and not only in its salvific effect. This presence occurs throughout the cult, especially in the sacraments and *above all in the sacramental sacrifice of Christ.*[67]

Söhngen did not, however, see this position as being contrary to classical Thomism but more of a valorization of certain elements of classical Thomism that were obscured in late scholasticism. He praises St Thomas 'for connecting the *nova et vetera*, keeping the great achievements of the fathers alive, which is to be seen in the fact that the spiritual particularity of sacramental reality as a symbolic reality was profoundly grasped'.[68] Moreover, he declared:

> St. Thomas did not allow himself to be blinded by the newly lit torch of efficient causality; efficient causality was not permitted to marginalise the significatory side of the sacrament and push it into the shadows.

---

65. Graf, 'Gottlieb Söhngen' in *Kölner Theologen: Von Rupert von Deutz bis Wilhelm Nyssen*, p. 463.
66. Söhngen, *Symbol und Wirklichkeit im Kultmysterium*, p. 52.
67. Graf, 'Gottlieb Söhngen' in *Kölner Theologen: Von Rupert von Deutz bis Wilhelm Nyssen*, p. 463.
68. Söhngen, *Symbol und Wirklichkeit im Kultmysterium*, p. 62.

It was precisely Thomas who retained the instrumental causality of the sacraments in vibrant and inherent connection with signification or symbolisation; the principal conceptual determination of the sacraments within Aquinas is that they are signs. And it is from the fact that the sacraments are bound to signs that their causality or effectiveness are to be understood, otherwise their supernatural, spiritual sense – the mysterium – will be lost.[69]

St Thomas is here presented as a typical champion of the both/and hallmark of Catholic theology. While sacramental theology can veer to extremes where either the significatory or symbolic side of the sacrament is emphasized or alternatively the causal or instrument-of-grace side is valorized, Söhngen, who was writing in an era when the causal side tended to predominate, applauds St Thomas for not ignoring or otherwise muting the symbolic dimension.

As Jean Borella concluded in his work *The Sense of the Supernatural*, the 'loss of the sense of the supernatural is but the religious aspect of the loss of the sense of the ontological, or the intuition of being', and in order to have this capacity awakened in us we need to have an experience of forms, which, by themselves, 'refer to nothing of the mundane'.[70] These experiences are in turn given by liturgical symbols through which the invisible transcendent renders itself more visible.[71] Borella explains that these elements are of course borrowed from the physical world otherwise no human experience of it would be possible – but they are set aside, separated from the natural order to which they originally belonged and to which they refer and consecrated in order to render present realities of another order. These forms became the realm of the sacred, and the realm of the sacred becomes the mediator between the natural and supernatural orders. The sacred forms, however, are not mediatory by themselves, they realize their mediatory function only if they are 'full of grace', that is, only if they serve as a mode of expression for the ritual activity by which the first mediation, that of the divine activity of Christ, is rendered present among us.[72] Thus, Borella concludes that we can distinguish three kinds of mediations:

69. Ibid., p. 57.
70. Jean Borella, *The Sense of the Supernatural* (Edinburgh: T&T Clark, 1998), p. 38.
71. Ibid., p. 59.
72. Ibid., p. 60.

The first is that of Christ in his redemptive Incarnation: this proceeds from the supernatural to the natural; the second is that of ritual action, the actual performance of a rite which is mysteriously identified with the divine action; the third is the mediation of those sacred forms which the ritual action signifies and without which is cannot be accomplished. This third mediation proceeds from the natural to the supernatural, while ritual activity realises something like a mediating fusion of the one with the other (the priest at the altar acts *in persona Christi*), a fusion which only an act and not an element of the world can realize.[73]

Getting all these mediations perfectly balanced and interrelated in sacramental pastoral practices can be challenging and was thus one of those issues that occupied the members of the early-twentieth-century new liturgical movement of which both Söhngen and his student, Fr. Ratzinger, were heirs.

Of all the judgments that have been made about the six scholars profiled in this collection, one of the highest is the assessment of Emery de Gaál that 'in a certain way, [Joseph] Ratzinger's theology is but a grand expansion on Söhngen's vision'.[74] De Gaál argues that 'the Cologne priest and Munich professor's influence on Ratzinger in 1947–1958 for fundamental theology and philosophical propaedeutics can hardly be overstated'.[75] Muth mentored the Scholls and befriended Haecker. Haecker also mentored the Scholls. Steinbüchel taught Alfred Läpple and Läpple introduced Ratzinger to the theology of Newman. Guardini inspired Josef Pieper, and Josef Pieper introduced Joseph Ratzinger to Karol Wojtyła. Przywara mentored St Edith Stein and Hans Urs von Balthasar, but it was Söhngen who was Ratzinger's *Doktor Vater*. Thus, while Söhngen is one of the least well known of the six authors profiled in this book, and the one with the shortest list of publications, his influence may in the long term be the greatest since it was his approach to fundamental theology that set the course for the future Prefect of the Congregation of the Doctrine of the Faith and his intellectually creative papacy.

73. Ibid.
74. Emery de Gaál, *O Lord. I Seek Your Countenance: Explorations and Discoveries in Pope Benedict XVI's Theology* (Steubenville: Emmaus Academic, 2018), p. 37fn41.
75. Ibid.

Chapter 5

ROMANO GUARDINI
(1885–1968)

If Europe detached itself completely from Christ – then, and to the extent that this happened, it would cease to be.[1]

Romano Guardini was ordained a priest in 1910 and after working briefly in a pastoral position he took up his doctoral studies under the supervision of Engelbert Krebs (1881–1950) in Freiburg im Breisgau, a city on the edge of the Black Forest. Krebs was an authority on medieval scholasticism, and he was also known for his opposition to the neo-Kantianism of the Baden school that was influential in the last three decades of the nineteenth century but began to wane at the end of the First World War. This probably explains Guardini's choice of St Bonaventure as the focus of both his doctorate – *Die Lehre des heiligen Bonaventura von der Erlösung* – and his *Habilitationsschrift* – *Systembildende Elemente in der Theologie Bonaventura* – the latter undertaken at the University of Bonn under the direction of Gerhard Esser, the Professor of Dogmatic Theology. From 1923 until 1939 Guardini held the Chair of Philosophy of Religion and Catholic *Weltanschauung* in Berlin. During this time, he dedicated many of his courses to anthropological themes. He was also heavily involved in the leadership of Quickborn – a Catholic youth movement – contributing articles to its journal *Die Schildgenossen* and working as one of the journal's editors.[2] However, in 1939 the National Socialists forced him to resign from the University of Berlin on the grounds that the state itself had a world view that was valid for everyone, and therefore his

---

1. Romano Guardini, *Europa: Compito e destino* (Brescia: Morcelliana, 2004), p. 44.

2. For an in-depth history of the journal see Katja Marmetschke, 'Nicht mehr Jugendbewegung, sondern Kulturbewegung: Die Zeitschrift *Die Schildgenossen*

Catholic world view was no longer needed. He himself at a general meeting of Quickborn's leaders voted to dissolve the organization to avoid a Nazi takeover of its youth education programmes.[3] Just as the British bombed the French fleet berthed at Mers-el-Kébir in Algeria in 1940 and the French themselves scuttled some of their remaining fleet at Toulon so that the Nazis could not take control of their ships, Guardini disbanded a movement he had done more than anyone else to form so that it did not become subject to Nazi control. He remained living in Berlin until 1943, writing books and taking evening classes in the Church of St Canisius. When sustained Allied bombing forced evacuations in 1943, he went to live in Mooshausen with his friend Fr Josef Weiger (1883–1966) who was a renowned liturgical scholar and also a friend of Carl Muth. After the Second World War he returned to teaching, first at the University of Tübingen, and then from 1948 to 1962 at the University of Munich. In 1965, three years before his death, Pope Paul VI offered to make him a cardinal but he declined the honour. In a speech delivered on the occasion of his seventieth birthday, he reflected:

> I was born in Italy, in Verona, and precisely, if it is legitimate to add it, in the vicinity of the Arena, whose powerful oval speaks of a long historical context and at the same time the vigor of the *forma* typical of classical antiquity ... For professional reasons my family moved to Germany; and while at home we spoke and thought in Italian, I grew spiritually within the German language and culture.[4]

In his afterword to a collection of Guardini's lectures on the subject of Europe, Silvano Zucal wrote:

> Guardini therefore carried within himself, as Albrecht Goes wrote, a double fragment: a fragment of Italy and a fragment of Germany. Latin clarity and all-German sensitivity to the unfathomable. He

---

in der Weimarer Republik', in *Le Milieu Intellectuel Catholoique en Allemagne, sa Presse et ses Réseaux (1871-1963)/Das Katholische Intellektuellen-Milieu in Deutschland, seine Presse und seine Netzwerke (1871-1963)* (Bern: Peter Lang, 2006), pp. 281–319.

3. Elisabeth Reinhardt, 'Romano Guardini, amigo y maestro de la juventad', *Scripta Theologica* 50 (Diciembre 2018), pp. 591–610 at 601.

4. Guardini, *Europa: Compito e destino*, p. 32.

loved Munich (city of great freedom of life, art and music) because he perceived it as a bridge between his two souls and his two homelands. It was in fact – according to him – among the German cities the most similar to the Italian world. Yet this double belonging – even beyond the existentially tormented vicissitudes of military service – was not for Guardini free of conflict and lacerations. Perhaps it was precisely from this interior oppositional duality, from this lived conflict, that his philosophy of the 'polar opposition' (*Gegensatz*) given to the most important of his philosophical works drew inspiration.[5]

Zucal went on to explain Guardini's concept of 'polar oppositions' as the idea that there are contrasts that cannot be eliminated because they each have their own specific wealth. They are not therefore contradictions (*Widersprüche*) but rather polar oppositions (*Gegensätze*) that need to be held in tension because one complements the other. He gave the example of 'Italian spontaneity' and 'German reflective torment' – 'the vital spontaneity not to fall short of superficiality, the reflective torment not to become a rarefied and abstract cerebral philosophy'.[6] In Guardini's own words, 'what matters is that the sides in a question are seen in relation to the rest and thus have the character of integrity'.[7]

In her study of Guardini's anthropology, Ursula Berning-Baldeaux added the insight that Guardini's theory of *Gegensätze* is fundamentally different from that of Kierkegaard. With Guardini, 'the opposites are organically correlated to one another and join architectonically – without a rupturing leap – to a living whole'.[8] In Guardini's theology there is no tragic either/or, but a very synthetic both/and.

Berning-Baldeaux also noted that Guardini stands in the tradition of the *Philosophia und Theologia cordis*, as it is found in the works of Plato, Augustine, Dante, Pascal, Dostoyevsky and Rilke. For Guardini 'the heart is the scene of the substantive unity of man and it is also the location of the conscience'.[9] In her roll call of scholars for whom the heart is the central locus of all operations of the soul, she omitted to

5. Silvano Zucal, preface to Romano Guardini, *Europa: Compito e destino*, p. 85.

6. Ibid., p. 86.

7. Romano Guardini, *L'opposizione polare. Saggio per una filosofia del concreto vivente* (Brescia: Morcelliana, 1997), p. 191.

8. Ursula Berning-Baldeaux, *Person und Bildung im Denken Romano Guardinis* (Würzburg: Echter, 1968), p. 44.

9. Ibid., p. 48.

mention St Bonaventure, the subject of Guardini's earliest studies, and St John Henry Newman whose episcopal motto was *cor ad cor loquitur* (heart speaks to heart).

Hans Urs von Balthasar regarded St Bonaventure as an important source of Guardini's understanding of polar oppositions, not in the sense that Bonaventure consciously addressed the theme, but insofar as his analysis of Bonaventure led Guardini to see that there were valuable polar themes at play in the ideas of the Greek patristics, and the medieval scholastics, both having a contribution to offer.[10] Balthasar also made the point that Guardini's understanding of the heart as the centre of perception and decision, in the tradition of Dante, among others, by no means stands opposed to the intellect.[11]

In a short monograph on the polarity theme, published in 1925, Guardini emphasized that in both the classical and medieval worlds there was not a sharp either/or cleavage between intuitive thought and conceptual thinking. He wrote:

> We tend to think that intuition close to life and the abstract formation of concepts are contradictory, that conceptual thinking must destroy living intuition; and this in turn distorts thought. But it is not so. What was going on from this point of view in Greek thought? It enhanced the concept and led abstraction to the extreme. But how strong were the forces of mystical lived experience and symbolic intuition in ancient Greece! A line runs from the Orphic cults to the Hellenistic mystery religions; the Eleusinian feasts manifestly culminated in a symbolic knowledge supported by a religious transmutation. However these 'mysteries' were not considered superstitious in contradiction with scientific seriousness; instead they stood within the overall framework of what constituted an accomplished personality. And the Greek people themselves did not feel hindered by the intellect in their creation of artistic work. It is evident that the abstract formation of concepts and the shaping forces of intuition and feeling did not cause any mutual harm here.[12]

---

10. Hans Urs von Balthasar, *Romano Guardini: Reform from the Source* (Communio: Ignatius, 2010), pp. 59–65.

11. Ibid., p. 67.

12. Romano Guardini, *L'opposizione polare. Saggio per una filosofia del concreto vivente* (Brescia: Morcelliana, 1997), p. 19.

Guardini concluded that rationalism, like its counterpart, intuitionism, are 'specifically modern attitudes'.[13] The medievals, he claimed, were intellectual without being rationalistic. While they valued thought and conceptual thinking, they never disconnected these from life and from the imagination. The greatest of the scholastics were also at the same time great mystics. Guardini came to distinguish what he called 'living concepts' which remained linked to intuitive thought and 'conceptual concepts' which are severed from the powers of intuition and have their criterion of perfection in mathematical formula. Throughout his life, Guardini stood opposed to university practices that placed each discipline into distinctive 'silos', effectively severing the interaction of conceptual and intuitive thinking. His idea of a university was more 'Newmanian' than Kantian or Humboldtian.

Guardini was a typical German of his generation in finding the theology of Newman attractive. He was especially attracted to Newman's work on conscience. In 1933, the first year of the Nazi regime, Guardini published a small monograph consisting of three lectures titled *Das Gute, das Gewissen und die Sammlung* – the good, conscience and inner composure. He began the collection by saying that he hoped to offer some aid to the Christian conscience in the struggle around the foundations of a moral life, especially as this struggle is conditioned by the spiritual situation in Germany. Rhetorically he asked, 'Fight: but who are our enemies?'[14]

The first name on his list of enemies of the moral life was Immanuel Kant. To Kant he attributed the notion of the absolute autonomy of conscience. The second on his list was Friedrich Nietzsche according to whom Christianity is a form of slave morality that excludes believers from greatness. In his preface to the Italian translation of Guardini's *Welt und Person* (*Mondo e persona*), Silvano Zucal put forward the idea that Nietzsche is the secret sparring partner of Guardini with whom he, despite the diversity of conclusions, maintained an empathetic relationship.[15] Thirdly, in the roll call of enemies, Guardini listed Bolshevism. Bolshevism 'suffocates the living spirit, and destroys the free personality in the collective and in the process of history, diminishing

13. Ibid., p. 21.
14. Romano Guardini, *La coscienza* (Brescia: Morcelliana, 2009), p. 5.
15. Silvano Zucal, Preface to Romano Guardini, *Mondo e persona* (Brescia: Morcelliana, 2015), p. 9.

it to a mere organ for the realization of super individual needs'.[16] Other enemies, he noted, could be named, but these were his top three.

Guardini went on to speak of a 'moral disorientation'. He suggested that 'in the judgement of many, the moral act does not compensate for the serious effort it requires', while for others, who would be ready for such an effort, they simply do not know where to start. They feel 'lost in chaos'[17]. The conscience, he argued, is not a 'mechanical instrument, a magnetic needle that puts itself in place, but something alive, and everything that is living is prone to error'.[18] While our conscience is our supreme compass, it can nonetheless, lose its own compass. This he argued can happen in three ways:

> [First], the conscience can become superficial, reckless, obtuse. Consciousness makes life more burdensome. It makes life richer in content, more dignified, but this also means heavier. As a consequence we have a tendency to seek the easy ways and free ourselves from the burdens. There is an internal operation that aims to cushion the need for conscience. It is not always a conscious desire; it may be that the sphere of the subconscious acts. This can happen in a thousand ways: by doing so, for example, that the gaze is distracted by the unpleasant lines of what we are dealing with; that the most important point remains veiled; that the situation with its fatiguing unicity and unrepeatability is flattened on a more comfortable general scheme ...
>
> [Second], consciousness may also be refined excessively. A person may see duties where there are none; to feel responsibilities which do not exist; to exaggerate obligations beyond the limits of what is right and possible ... Within the human person the secret instinct to torment oneself is deeply rooted, and in certain temperaments this instinct works with particular force. If it is not cured with prudent care it can degenerate into melancholy.
>
> Thirdly, consciousness can also be altered in its contents. Our knowledge is not a mirror which simply reproduces what is in front of it. We do not view a situation the way that a camera photographs an object. In our view we are present ourselves. We ourselves, with our temperament, with our desires, with our secret and overt motives, are already contained in the gaze, which we direct on things: thus,

---

16. Guardini, *La coscienza*, p. 5.
17. Ibid., p. 21.
18. Ibid., p. 29.

by looking at them, we shape them. We do not take them as they are in themselves, but as we wish they were, that is, to find a welcoming environment for our desires and our feelings. We would like to see the confirmation of what we are in the situation.[19]

Not only is the conscience not a mirror or a camera, or a magnetic needle or any other kind of mechanical instrument, Guardini also argued that it is not a 'law that hangs somewhere', 'not a simple idea', 'not a concept in the air' but rather 'the living voice of God's holiness in us'.[20] This means that as soon as a person starts to engage with his conscience, he 'strikes a religious ground'. In the Old Testament this was described as 'walking in the sight of God' or 'walking in the presence of God'. Guardini believed that to those who pray, 'thy will be done on earth as it is in heaven', God will give the grace of a clear conscience.[21]

While three enemies were listed at the beginning of the book, the weight of the argumentation is against the Kantian enemy. Guardini spent several paragraphs firing canons into the idea that a person who looks to God for knowledge of what is good and moral is a slave to others and fails the autonomy test. God, he stated, 'surrounds us, envelopes us, penetrates us'.[22] He is 'present in our intimacy'. He 'speaks within us'. He 'speaks from the inside with the raising of the conscience, from the outside with the disposition of things'.[23] The word of the one is clarified by the word of the other. 'Man is regenerated, from God the Father, in Christ, by the work of the Holy Spirit, to participate in the divine life'.[24] Therefore the moral law is not a law of my 'I'. Guardini described the Kantian belief that the moral law is a law of my 'I' as 'an inner optical illusion' and an 'incorrect thesis' both philosophically and theologically.[25] God, he declared, is *not* an 'other'. Rather, 'my religious relationship with God is determined precisely by that unique phenomenon that is not repeated elsewhere'.[26] The fact is that 'the more deeply I abandon myself to Him, the more fully I allow Him to

19. Ibid., pp. 28–32.
20. Ibid., pp. 32–3.
21. Ibid., p. 35.
22. Ibid., p. 36.
23. Ibid., p. 37.
24. Ibid., p. 38.
25. Ibid., p. 39.
26. Ibid., p. 40.

penetrate me, the greater the force the Creator asserts in myself, the more I become myself'.[27]

Having dealt with Kant's optical illusion, Guardini then deepened his theological analysis by suggesting that people often forget that there is a sacrament of the Christian conscience called Confirmation which comes with some seven gifts – those listed in the Book of Isa. 11. 1-2 as wisdom, understanding, counsel, knowledge, fortitude, piety and fear of the Lord. He also endorsed the prayer of John Henry Newman for clarity of conscience against ears that are deaf to the voice of God and eyes that are blind to the signs of God. In another work *Antropologia cristiana*, he described the conscience as an organ for God – *das Organ für Gott* – which finds its sanctification in the sacrament of Confirmation.[28]

In an address to honour the White Rose Martyrs, the students of the University of Munich who scattered anti-Nazi leaflets like rose petals, Guardini offered another reflection upon the claim of the moral autonomy of the human person and what he called the 'desperate freedom' of existentialism. He wrote that the effort to realize moral autonomy caused something to occur within the human person 'without which the events of the last three decades cannot be understood'.[29] This 'effort', he argued, or the great moral project of German Idealism, left its subjects 'exhausted right down to their inner selves, to the point where this exhaustion became a determining factor in history'.[30] As a consequence, man suffered 'an existential collapse'. Moreover, 'the effect of this collapse was, on the objective level, the dictatorship: on the subjective level, the desire to be supported in the exercise of one's own responsibility, that is, to be crushed by the dictatorship, be it direct or indirect'.[31] From these empirical observations he concluded:

> Man can be weaned from the exercise of freedom. Those whose personal formation had its roots in the years before the First World War found it almost impossible to realise how short a period was required to do away with free values and attitudes. From those who thought historically it had become axiomatic that our modern age

27. Ibid.
28. Romano Guardini, *Antropologia cristiana* (Brescia: Morcelliana, 2013), p. 115.
29. Romano Guardini, *La Rosa Bianca* (Brescia: Morcelliana, 2014), p. 58.
30. Ibid.
31. Ibid.

had established freedom as the indispensable basis of civilisation. Experience in Germany since 1933 has shown that this basis cannot merely be eradicated from the social and political structure, but it can be removed from the general frame of mind of the people. For many in this period freedom had lost its character of a value and was even regarded as contemptible bourgeois selfishness. [32]

Such a dereliction of responsibility for the exercise of one's own freedom was, for Guardini, profoundly anti-Christian. It was a mentality that struck at the very root of the Christian idea of the person as a being made with a rational intellect and a free will and it was also an exhibition of herd behaviour beyond anything imagined by Nietzsche.

In a manner similar to Haecker, Guardini held a high level of respect for the achievements of pre-Christian classical culture wherein notions like reason, rationality and personal responsibility for one's behaviour were held in high regard. Although he did not write whole works on the classical heritage, such as Haecker's book on Virgil, he did declare that 'antiquity was for Christ and His Kingdom as Dante well understood'.[33] Nonetheless, notwithstanding his acknowledgement of the valuable preparatory work of classical culture, Guardini argued that the 'European image of man is determined in the deepest way by Christianity'.[34] The Christian contribution is the deepest because 'it rests on the influence of the saving action of Christ, who has freed man from the spell of nature and has given him an independence from nature'.[35] Moreover, 'the man of the Christian era has, in front of the ancient man, an extra dimension of spirit and soul; an ability to feel, a creativity of the heart and a strength to suffer, which do not proceed from natural talent, but from custom with Christ'.[36] Guardini concluded that this 'extra dimension' means that the Christian person has a much higher level of potentiality for goodness than that of the pre-Christian virtuous pagan, and conversely, if those who live after the Incarnation follow the path of evil, their evil will be far deeper than that of the classically pagan.[37]

---

32. Romano Guardini, *Freedom, Grace and Destiny* (London: Harvill, 1961), pp. 22–3.
33. Guardini, *Europa: Compito e destino*, p. 42.
34. Ibid.
35. Ibid.
36. Ibid., p. 43.
37. Ibid.

This is because 'as soon as God, in the incarnation, entered history, ready to assume destiny for man, a possibility of evil emerges, for which nothing remains but to call it ... the will to annihilate God – and with God what comes in man from God'.[38] Guardini also argued that this 'extra-dimension' is responsible for 'the intensity of western historical consciousness'.[39] He acknowledged that such consciousness is in part a consequence of the 'ancient force of acting and founding as, [for example], the boldness and creative force of the Germanic tribes', but he nonetheless believed that the decisive element in Western historical consciousness is derivative from the Christian cultural components since, *pace* Nietzsche et al. it determined that 'the pattern of historical existence is not the eternal return of things, the cycle of becoming, passing and becoming again, but that non-repeatability of person, of decision and action, which Christianity teaches and which determines not only time, but through it also eternity'.[40]

The 'extra dimension' of the Christian soul was, however, systematically oppressed in Nazi Germany. Planning referred not only to things and institutions but also and above all to the living human being himself. The ideology that undergirded all of this was found 'in the idea of blood and race, for which every essential and important moment comes from the biological constitution of man', including his 'personality, character and moral qualities'.[41] Guardini declaimed, 'All that is called autonomous capacity for judgment, conviction, conscience, freedom of the individual, and right truth was discredited and removed; in a word, everything that is rooted in the dignity and responsibility of the person, the whole of thought was biologized'.[42] Spiritual judgements, personal convictions, ideas about the responsibility for one's own conscience, the awareness of the eternal value of each person was presented as 'alien to the species', as 'Christian-Jewish depravity', as 'misuse of the sacred forces of nature', as 'hostile to life'.[43] Biology thereby became the basis 'not only of anthropology, but also of civilisation, of the state and of religion'.[44] Guardini went on to suggest that this ideology was not even

---

38. Guardini, *Mondo e persona*, p. 205.
39. Guardini, *Europa: Compito e destino*, p. 43.
40. Ibid.
41. Ibid., p. 46.
42. Ibid., p. 48.
43. Ibid., p. 50.
44. Ibid., p. 46.

original to the Nazis but could be found in the fourth chapter of the first part of Nietzsche's *Thus Spake Zarathustra*. He concluded:

> Where these efforts were successful, thinking and feeling about sexual things as well as the relationship of the sexes between them slipped more and more into the atmosphere of the breeding barn. More and more, what gives man support in himself disappeared: the feeling of spiritual dignity, the capacity for personal judgment, the awareness of the eternal value of the individual. Man was thus increasingly abandoned at the mercy of power that governed him and used him for its own purposes.[45]

In the same speech, Guardini described Hitler and Goebbels as 'renegade Catholics'.[46] Hitler was presented to the public as a 'Saviour', as a pseudo-Christ figure. He was 'capable of judging all things, political and military, scientific and artistic. He knew and could do everything.'[47] He was 'the creator of the perfect state, the greatest leader of all time, the one who solves all social and economic problems, the infallible art critic', notwithstanding the fact that he had 'never gone through any serious course of study'.[48] Like Theodor Haecker, Guardini noted the way that Hitler and Goebbels and other Nazi propagandists exploited the destiny theme in German culture. In his *Freedom, Grace and Destiny* Guardini wrote:

> Pedagogy did its best to educate youth in a readiness to embrace destiny. Poetry presented the picture of the heroic man filled with an awareness of his destiny. In public speeches, the press, and the general interpretation of life a Germanic mentality, inspired by the force of destiny and of bravery in the face of destiny, was lauded as a counterbalance to Jewish calculation and Christian tender-heartedness. Enthusiastic because of the splendour of the 'Reich', the new man must feel he is summoned to encounter danger and the threat of death and to rise to loftier planes of being through this willingness to meet destiny.[49]

---

45. Ibid., p. 49.
46. Ibid., p. 52.
47. Ibid., p. 51.
48. Ibid.
49. Guardini, *Freedom, Grace and Destiny*, p. 186.

While the Nazi regime represented a totalitarianism 'from above' Guardini also detected a totalitarianism 'that comes from within' and 'flattens the personality'. There is, he argued, an indirect form of coercion that is exercised through the apparatus of technological culture that includes 'the scientifically studied manipulation of the unconscious of man by the economy'.[50] He drew special attention to the fact that 'economics studies the ways in which the apparently unnoticed stimuli of advertising are internalized in the motivation of the individual and develops the results of these researches in a technique of constant influences, not perceived by the interested party himself'.[51] Here Guardini's social criticism comes close to that of Herbert Marcuse's ideas expressed in Marcuse's *One Dimensional Man* (1964). Guardini argued that advanced industrial society created false consumer needs that integrated individuals into a system of media-driven mass consumption. Although the Catholic Guardini and the Marxist Marcuse clearly had different readings of the root cause of this problem and different solutions for it, they were similarly concerned about this social pathology.

In his collection of essays *The End of Modern World* (1950), Guardini drew a connection between the character of 'mass man', (his analogue for Marcuse's 'one dimensional man') and the problems of evangelization in the contemporary world. He described 'mass man' as having 'no desire for independence or originality in either the management or the conduct of his life'.[52] Mass man simply accepts 'the gadgets and technics forced upon him by the patterns of machine production and of abstract planning', and 'to either a greater or a lesser degree [he] is convinced that his conformity is both reasonable and just'.[53] This propensity to conform is related to what cultural historians have identified as the 'bourgeois', rather than 'aristocratic' character of the culture of modernity. The bourgeois temperament is calculating, pragmatic, focused on efficiency and predictable outcomes. It discourages moral heroism as unreasonable and gives priority to the 'bourgeois' goods of efficiency over the 'aristocratic' goods of excellence. It both levels and narrows horizons. When this mentality is fused with Christian

---

50. Guardini, *La Rosa Bianca*, p. 56.

51. Ibid.

52. Romano Guardini, *The End of the Modern World* (Wilmington Delaware: Intercollegiate Studies Institute, 1998), p. 60.

53. Ibid.

elements, the end result is the bourgeois Christianity ridiculed and condemned by the atheists Feuerbach, Marx and Nietzsche, on the one side, and Kierkegaard, Newman, Steinbüchel, Haecker and others, on the theistic side.

In his later *Freedom, Grace and Destiny* (1956), Guardini returned to the subject of mass man's incapacity for personal responsibility. He asserted that the 'emphasis on authority, however necessary, and on the obedience due to it, has diverted men's attention from the responsibility of individual judgment, moral decision and personal participation to an extent that might well disturb us'.[54] Here the diagnosis is consistent with Georges Bernanos's distinctions between the dispositions of the imbecile and the *honnête homme*, between a technocratic servility and an 'aristocracy of the spirit'. In *We, the French*, Bernanos wrote:

> The more a sense of Christian honour becomes debilitated, the greater the abundance, indeed superabundance, of casuists. At the very least, the man of honor offers you the following advantage: he spares the casuist all his labor … The moment a person feels the need to consult the casuists in order to know the amount starting from which stealing money may be considered a mortal sin … we may say that his social value is nil, even if he abstains from stealing.[55]

Commenting on this passage, Balthasar suggested that 'the person who does not come to terms with his drives and whose religion risks becoming an endless struggle between duty and inclination – the threat of a Kantian Jansenism – is precisely the person who will most readily accept casuistry', and further, against such a 'bourgeois morality and a despairing moralism, Bernanos proposed the ethos of chivalry, which for him was intimately related to the ethos of the saint'.[56] The chivalrous person and the saint both go beyond what is required by duty. They are not constrained by notions of what is normally expected of people in this circumstance, or by what people are required to do by the law. Their moral code is not limited to the horizons of 'mass man'.

---

54. Guardini, *Freedom, Grace and Destiny*, p. 231.
55. Georges Bernanos, *Nous autres Français* (*We, the French*), cited by Hans Urs von Balthasar in *Bernanos: An Ecclesial Existence* (San Francisco: Ignatius, 1996), pp. 298-9.
56. Ibid., p. 298.

Bernanos was concerned about the issue of casuistry because of what he, Balthasar and other Catholic writers of the era, perceived to be a kind of Kantian-Jansenism at work in the field of Catholic moral theology. They opposed a Prussian 'duty-parade Catholicism' with its 'tax lawyer morality' always searching for loop-holes and exemptions in the manuals of the casuists. What Balthasar called a Kantian-Jansenism, Guardini simply called 'moralism'. He was highly critical of the Kantian narrowing of Christianity to a mere moral code. Time and again he exhorted his students to understand that Christianity is not primarily a moral code but a relationship with a Person. This exhortation was not lost on the young Fr Ratzinger who began a series of sermons at the Cathedral of Münster in 1964 with the question, 'What actually is the real substance of Christianity that goes beyond mere moralism?'[57] As Pope he followed up these lectures with his encyclical *Deus Caritas Est* that begins by emphasizing that God is a person. He then situated Catholic morality within the context of this very dialogical I–Thou relationship which is based on love not upon adherence to a moral code. The moral code, to the extent that it exists (and the Ten Commandments are obviously a moral code, as are Christ's Beatitudes), is secondary to the primacy of the I–Thou relationship. Even the Ten Commandments begin with a declaration about this relationship – I am the Lord your God!

Thus, while Guardini's whole approach to the relationship of the human person to his Creator was anti-Kantian and decidedly personalist and oriented by the theological virtues of faith, hope and love, rather than by any system of casuistry, the situation of the German Catholic of the first half of the twentieth century was not merely that of having to contend with the prevalence of a warped Kantian-Jansenist spirituality, a problem named and shamed by Bernanos and Balthasar. They were also contending with the social coercion of the Nazi era that directly attacked their freedom, dignity and nobility. They were in a sense being ground down by the Kantian spirit coming at them from two different directions: the direction of casuistic moral theology and the direction of fascist conceptions of civic duty.

Like Bernanos and Steinbüchel, Guardini was interested in the courtly *Menschenbild* and he went so far as to compare the Quickborners with Parsifal. In her article '*Romano Guardini, amigo y maestro de*

---

57. Joseph Ratzinger, *What It Means to Be a Christian* (San Francisco: Ignatius, 2006), p. 47.

la juventud', Elisabeth Reinhardt drew attention to this chivalrous dimension of Guardini's thought:

> Rothenfels, dating from the twelfth century, was from the outset a source of inspiration for Guardini in his educational activity with young people. The fortified complex with the great tower is built on a high place, at the foot of a large reddish rock (hence Rothenfels), overlooking the Main River in the bottom of the valley. Inside, buildings, walls, squares, meeting places and also some activities had medieval names. All of this recalled the legend of Parsifal and the ideals of medieval life that had perennial value and could be attractive to young people. At a meeting in 1922 he told them that they were like Parsifal, who had gone in search of the castle where the Grail was guarded. 'The Grail is truth and love with the strength that Christ gives. This is what Quickborn is looking for, like in the past Parsifal ... Anywhere where brothers and sisters are united, loyal to each other and Quickborn's mission, in common sense and self-forgetfulness, there is the castle and within it the Grail.'[58]

The contrast between Parsifal and 'mass man' could not possibly be starker. One is content to be told how to exercise one's freedom, to be a part of the 'herd', the other views life as a quest for the highest, most excellent. In his analysis of 'mass man' Guardini argued that this social type has been fostered by two apparently opposite philosophical movements, that of determinism and absolutism. Determinism denies the existence of freedom while absolutism identifies it with complete autonomy. Determinism reduces the human person to a purely natural being while absolutism identifies the person with God.[59] Determinism denies each person's uniqueness and unrepeatability and freedom, while, from a different angle, absolutism similarly overlooks the person's relationality, his or her place within a family and a community, by treating him as a self-sufficient miniature god. Jansenism was the theological shadow side of determinism while Kantianism was the philosophical shadow side of political projects aimed at replacing piety with autonomy and thus turning man into a god. Determinism was also aided and abetted by what Guardini identified as 'the unparalleled use

---

58. Elisabeth Reinhardt, 'Romano Guardini, amigo y maestro de la juventad', *Scripta Theologica* 50 (Diciembre 2018), pp. 591–610 at 603.
59. Guardini, *Freedom, Grace and Destiny*, p. 62.

of the notion of destiny in Germany during the twelve years of Nazi leadership'.[60] In such cultural conditions, Guardini argued that the believer is faced with a twofold danger:

> The first, [is] that of toning down and secularising Christ's will in order to conform to the community in which he lives, the second, [is] of taking Christ's will earnestly but lapsing into a mood of pessimism that abandons all control of the world or even [lapsing] into a ghetto mentality, the outlook of a despised minority.[61]

In contrast to neopagan conceptions of fate and destiny, Guardini countered that the Christian concept of providence develops from the harmony of the believer with God's active and creative will.[62]

In addition to the philosophies of determinism and absolutism, Guardini also identified a third philosophical position that undermines the power of truth and its freedom. In *The Spirit of the Liturgy* he devoted an entire chapter to what he called *Der Primat des Logos über das Ethos*, or, the primacy of *Logos* over *Ethos*, of reason over will. In this section he traced the transition from the wisdom of the medieval era which gave primacy to *Logos* over *Ethos*, to the reversal of this priority in the philosophy of Immanuel Kant and his followers. Kant's priority of the 'pure will' morphed into the priority of the psychological will of Fichte and Schopenhauer until finally it found its clearest expression in Nietzsche's will to power. In his *End of the Modern World*, Guardini predicted that the final outcome of this trajectory would be a 'non-cultural culture', accompanied by a 'non-human man' and a 'non-natural nature'.[63] Similarly, in *Freedom, Grace and Destiny*, he linked the indifference to both freedom and truth to the trend towards prioritizing 'outcomes' over truth, of giving priority to *ethos* over *logos*. He wrote:

> One very disastrous error of recent times, propagated by Nietzsche and Pragmatism, was the belief that truth consisted essentially in its effect upon life, in so far as it imparted to it assurance, energy, and intensity. According to this theory, thought which assisted life was accepted as true; what impeded life was rejected as untrue. And so

---

60. Ibid., pp. 186 fn 83.
61. Ibid., p. 220.
62. Ibid., p. 212.
63. Guardini, *The End of the Modern World*, p. 87.

truth was subordinated to life and its essential character was lost. But truth contains its significance within itself in its intrinsic validity and dignity. Truth is not utility; it is precisely truth.[64]

In his work of tribute to Guardini – *Reform from the Source* – Balthasar highlighted this particular dimension of Guardini's thought, saying that Guardini took a stand against the primacy of *ethos* over *logos* early in his life and that he also opposed the practice of making dogma dependent on its 'existential value' or *Lebenswert*.[65] The reversal of the primacy of *Logos* over *Ethos* became the signature tune of late-twentieth-century liberation theology, in many cases propounded by theologians whose doctoral dissertations were undertaken at universities in Germany and Belgium. As an early critic of liberation theology wrote in 1976, it carries the label 'made in Germany'.[66] One of the fascinating questions in Catholic intellectual history is therefore, 'What caused such a rupture in the sensibilities of the generation(s) who lived through the Nazi era and the immediate post-War generation that came of age in the 1960s, such that the priority of *logos* over *ethos* was rejected and flipped?'

As a generalization one might say that the post-war generation dropped the philosophy of classical Greece and replaced it with the critical theory of the Frankfurt School. Even if this is so, it still raises the question of why so many German Catholic scholars of the post-war generation preferred Horkheimer et al. to Guardini. The standout exceptions are Joseph Ratzinger and Robert Spaemann, though in each case they are not so much representative of the post-war generation as men who arrived on the tail end of one generation and reached maturity at the beginning of the next. They were born nineteen days apart in 1927 and were thus children when the Nazis came to power in 1933 and men in their late teens when the Second World War ended. They were intellectual leaders of the post-war era but stood apart from others who represented the 'Generation of 1968' – the 'priority of praxis' generation – in the realm of Catholic theology. One theory is that members of the post-war generation desperately desired a 'narrative' that could explain the behaviour of their parents and grandparents,

64. Guardini, *Freedom, Grace and Destiny*, p. 37.
65. Hans Urs von Balthasar, *Romano Guardini: Reform from the Source* (San Francisco: Ignatius, 2010), p. 25.
66. P. André-Vincent, 'Les théologies de la liberation', *Nouvelle Revue Théologique* (February 1976), p. 110.

their submission to tyrants and psychopaths, and this was not provided by Catholic leaders but by Theodor Adorno's 1950 publication *The Authoritarian Personality*. Adorno's analysis, rather than a more multicausal and interdisciplinary analysis, including an analysis of the existential crises suffered by the First World War generation – their spiritual exhaustion, as it were – came to define the generation of 1968.

Returning to the issue of Guardini's analysis of the social pathologies associated with 'mass man', in a work written during his Berlin years titled *Der Mensch: Umriss einer christlichen Anthropologie*, but published posthumously in 2009 as *Antropologia cristiana*, Guardini made the following observation:

> Humility means recognising that what one must want to be is not and cannot be reached by one's own power, but one can only receive it; that it is constituted not from the bottom to the top but from the top to the bottom, or better still starting from the mystery of the love of God; that one lives as a result of a gift, following grace.[67]

This kind of understanding avoids the extremes of the isolated superman with his will to power and the bland, uniform, 'mass man' shackled to the herd without a unique personality or a sense of personal responsibility. In this early anthropological work, Guardini also emphasized revelation's role as the hermeneutical key to understanding human nature. He described revelation as 'not only a reliable truth, which we try to grasp for the sake of knowledge, but a living and holy truth; a wisdom to which we turn with a docile heart to receive meaning and indications'.[68] An explicitly theological anthropology reliant upon revelation delivers up a very different image of man from the disciplines of psychology and sociology which Guardini described as being 'distinctly functional'. According to Guardini the purely natural being to which modern science refers would be unrecognizable by the author of the Book of *Genesis*. Long before de Lubac challenged the baroque idea of 'pure nature', Guardini was expressly critical of the concept. He wrote:

> In a strict sense, man has no 'nature' in the sense of the natural ontological closure and sensorial self-subsistence of the animal. And he has no autonomy of spiritual-value existence, or any 'culture'

---

67. Guardini, *Antropologia cristiana*, p. 116.
68. Ibid., p. 17.

in the modern sense. Rather man exists, in his essence, as a being 'turned towards'. It is for this reason that only in love and grace does human nature ultimately become itself ... Only in the love and grace of which the kingdom of God is made does the existential and cultural world of man attain authenticity. If however, he refuses to reach the right objective, the one to which he is ultimately turned, what happens is not that man gains access to himself, or acquires an autonomous personality in his own nature and in his own cultural creativity; on the contrary, he continues to exist 'facing', and it cannot be otherwise, only that he now exists facing the void.[69]

While Guardini cited *Genesis* as the starting point for an understanding of the human person based on revelation, it is not in the Old Testament that he found the most significant insights, but in the New Testament with the revelation of the Trinity and in St Paul's *First Epistle to the Corinthians*, wherein the importance of the theological virtues of 'faith, hope and charity' is explained. Guardini described Christ as the key to the knowledge of man. This proposition was later to appear in paragraph 22 of the Conciliar document *Gaudium et spes*. This document has been widely criticized for not integrating an account of the human person based upon the Book of *Genesis*, which features in its first half, with an account based on the revelation of the Trinity, which appears in its second half. Throughout the pontificate of Karl Wojtyła/John Paul II, the scholar-pontiff made it clear that the explicitly Trinitarian account was his preferred approach, and he even released a trilogy of encyclicals to unpack this theological proposition. *Redemptor Hominis* (1979) dealt with God the Son, *Dives in Misericordia* (1980) addresssed the subject of God the Father and *Dominum et vivificantem* (1986) explained the role of the Holy Spirit. In this sense it is often said that Guardini was one of the precursors of the Second Vatican Council and especially of the trinitarian anthropology that followed so strongly in its wake, particularly in the pontificate of St John Paul II. In this publication written in the 1930s, Guardini adds a caveat to the effect that it is not simply a matter of 'assuming Christ as the starting point of a new theory', rather one needs to enter into a relationship with Christ. It is only when one enters into a relationship with the Persons of the Trinity that the faculties of the soul acquire an understanding of such concepts as original innocence and original sin and the possibilities

---

69. Ibid., p. 56.

of redemption. He exhorted his readers to try and penetrate the Christian mysteries, not so much by thought but by living them. He wrote, 'We must let Christ put our thoughts in order', 'Christ must be taken as a category of existence, of thought and of Christian axiological judgment'.[70] He acknowledged that 'all scientific and philosophical knowledge is helpful, but none of it remains as and in itself, rather it is modified by one's relationship to Christ'.[71] Guardini was thus a proponent of a theological anthropology built upon a Christocentric Trinitarian foundation. Silvano Zucal has described this theology as a fusion of Johannine Christology, the 'Cosmic Christ of St Paul' and St Bonaventure's vision of Christ *'tenens medium in omnibus'* (the medium holding all things).[72]

In *Antropologia cristiana* Guardini also told the story of how he came across a book on the subject of the development of humanity and discovered in it a chapter on the theme of 'Homination' (*Menschwerdung*). The author was using the expression to refer to the process by which monkeys or other species of higher primates developed into human beings. Guardini noted that the same word is used in theological parlance to refer to the Incarnation of Christ – *die Menschwerdung Gottes* rather than *die Menschwerdung des Affen*.[73] The first use of the word explains the human person from above, the second usage explains the human person from below. Guardini argued that no compromise between the positions is possible, only a decision in favour of one or the other. He also exhorted his readers to take a stand against the 'secularisation and correlated corruption of Christian concepts' – a process he claimed began in Italy in the thirteenth century and spread to the rest of Europe in the sixteenth.[74] In sounding this warning Guardini had anticipated what was to become a major theme in the works of genealogists of modernity in the late twentieth century. Alasdair MacIntyre tracked the secularization of the concept of virtue, Louis Dupré tracked the secularization of the concept of nature, and Charles Taylor similarly argued that modernity is not a completely new culture but rather a

---

70. Ibid., p. 36.
71. Ibid., p. 77.
72. Silvano Zucal, Afterword to Romano Guardini, *La Visione Cattolica del Mondo* (Brescia: Morcelliana, 2018), p. 84.
73. Guardini, *Antropologia cristiana*, p. 58.
74. Ibid., p. 60.

culture that was created by the transformation in meaning of several key Christian concepts.

In the conclusion of *Antropologia cristiana*, Guardini suggested that three questions needed to be answered: is redemption necessary, is it possible and do we want it? He noted that modernity answered no to the first question in the following series of historical moments:

> The Enlightenment outlined the first major project of the autonomous order of human existence and the French Revolution was the first to draw its political consequences. Then both liberalism and socialism have begun to change the whole existence, to build a cultural, economic and social system. With Nietzsche, the thought bursts that it is possible to 'raise' a superior man. Bolshevism [then] treats the human being as the chemical substances of laboratories and factories; it shatters, assembles, experiments, builds.[75]

In relation to the further two questions, Guardini observed that the scholars of the nineteenth century often took the attitude that they did not want to be redeemed if they had to first acknowledge their need for redemption. He concluded that 'every form of humanism that is not Christian is destined to fall back into the sub-human'.[76]

While *Gaudium et spes* paragraph 22 is usually interpreted as making precisely this point, that any form of humanism that is not Christocentric will collapse into the subhuman, *Gaudium et spes* paragraph 36 affirms the concept of 'the autonomy of culture'. One of the unresolved theological issues of post-Conciliar theology is how these two sections of *Gaudium et spes* relate to each other. If culture can be autonomous, does that mean that it has no need of Christ, and if it needs Christ, in what sense is it autonomous?

In his *Welt und Person* (1939), later published in English as *The World and the Person* (1965) and in Italian as *Mondo e persona* (2000), Guardini drew attention to the problem of the autonomy of culture which 'progressively detaches science, politics, economics, art, pedagogy, etc from the bonds of faith, but also from any universally binding ethics and bases them on themselves'.[77] He lamented that 'the whole modern view of the autonomy of the world and of man ... seem to rest ultimately on the notion which made of God the "other" '.[78]

---

75. Ibid., p. 61.
76. Ibid.
77. Romano Guardini, *Mondo e persona* (Brescia: Morcelliana, 2000), p. 33.
78. Ibid.

The end result of this mentality is that the world becomes an idol. Guardini concluded that this concept of autonomy 'is a kind of tetanus in which the world suffocates'.[79] In his autobiographical work, *A Theologian's Journey*, Thomas F. O'Meara suggested that much conflict in the post-Conciliar era would have been avoided if Guardini's perspectives on modernity had been read by the Conciliar Fathers and their *periti*.[80]

The two Conciliar paragraphs may be capable of a harmonious reconciliation if one understands 'autonomy' in the sense in which St Thomas, in *Summa Theologiae* I, q. 85, speaks of all things being endowed with their own stability, goodness and order. This is an echo of St Augustine's comments in *De Trinitate* 6: 12, that all things which are made by divine skill, show in themselves a certain unity and form and order. This interpretation presupposes some form of the analogy of being and a related hierarchy of goodness. This notion of autonomy means something like an internal coherence and order which runs on its own principles, however even the internal principles were initially put into place by the Creator of all things. This Augustinian-Thomistic idea of all things having their own internal coherence and order is not a recognition of an ontological space completely disconnected from the graces of creation and redemption. It is nothing like the Lutheran 'Two Kingdoms' theory.

Guardini offered three examples of how culture can be problematically construed as an autonomous order according to different non-Christian cosmologies. As he explained:

> A problem with the psychological structure or situation in the history of the spirit lies in how the original data of nature, subject and culture are related to each other ... The center can be fixed in nature and the subject can be felt as an organ of it; so it happens in the philosophy of nature of the Renaissance and Romanticism. Then culture also becomes an emanation of nature; as a spontaneous building of itself with the mediation of the reflective subject. Or the point of gravity moves into the ego, and nature then becomes the chaotic mass of possibilities, from which the subject, operating with autonomous energy, produces the world of culture, as developed

---

79. Romano Guardini, *The World and the Person* (Henry Regnery: Chicago, 1965), p. 204.

80. Thomas F. O'Meara, *A Theologian's Journey* (Boston: Paulist Press, 2002), p. 218.

in Kant's philosophy. Finally, nature and subject can be considered equally important supports of the relationship, and between them there is then the process, superior to that of a natural and personal character, of the formation of culture: thus in Hegel.[81]

With each of these constructions the religious aspect of culture is automatically affected: 'The divine is absorbed in nature and made to coincide with the creative depth of it; or it is drawn into the interior of the person, into the soul, into the genius, of which the arcane source appears; or it is regarded as the spiritual and dynamic principle of universal existence, which unfolds in the process of creative culture.'[82] Guardini added that 'the religious relationship can also be conceived in the sense of distance or separation, as deism and rationalism do. "God" is relegated to such a distance from the world that He can no longer have any impact on nature or on the subject and on their autonomy and on the creative work of culture in its unfolding by its own force.'[83] Finally, this 'God who has nothing to do', as Joseph Ratzinger was later to call him, can come to be seen as a danger to freedom and thus as someone or thing that needs to be set aside, as with various versions of positivism and materialism.[84]

The 'autonomy of culture' construction on its plain non-Augustinian-Thomistic surface meaning is clearly related to the kinds of issues discussed by Söhngen in relation to Kant's ideas on the autonomy of each of the university's faculties. This issue could be described as one of the great existential problems of Guardini's life. His whole approach to scholarship was a rebellion from the strait-jacket of the autonomy of the disciplines hermetically sealed from each other. As Robert A. Krieg remarked:

> Guardini's writings were unconventional within the academy. He refused to delve into narrow doctrinal topics and rejected the neo-Scholasticism that church officials and most Catholic theologians took for granted during the period form Vatican I to Vatican II. Also, he had no interest in becoming a specialist in one scholarly area but took a phenomenological approach to a wide range of topics. As a

81. Guardini, *Mondo e persona*, p. 33.
82. Ibid.
83. Ibid.
84. Ibid.

result of his unusual scholarship, he never participated in a Faculty of Theology.[85]

Kreig went on to explain how the University of Berlin got around the bureaucratic regulations by formally appointing Guardini to the Faculty of Catholic Theology at the University of Breslau with an agreement that he remain at the University of Berlin as a guest professor. At the University of Munich, he was formally associated with the philosophy department and for this reason not allowed to direct doctoral dissertations in the theology department. Kreig noted that in Berlin his name did not even show up on the *Vorlesungsverzeichnis* (timetable of lectures) but among the students who nonetheless came along were Elisabeth Schmitz, a member of the Confessing Church, and a young Hannah Arendt.

By holding positions with the bi-line 'Catholic *Weltanschauung*' (Berlin) or "Christian *Weltanschauung*" (Munich), Guardini was able to work within the border zones of more than one discipline, even if this was, from a Kantian perspective, an academic mortal sin. Guardini did not, however, hold Kant solely to blame for this state of affairs, as is clear from the following passages:

> Early Christian thought had [a] universal view. Augustine draws no methodological division between philosophy and theology or, in philosophy, between metaphysics and psychology, within theology, between theoretical dogma and practical application to life but his mind proceeds from the whole of Christian existence to consider the total pattern and its different parts. The position remained fundamentally the same till the peak point of the Middle Ages had been passed. Thomas Aquinas took considerable trouble to draw critical distinctions as well as to give a comprehensive synthesis. But the basis of his thinking was, none the less, the living consciousness of the unity of Christian existence, as world and grace.
>
> Then the division sets in. Philosophy is separated from theology, empirical science from philosophy, practical instruction from knowledge of reality. The effort was not unjustified and has resulted in numerous valuable consequences, but it has its perilous side because it deepens and solidifies the disintegration of modern man.[86]

---

85. R. A. Krieg, 'Romano Guardini's Theology of the Human Person', *Theological Studies* 59 (1998), pp. 457–74 at 462.

86. Guardini, *Freedom, Grace and Destiny*, p. 9.

The statement 'then the division sets in' may be a reference to the *Ratio Institutio Studiorum Societatis Iesu* (the curriculum for Jesuit formation) which treated philosophy as an autonomous discipline for the first time since antiquity and is therefore part of the backstory of the rise of secularism.[87] The sharp separation of the two disciplines, running parallel to sharp separations between nature and grace, faith and reason, history and ontology, ends up unwittingly marginalizing revelation, grace, faith and ontology, as scholars place these components of a Christian world view into a basket labelled 'for Christian consumption only' and otherwise get on with the Kantian-style project of understanding the human person by reference to reason alone, nature alone and ultimately, in the postmodern era, by history alone. As Joseph Ratzinger later noted in his long essay analysing the treatment of human dignity in *Gaudium et spes*, this academic practice of a sharp separation invites the question of why burden people with the story of Christ if the *humanum* can be understood without Him?[88]

The man who was born within the vicinity of the Arena di Verona and who was the recipient of the Erasmus Prize not only thought that there was no possibility of truly understanding the *humanum* without Christ, he also thought that if Europe detached itself completely from Christ – then, and to the extent that this happened – Europe would cease to be Europe.[89] For Guardini, Europe was not a purely geographical complex, or just a group of peoples, but 'a living entelechy, an active spiritual figure'.[90] When reflecting upon the future of Europe, Guardini observed that for all their greatness the Greeks failed to create a state that would embrace the 'vital wealth of all the different ethnic groups' and that while the Romans did create a kind of unity, they did so in the absence of freedom.[91] He warned that any attempts to make Europe as a whole a unifying force could risk a fall into a new common servitude. He concluded that 'the formation of [a new] Europe presupposes that each of its nations rethinks its history and that it understands its past in

---

87. D. D. Novotný, 'In Defense of Baroque Scholasticism', *Studia Neoaristotelica* 6 (2) (2009), pp. 209–33 at 222.
88. Joseph Ratzinger, 'The *Dignity of* the Human Person', in *Commentary on the Documents of the Second Vatican Council*, Herbert Vorgrimler (ed.) (New York: Herder and Herder, 1969).
89. Guardini, *Europa: Compito e destino*, p. 44.
90. Ibid., p. 57.
91. Ibid., p. 29.

relation to the establishment of this great vital form. But what a measure of self-overcoming and self-reflection that means!'[92]

In conclusion, it is not difficult to find declarations of esteem for Guardini from among the most outstanding of his students. In his reflections on his youth in interwar Germany, Josef Pieper remarked that Guardini helped members of his generation to understand that 'beyond all the stifling crassness of moralistic and doctrinaire talk, something real takes place in the sacramental/cultic celebration of the mysteries ... we came to realise that this is the core of all intellectual and spiritual life'.[93] In his homily at the Requiem Mass for the writer Countess Ida Friederike Görres, Joseph Ratzinger said that through Görres's involvement in Guardini's movement, 'she realized that the Church is not just an organization, a hierarchy, an administrative office, but an organism that grows and lives through the centuries'.[94] This realization was to form the centre of her thought and work. Hans Urs von Balthasar wrote, Guardini 'built shelters for entire generations, indeed bulwarks against the encroaching desert'.[95] The final words, however, go to Heinz R. Kuehn:

> The secret of his popularity was simply: Here was a man who, after Europe's bloodiest and most turbulent era, penetrated in his lectures to the essence of a truly Christian vision of the world. He did not lecture in terms of abstract theological or philosophical principles but in terms of the stark and often violent realities of our world, connecting them with the traditions of the western world in religion, art, literature, and architecture, and persuasively demonstrating the life-giving validity of the old, yet ever-young, verities of Christianity for a generation trying to come to terms with the Second World War and its consequences.[96]

---

92. Ibid., p. 57.
93. Josef Pieper, *No One Could Have Known* (San Francisco: Ignatius, 1987), p. 39.
94. Joseph Ratzinger, 'Eulogy for Ida Friederike Görres', *Logos: A Journal of Catholic Thought and Culture* 23 (4) (Fall 2020), 148–56 at p. 149.
95. Balthasar, *Romano Guardini: Reform from the Source*, p. 8.
96. Heinz R. Kuehn, *The Essential Guardini* (Chicago: Liturgy Training Publications, 1997), p. 9.

Chapter 6

ERICH PRZYWARA
(1889–1972)

The distinguished atheism [of the nineteenth century] has turned into a satanic contra-theism, a religiosity that hates God.[1]

Erich Przywara was born in 1889 in Katowice, Poland, of a Polish father and a German mother. He joined the Society of Jesus in 1908 and pursued his studies in Holland since at that time the Society was banned in Germany under Otto von Bismarck's *Jesuitengesetz* of 4 July 1872, a ban that was not lifted until 1917. Ordained a priest in 1920, he worked from 1922 until 1941 in the editorial office of the Jesuit magazine *Stimmen der Zeit* (*Voices of the Time*), the Catholic alternative to the Barthian journal *Zwischen der Zeiten* (*Between the Times*). *Stimmen der Zeit* was shut down by the Nazis in 1941; one of its editors, Alfred Delp SJ, was executed for his membership of the Kreisau Circle resistance group. The journal reopened in 1946 and continues to this day. During the time of Przywara's involvement its office was located in Munich; he contributed some 120 essays to its volumes. Besides his journalism, he delivered sermons and lectures in Munich, Berlin, Vienna and the university cities of the Rhineland. His two most famous foundational works were *Polarity* (1927) and *Analogia Entis* (1931) in which he attempted to present a unity 'of theology and philosophy within the framework of a metaphysics' while two of his most significant works of theological anthropology were his *Crucis Mysterium: Das christliche Heute* (1939) and *Humanitas: Der Mensch gestern und Morgen* (1952).

---

1. Erich Przywara, *Vier Predigten über das Abendland* (Einsiedeln: Johannes-Verlag, 1948), p. 47.

His *Deus semper maior: Theologie der Exerzitien*, a reflection on the Spiritual Exercises of St Ignatius, has been described as 'unsurpassed' in this field.[2] These anthropological works do not, however, stand alone, methodologically speaking, but are built on the foundations established in *Polarity* and *Analogia Entis*. Indeed, Aaron Pidel has remarked that if one were to apply Isaiah Berlin's fox and hedgehog metaphor to Przywara (the fox knows many things, the hedgehog knows one big thing), Przywara definitely belongs to the class of hedgehogs because the *analogia entis* and the theme of polarity underpin everything he wrote.

Although Przywara lived until 1972, the high point of his influence was the interwar years. He was a dialogue partner of Karl Barth and Martin Buber; he was engaged with the ideas of Edmund Husserl, Max Scheler and Martin Heidegger; he was instrumental in opening up the thought of St John Henry Newman to German readers; and he mentored many of the Catholic leaders of that period. In 1934 he delivered a much-acclaimed keynote lecture on 'Religion and Philosophy' at the International Philosopher's Conference in Prague. During and after the war, however, his health declined severely and along with it his active influence. Today he would probably be diagnosed as suffering from post-traumatic stress disorder occasioned by his experiences in Nazi Germany. He spent the last two decades of his life living quietly in Hagen near Murnau am Staffelsee, a town some seventy kilometres south of Munich. In 1967 he was awarded the Upper Silesian Culture Prize for which the *laudatio* was delivered by Karl Rahner. In his speech, Rahner spoke of the 'dark fire' of Przywara's theology and lamented that it was not more popular with the post-Conciliar generation of theologians. The 'fire' theme is strong in Ignatian spirituality. St Ignatius is said to have told the great missionary St Francis Xavier to 'Go and set the world ablaze' ('*ite, omnia incendite et inflammate*'). The 'fire' metaphor so often appears in Przywara's works it could form the subject of a research project on its own. Przywara used the metaphor to highlight what Balthasar called the 'theo-dramatic' nature of human existence. For example, Przywara described Nietzsche as a person facing the 'lightning and fire of God at the highest level in the pride of naked finiteness' – Nietzsche wanted to 'steal this lightning and fire and pour it into his

---

2. Johannes B. Lotz, 'Erich Przywara zum Gedächtnis', *Stimmen der Zei* 189–90 (1972), pp. 289–90 at 290.

own heroic heart'.[3] Przywara also spoke of the 'fire in the fire of God' and 'fire in the fire of the light bearer (Lucifer)'.[4]

Another recurring theme throughout his publications is the notion of a 'unity-within-the-rhythmic-interplay-of-opposites' in polyphonic musical forms.[5] This is an idea similar to Guardini's *Gegensätze*, though Przywara ties his conception directly to his theory of the *analogia entis*. As noted by Aaron Pidel and Eva-Maria Faber, among others, the *analogia entis* pervades Przywara's entire theology. It was thus a more pervasive melody across the works of Przywara than was the *Gegensätze* theme for Guardini's ouevre. Faber also suggests that the centrality of the *analogia entis* for Przywara was responsible for the fact that his publications have a characteristic restlessness. Just when one thinks that he has reached a conclusion, the train of his thought moves off in a different direction in pursuit of some polarity. Faber concluded that 'the rhythm of the *analogia entis* by far exceeds the internal tension of Guardini's "contrast" in terms of explosive power'.[6]

In section two of his *Analogia Entis*, Przywara offers a tantalizing paragraph in which he compares his own approach to polarity with Guardini's notion of *Gegensätze* – but unfortunately the remark is brief and undeveloped. Specifically he claimed that Guardini preserves a tension between antitheses to the point of creating, on the one hand, 'a structure that ultimately oscillates only within itself; and does so in such a way, that on the other hand, supernature and theology threaten to become but one side (the personalistic) of the antithesis'.[7] In the same paragraph he affirms Haecker's endorsement of an *Analogia trinitatis*, but he is nonetheless critical of Haecker for allegedly portraying the finitude of human nature as a fall.[8]

3. Erich Przywara, 'Kierkegaard-Newman', in *Newman Studien* 1 (1948), pp. 77–101 at 87.

4. Ibid., p. 87.

5. For an analysis of this concept see Michael Dominic Taylor, *The Foundations of Nature: Metaphysics of Gift for an Integral Ecological Ethic* (Eugene: Cascade, 2020), pp. 143–54.

6. Eva-Maria Faber, *Kirche zwischen Identität und Differenz: Die ekklesiologischen Entwürfe von Romano Guardini und Erich Przywara* (Echter: Würzburg, 1993), p. 120.

7. Ibid.

8. Erich Przywara, *Analogia Entis: Metaphysics: Original Structure and Universal Rhythm*, trans. John R Betz and David Bentley Hart (Grand Rapids: Eerdmans, 2014), p. 349.

Without doubt, the distinctions in thought between Przywara and Guardini would make an interesting doctoral dissertation but are beyond the scope of this monograph, focused as it is on the response of the inter-war generation to the denouement of German Idealism and Nietzsche's challenge to the whole Christian tradition. The shades of grey and their significance for fundamental theology are certainly worthy of a deeper analysis in another place. The similarities, rather than the distinctions, between Guardini and Przywara, are, however, palpable. Perhaps because they were both bi-cultural, with Guardini Italo-German, and Przywara Germano-Polish, one shared dominant hallmark of the intellectual culture of the pair was an ability to pinpoint the significant historical and cultural dimensions of any issue. Przywara was also on a similar wave-length to Guardini in so far as he argued that 'being a Christian is not simply something ethical or moralistic in the sense of following or imitating the virtuous figure of Christ, but fundamentally something existential (*etwas Seinshaftes*)'.[9] A third point of comparison between the two priests, one a diocesan and one a Jesuit, is that while Guardini had in effect his own personal youth movement about him, Przywara mentored some of the greatest names in mid-to-late twentieth century philosophy and theology, including Edith Stein – who became St. Teresa-Benedicta of the Cross who was martyred in Auschwitz – Hans Urs von Balthasar, Josef Pieper and Karl Rahner. One was a spiritual father to scholars, the other a spiritual father to the youth, some of whom later became scholars. Symbolically the spiritual link between them is expressed by the appropriation of Przywara's hymn '*O Du mein Heiland hoch und hehr*' (O Thou my Saviour Glorious) as the unofficial anthem of Guardini's Quickborn youth movement.

Edith Stein acknowledged Przywara's influence in her preface to *Finite and Infinite Being*. Josef Pieper praised Przywara for 'ingeniously managing to combine historical and systematic details into a universal overview',[10] and also credited him with helping him to understand that 'every attempt to devise a self-enclosed system of truth actually

---

9. Erich Przywara, *L'Idea d'Europa: La "crisi" di ogni politica 'cristiana'* (Trapani: Il Pozzo di Giacobbe, 2013), p. 111.

10. Josef Pieper, 'Philosophie in Selbstdarstellungen', in *Werke*, Ergängzungsband 2 (2003), pp. 1–25 at p. 5; cited in Bernard N. Schumacher, *A Cosmopolitan Hermit: Modernity and Tradition in the Philosophy of Josef Pieper* (Washington, DC: Catholic University of America Press, 2009), p. 6.

contradicts the real existential situation of the finite mind, its creatureliness', and further, that this situation 'resists all attempts to reduce the thinking of Thomas Aquinas to a school of thought consisting of teachable propositions'.[11] Although Pieper became a world-renowned philosopher in the Thomist tradition, his academic style was completely different from those trained in seminaries to construct systems of propositions. Pryzwara counselled a young Balthasar to endure such seminary lectures in 'sawdust Thomism' with a disposition of spiritual detachment. Later Balthasar would remark that Przywara's oeuvre cannot be classified, that it is difficult to encompass, and so most have chosen to ignore it. Nonetheless Balthasar was of the view that those who took the trouble to go through his school 'may later settle here or there', with their thinking and life forever marked by this encounter.[12] Balthasar also observed that 'Augustine remains the ever-living primeval impulse in Przywara's entire thinking, in him he sees the real father of all the spiritual currents of the West, although he has understood how to read and interpret him in a range that surpasses all the usual depictions of Augustine'.[13] James V. Zeitz SJ explained that for Przywara, John Henry Newman (the Augustine of his time) was 'a counter-balance to Thomas Aquinas, whose work speaks only of the objective, logical *in se*', while Newman 'better emphasizes the concrete and the living in the Catholic tradition'.[14] A counterbalance is not, of course, an opponent but simply someone who represents the other pole, the complement of the qualities of the one for whom he is the counterbalance. There is nothing fundamentally anti-Thomistic in Przywara, notwithstanding his empathy for Balthasar's boredom with what some had made of the Thomist tradition in the 1920s. Przywara regarded his own account of the *analogia entis* as consistent with that of St Thomas.

In his foreword to the collection of essays titled *Müller: Schriften zur Staatsphilosophie*, edited by Rudolf Kohle, Przywara offered the

11. Schumacher, *A Cosmopolitan Hermit*, p. 6. See also Josef Pieper, *No One Could Have Known: An Autobiography: The Early Years 1904–1945*, trans. Graham Harrison (San Francisco: Ignatius, 1987), p. 68.

12. Hans Urs von Balthasar, *Einführung zu Erich Przywara: Sein Schriftum 1912-1962*, Leo Zimny (ed.) (Einsiedeln: Johannes Verlag, 1963), p. 18.

13. Ibid., p. 12.

14. James V Zeitz, 'Erich Przywara: Visionary Theologian', *Thought: A Review of Culture and Idea* 58 (229) (June 1983), pp. 151–64 at p. 157.

following succinct explanation of his understanding of polarity, in contrast to that of several others (though not in contrast to Guardini's):

> Polarity can mean a unity of the opposites of the human in man, and this may well be the sense of Goethian and Görressian polarity. But it can also mean the polarity between the needy person and the fulfilling God, and this formula corresponds more to the polarity of Novalis, Schlegel and Deutinger. In Pascal's ideas of polarity, however, the two views of polarity intersect in a strange, unsolvable conflict, while in Newman they weave together unharmed through the correspondence between the 'incomprehensible God' and the unity of opposites of longing and awe. Both styles of polarity, taken in isolation, have their inner dangers if they are not measured against the calm, classic Christian version of the relationship between God and creature. The polarity which structures humanity may push us to make man independent of God and thus ultimately to divinize him. However, the polarity directly dependent on God robs the creature of its justified independence, so that God becomes a piece of the creature, – and again the specter of divinization arises, only from the other side.[15]

The solution, for Przywara, was found in the *analogia entis* insofar as it operates as a principle of dynamic polarity between the essence and existence of the person and the immanence and transcendence of God. This understanding of the relationship between God and His creatures was found in the patristic-scholastic concept of 'God above us and in us', but this principle was one of the casualties of late scholasticism. It was one of the sections of the Thomistic tapestry that started to unravel with the rise of nominalism in the fourteenth century. The inner dialectic of the Lutheran concept of God then developed from a combination of 'Areopagitic mysticism and Occamistic nominalism'.[16] The end result as diagnosed by Przywara was the manifestation of two extremes. As Raczyński-Rożek explains:

---

15. Erich Przywara, 'Die Polarität zwischen Individuum und Gemeinschaft: Ein Vorwort', in *Adam Müller: Schriften zur Staatsphilosophie*, Rudolf Kohler (ed.) (München: Theatiner-Verlag, 1954), pp. vi–vii.
16. Ibid., p. vii.

The first [extreme] defines the idiom "God alone" (theopanism) because it minimizes the role of creatures. Such a process Przywara observes in German Idealism, Neoplatonism and eastern philosophies, where the world is only a manifestation or emanation of the divine ideal, and also in Lutheran and Reformed theology, where the role of creatures, contaminated by original sin, is reduced to a minimum because it is marked by a lack of all integrity and possibility of cooperation with God. The second extreme is defined by Przywara by the idiom 'world alone' (pantheism) because it divinizes the world. It is the dialectical opposite of theopanism. Examples of such an attitude are the materialisms of Western Europe. God is unreal in them and all reality is transferred to the world, making God a product of self-alienation (Feuerbach-Marx), mythopoesis (Nietzsche) or the desire for self-fulfilment (Freud).[17]

In summary, it has been said that the primary message of Przywara's theology is that if you get the *analogia entis* wrong, you find yourself living in a gulag.

Numerous case studies of Przywara's application of the polarity principle can be found across his essays, including those on Augustine and Aquinas. In his book *Augustinisch: Ur-Haltung des Geistes* (*Augustinian: The Primal Attitude of the Spirit*), Przywara spoke of a 'triple Augustinianism', or three dominant ways in which Augustine has been appropriated. First, there is an Idealist Augustine whose accent on truth and an intelligent world would appear to make him a kindred spirit of Descartes and Kant. There is also an affinity between Augustine and Goethe in their mutual contemplative openness to the truth of light and an affinity between Augustine and Hegel in their mutual appreciation of the pathos of wholeness as one finds in the following fragments from Augustine: *Deus sub quo totum, in quo totum, cum quo totum* – Solil I 1.4; *contrariorum oppositione saeculi pulchritudo componitur* – de Civ Dev XI 18 and *Deus, per quem universitas etiam cum sinistra parte perfecta est* – Solil I 1,2. Przywara argues that this 'idealist Augustine' falls, however, into 'second place' when it receives measure and judgement from the 'Augustinianism of the "supernatural eye": the Augustinianism of hereditary sin and redemption', found

---

17. M. Raczyński-Rożek, 'The Church as the Realization of the Nature of Man in *Deus Semper Maior* by Erich Przywara', *Bogoslovni vestnik/Theological Quarterly* 79 (2019), pp. 3, 752–85 at 754.

in Augustine's *Retractationes* treatise. In this work the Augustine 'of critical and Idealist truth, that is, the Augustine of an ideal humanity of insight and freedom, is inwardly transformed by the more critical Augustine of the *prevaricatores redite ad cor*', that is, the Augustine of the 'repentant retreat from the abyss of unsoundness that oozes from the wound of original sin'.[18] Similarly, the correlation between sight and light in the contemplative Augustine knows that the 'smoke of greed' can cloud one's vision and therefore that the true light of grace must burn fiery bright. Finally, the Augustine who appreciates the pathos of wholeness is inwardly transformed by the more comprehensive Augustine who acknowledges the incomprehensibility of the relation between *iustitia* and *misericordia* and between heaven and hell, 'which do not enter into any aesthetically shimmering formula', because these relationships belong inside the territory of divine prerogatives. They are, in Przywara's idiom, 'the crown prerogatives of God' who said, 'My Thoughts are not your thoughts, and My ways are not your ways.'[19]

Summarizing these juxtapositions, Przywara concluded that when compared to the critical idealistic Augustinianism of the 'spirit', the deeper Augustinianism of the curse of the 'flesh' remained conscious of the effects of original sin. However this second Augustinianism, the Augustine who is acutely conscious of the reality of concupiscence, is still not as deep as the third Augustinianism, the Augustine of the *Verbum-Caro*, 'the Eternal Truth that became flesh and lives on in the flesh of humanity as the body of Christ'.[20] Consistent with his polyphonic counter-point metaphysics, Przywara concluded that it is not merely that the Augustinianism of the spirit is humiliated by the Augustinianism of the flesh or that the Augustinianism of light is humiliated in the Augustinianism of the night. While these humiliations are a fact, the story does not end here on a low note with paradise lost, death entering the world and a serpent looking smug. Rather the diminuendo of the fall is followed by the crescendo of the redemption. In Przywara's words, 'It is not the torn state of the human being in this night of struggle that is the deepest, but the deeper Augustinism of the night that raises its head in the middle, the Augustinism of the "light of the world" that rose into the "darkness" where the darkness is finally overcome in the Eternal

---

18. Erich Przywara, *Augustinisch: Ur-Haltung des Geites* (Einsiedeln: Johannes Verlag, 1970), p. 93.
19. Ibid., p. 94.
20. Ibid., p. 95.

Light of Easter'.²¹ This third Augustinianism is the Augustinianism of glory. Przywara reads this third form of Augustinianism as the solution to the contrast or polarity between ecstatic Neoplatonism and demonic Manicheanism and between an Antiochene Christianity of an ethical-rational perfection (right down to Pelagianism) and an Alexandrian Christianity of the merciless absorption into the life and work of God (until one falls into Jansenism and Docetism).²²

Towards the end of his analysis of Augustinian polarities, Przywara could not resist finding one last paradoxical contrast to entice the interest of an already intellectually dizzy reader. He noted that owing to the fact that Augustine became the one in whom all the theology of the Holy Scriptures and the Fathers culminated, and from whom all the theology of scholasticism emanated, he was at the same time humiliated as the source from which all the great heresies of the subsequent period derived, so that the condemnations of the church seemed directed against him.²³

Having offered an account of the hallmarks of the three appropriations of Augustine and their internal polarities, Przywara then moved on to examine the poles represented by the names Augustine and Aquinas. Here he suggested that the two poles need to be studied from the perspective of three questions: does perception go from top to bottom or from bottom to top, that is, in *a priori* intuition or in real experience? Second, does perception go from the inside out or from the outside in, that is, in primary self-knowledge or in primary knowledge of the world? Third, does perception go from beyond to beyond or from this side to beyond, that is, is it primarily theological or primarily philosophical?²⁴

In Augustine, especially in his *De Trinitate*, Przywara found a 'looping duality of intuitive wisdom and inductive science' (de Trin XII 2; 2–14; 22), just as St Thomas distinguished between the indirect way of factual perception through the senses and the immediate intuition of pure truth in the judgment.²⁵ Conversely, Przywara found that the abstraction of St Thomas 'seems to so decisively bind the mind to the limits of the sensory world, that the spontaneity of the mind (the *intellectus agens*) has the formal task of abstraction' and that the 'first

21. Ibid.
22. Ibid., p. 97.
23. Ibid., p. 114.
24. Ibid., p. 99.
25. Ibid., p. 102.

principles', in which all knowledge and all wisdom are contained are so decided in the senses that they have their 'instantiation' in it.[26]

Przywara also noted a polar difference in the temperaments of the two biggest names in the Latin theological tradition to which he gave poetic expression in the following paragraph:

> In Augustine [we have] the longing for bridal love, in Thomas its quiet celebration … in Augustine the burning, anticipating and the glad and fearful surpassing of such a longing (through highs and lows), – in Thomas the impersonal silence and daring sobriety of such a celebration, up to the rigidity of a 'ceremonial'; in Augustine, therefore, the fear of the night of the divine light in the midst of being swept away, – in Thomas, the quiet worship (*Adoro te devote, latens deitas*), until a formula of confession is said.[27]

Przywara also associated two different models of the *analogia entis* with Augustine and Aquinas: the Christian-platonic model associated with St Augustine, and the Christian-Aristotelian model, exemplified in St Thomas:

> The first is, on the one side, the type that chiefly affirms God as 'All in all', and yet, just because God is, so to speak, the foundation or Creator of the world, it is, on the other side, the type which chiefly affirms the comprehensible nearness of God. The second, on the one side, is the type which chiefly affirms the 'reality of the creature', but yet, just because in doing so it recognizes the difference between God and the world, it is, on the other side, the type which chiefly affirms the incomprehensible aloofness of God. Nevertheless … in the Augustinian *homo abyssus*, *Deus-caritas*, and *Deus incomprehensibilis* are given the fundamentals of the Christian Aristotelian type; while conversely in Aquinas the Augustinian passion for truth, with its 'ideas of life' and its *Deus-veritas*, lives on.[28]

In summary, notwithstanding the harmonious relationship between the two, they do represent two different emphases: the Platonic

26. Ibid.
27. Ibid., p. 111.
28. Erich Przywara, *Polarity: A German Catholic's Interpretation of Religion*, trans. A. C. Bouquet (London: Oxford University Press, 1935), pp. 116–17.

Augustinian on the relative *likeness* between God and the person, and the Aristotelian Thomistic on the relative *unlikeness* between God and creation. Przywara describes this situation as giving rise to a 'dual kind of rhythmical motion within the one *analogia entis*'.[29]

Yet another significant polarity identified by Przywara that gives rise to a dual kind of rhythmical motion is that between religion and culture. Beginning with Justin and Tertullian, Przywara defined these poles to be religion as the ultimate strength of culture and culture as religion's opponent. This polarity plays out in the medieval period in the different spiritualities of Cluny and Clairvaux, of Peter Abelard and St Bernard of Clairvaux. By the time of the Reformation, these polarities become part of the explosive problematic of the sixteenth century, with its contrast between the culturally resplendent church of the Renaissance and the Baroque and the iconoclastic 'imperceptible and invisible God' of the Protestants reaching its acme in the aesthetic astringency of Calvin. With the rise of the Romantic movement in the nineteenth century, the polarity then morphs into the choice between the 'autonomy of science and culture', and, indeed, 'science and culture *as* religion' and the ideas of the Catholic romantics for whom science and culture have their immanent ideals in religion, especially in Christendom. With respect to those for whom science and culture was their religion, there was a further trivision between 'a positivism of pure knowledge (Spinoza, Comte), an intellectualism of pure logical assertions (the rationalism of the Marburg School) and a voluntarism of pure will or pure values (Windelband, Rickert, Scheler)'.[30] In short, modern philosophy 'divided the Ur-platonic ternary among itself, since in nominalism it lost the internal unity of this ternary'.[31] Przywara's tracking of this polarity from Justin and Tertullian all the way through to Scheler prompts one to imagine what Przywara would have thought of the correlationist pastoral strategies of the 1970s that sought to 'hook-up' Catholic liturgical life with contemporary popular culture. He surely would have indicted these pastoral projects as a complete evasion of the polar tension.

The polarity theme also re-emerges in Przywara's analysis of Nietzsche. In an essay published in 1929, Przywara offered an

---

29. Ibid., p. 119.
30. Erich Przywara, *Religions-Philosophische Schriften* (Einsiedeln: Johannes Verlag, 1962), p. 503.
31. Ibid.

analysis of Nietzsche similar to that given by Steinbüchel. In accord with Steinbüchel, he rejected a facile libertine reading of Nietzsche, describing such a construal as 'an embarrassing misunderstanding of the great despiser of the "Pied-Cow".[32] The Pied Cow or '*Bunten Kuk*' was the name of a town in Nietzsche's *Thus Spake Zarathustra* where people have no higher horizons than the satisfactions of ordinary life such as drinking the milk of a cow. Przywara acknowledged Nietzsche's 'Luciferian defiance', but noted that this defiance was intermingled with a 'divine homesickness', with an 'undeniably genuine pathos'.[33] From this perspective he endorsed the readings of Justus Obenauer and Theodor Odenwald:

> Justus Obenauer interprets it [the defiance and the pathos] as a struggle of a self-unconscious religious heroism against the 'gentle, humble, life-denying, absolutely unheroic moralism' of contemporary Pietism. Nietzsche is the 'ecstatic nihilist', whose will to tragedy ('*Wille zur Tragik*'), understood as the highest dramatic tension in life, is his religiosity. Theodor Odenwald – in a kind of mediation between [Richard Heinrich] Grützmacher and [Ernst] Bertram – tries to understand Nietzsche within his historical context of life-denying Pietism and rationalism. Odenwald interprets Nietzsche's 'Dionysian spirituality', his enraptured affirmation of life, this world, the individual and the body, as a reaction against Pietism. Nevertheless, Nietzsche still remains a child of his rationalistic time, believing that he can address belief in God in a purely dialectical way. Nietzsche's 'religiosity' means a break with the existing forms of religion, with a 'narrowed Pietism' and a 'watered-down didactic religion in the sense of D. Fr. Strauss', and a departure thereby for a new religiosity. This new religion shows itself in the fast strengthening, 'über-empirical form' of his 'superhuman' and 'the eternal return'. This object of his religion ... grows into the super-empirical, becomes the super empirical reality of a belief.[34]

32. Erich Przywara, '*Ringen der Gegenwart*' I, *Gesammelte Aufsätze* (1922-27) (Augsburg: Benno Filsner-Verlag, 1929), pp. 169–96 at p. 170.

33. Ibid., 169.

34. Ibid. See also Theodor Odenwald, *Das Religionsproblem bei Friedrich Nietzsche* (Leipzig: J.C. Hinrichs'sche Buchhandlung, 1922. Derselbe, Die Verkündigung Nietzsches und die religiöse Krisis der Gegenwart [protest.], *Zeitschrift für Theologie und Kirche* N.F. 4 [1923] 449–66.

The polarities here are rationalism on the one side and piety on the other. Przywara concluded that there should be no doubt that the 'turning point of the spirit', to borrow a Hegelian phrase, was to a large extent, in the early decades of the twentieth century, as much a 'turning to Nietzsche' even as it seemed to announce itself as a 'turning to Hegel'. The 'turn to Thomas', he conceded, 'remained a secret background'.[35]

In his essay 'Dionysisches und christliches Opfer' published in *Stimmen der Zeit* (1934/5), Przywara expanded his analysis of Nietzsche to include a comparison with the Spanish Catholic political theorist and diplomat Juan Donoso Cortés (1809–1853). He noted that taken together the pair almost completely span the nineteenth century, and that their lives are almost consecutive, one beginning just a few years before the death of the first. While they were both irreconcilable enemies of liberalism, their anti-liberalism took different forms and offered different alternatives. Cortés regarded all appeals to 'pure reason' and 'pure freedom' and 'pure knowledge' and 'pure ethics' and 'pure philosophy' and 'pure culture' as nothing more than an uprising against reason and a retreat from the 'unity of the Cross'. He also wanted to enter the Society of Jesus though this never came about due to his early death at the age of forty-four. While sharing many of Cortés's negative judgments about the philosophy of the eighteenth century, Nietzsche, in his *The Birth of Tragedy*, preferred the 'incarnation of dissonance', to the unity of the Cross.[36] In the final paragraph of his article Przywara cited an 1879 letter from Nietzsche addressed to his musician friend and editor Heinrich Köselitz (1854–1918), whose pseudonym was Peter Gast. In this letter Nietzsche spoke of what he perceived to be the German preference for Martin Luther over Ignatius of Loyola (Bavarian and Swabian Catholicism notwithstanding). Przywara then concluded his reflection by drawing a pair of analogies between Loyola and Cortés, on the one side, and between Luther and Nietzsche, on the other. Connecting Loyola and Cortés with Nietzsche, there is a shared spirit of 'aristocratic radicalism'. This trio share an aristocratic disposition. They only want what is *most* perfect, *most* excellent, the very highest that can be obtained. They have no inclination to be satisfied with whatever is deemed to be 'normal' for your average 'Tom, Dick and Harry' in

35. Erich Przywara, '*Ringen der Gegenwart*' I, *Gesammelte Aufsätze (1922–27)*, p. 170.

36. Erich Przywara, 'Dionysisches und christliches Opfer', *Stimmen der Zeit* 65 (1934–5), pp. 11–24 at p. 20.

British parlance, or your 'Juan Pablo' in colloquial Spanish. In this sensibility they are united. However, with Luther and Nietzsche there is a shared 'No' to obedience to the Catholic Church. Przywara remarks that Luther's 'No' developed in the direction of religious individualism, which then became secularized over the centuries into all other individualisms, including the passive bourgeois form of Christianity Nietzsche so despised. Although Przywara did not didactically hammer home his point, his subtext was that Nietzsche should have followed the 'chivalrous Spaniard' (Cortés), who would have led him to the Spiritual Exercises of St Ignatius. Instead of remaining on the side of Luther he should have crossed the 'bridge' (the unity of the Cross) to Loyola and Cortés.

In *Humanitas*, Przywara offered the same counterpoint between Cortés and Nietzsche but this time added Jean Calvin into the frame. He summarized the sixteenth century as a battle between Loyola (1491–1556) and Calvin (1509–1564). As he made the point, 'throughout the entire century the Picard and the Basque fought over the world, over the soul; and perhaps even more centuries will be spent in this struggle'.[37] While Nietzsche shared Loyola's aristocratic disposition, his *amor fati* (love of fate) was, tragically, 'truly Calvinistic'.[38]

While *Humanitas* examined the many polarities across the spectrum of the world of ideas, the essays published in *Crucis Mysterium* were focused on intra-ecclesial polarities such as that between Ignatian and Thomistic spirituality, and Ignatian and Carmelite spirituality. The following paragraph is Przywara's summary of the Ignatian–Thomistic polarity:

> In Ignatius one sees the emphasis on the 'secular': an emphasis on the world, on becoming, on the self-actuality of the ego, and therefore on tangible practical religious purposes, on intra-worldly religious goals, on strictly organised activity as 'action', and hence the Church as a church of laws, duties and obligations and a militant church. In St. Thomas, on the other hand, one sees the emphasis on the 'sacred': all the world as a golden icon of heavenly glory, becoming like a light mist around the Eternal Being, the acting of the I as also the mysterious being acted upon by God, therefore praise and

---

37. Erich Przywara, *Humanitas: Der Mensch gestern und morgen* (Nürnberg: Glock und Lutz, 1952).

38. Ibid., p. 814.

worship of the mystery of God as a unified religious meaning, the freedom of the 'movement of the spirit' in the organic fruition of 'contemplation', the Church as the illumined body of Christ already on earth.[39]

Przywara concluded that these dispositions tended to stand opposed to each other: 'a Jesuit secularism of the *ecclesia militans* and the Thomistic theocentricism of the *Corpus Christi mysticum*'.[40] However, he wanted to reconcile the two by arguing that since the Ignatian mission is motivated by service of the Divine Majesty, it is a secularism that derives from a sacralism; whereas since for St Thomas the majesty of the supremacy of God is handed down in all things (*Ipsum Esse, Ipsa Forma, Causa Prima, Providentia Universalis et Finis Ultimus*), the authentic Thomist emphasis of 'heaven on earth' is only true to the extent that it is aimed at an earth that is independent of God to the utmost, that is to say that enjoys its own legitimate autonomy. In Przywara's reconciliation the traits of 'Thomistic sacralism' appear as fundamental in Ignatian spirituality, while conversely a 'Jesuit secularism' appears to be the outcome of Thomistic spirituality.[41] Whether, of course, contemporary Thomists and Ignatians would agree with this attempt at a reconciliation is a moot point, and one that could perhaps form the substance of a doctoral dissertation in the fields of spirituality and soteriology. The division between the transcendental Thomism of Karl Rahner SJ and the neo-Augustinian account of the grace and nature relationship proposed by Henri de Lubac SJ may well make any such reconciliation a more difficult project. Or to put the proposition in another way, while a reconciliation might be possible if de Lubac is taken to stand for the Ignatian position, or even Balthasar, it may be much harder to effect a reconciliation if Karl Rahner or Pedro Arrupe were to be the flag-bearers for the Ignatian position. How the nature and grace relationship is construed would seem to be an essential element of any such reconciliation process.

At the conclusion of his analysis of these Ignatian and Thomistic polarities, Przywara juxtaposed Nietzsche's 'drunken song' from *Thus Spake Zarathustra* with the *Adoro Te* (Godhead Here in Hiding) hymn

39. Erich Przywara, *Crucis mysterium. Das christliche Heute* (Schöningh: Paderborn, 1939), p. 65.
40. Ibid.
41. Ibid., p. 68.

of St Thomas and the *Tomad y recibid* (Take Lord, Receive) prayer of St Ignatius. The *Adoro Te* 'burns in the flames and flows in the flood of the inebriation of that divine love of which the "drunken cruelty" of the Dionysian is only a pallid afterimage and a hollow echo of the eating of God's flesh and drinking of God's blood'.[42] The *Tomad y recibid* contains something of the element of Dionysian excess in its levels of trust and generosity but also something of Apollonian peace and tranquillity in the aftermath of the act of self-surrender. It is typical of Przywara's style that he does not 'tie a bow' on his argument. He does not 'rub Nietzsche's nose' into the obvious conclusion. It is as if he wants to defend Nietzsche's dignity, the freedom of his will, his freedom to take the *non serviam* stance. However, the clearly visible subtext is that if you want Dionysian excess, if you want aristocratic radicalism, if you want a high humanity and life as an epic drama, then Aquinas and Loyola have more to offer than Nietzsche. This is his untied bow.

Backtracking from Nietzsche to Kant, Przywara addressed the tragic character of Kantian anthropology in his *Kant Heute*. He began by observing that Kant was confronted by 'the tortured extremes of an empiricism that denies the spontaneity of thought and asserts its receptivity alone, and of a rationalism that knows only spontaneity'.[43] Kant tried to unite the extremes as St Thomas had earlier done, but 'between Thomas and Kant there lies the fatal dissolution of the God-creature relation of the *analogia entis*'.[44] After the Reformation, there is a God who alone is holy and thus disconnected from a human being who wallows alone in a dejected state of sin. For Kant that which is divine in a person is the transcendental subject or the transcendental ideal, towards which the empirical subject strives without ever being able to reach it. Spontaneity comes to be associated with the absolute autonomy of the transcendental subject, and receptivity grows into what Przywara described as the complete bondage of the empirical will to duty. Przywara concluded that 'there then arises that frightful contradiction that yawns wide within the depths of Kantian man: the Olympian "divine humanity" and the inextirpable "radical evil", God and the devil encompassed within the one being', or, to put the proposition less poetically, within the one person there is an irreconcilable competition

---

42. Ibid., p. 88.
43. Erich Przywara, *Kant Heute* (München: Verlag von R. Oldenbourg, 1930), p. 10.
44. Ibid.

between the divine and the demonic.[45] This differs from what Aquinas called concupiscence, the difficulty that the will sometimes has in performing good actions. In Thomistic anthropology God and man are connected by the *analogia entis* such that human free will, though wounded by the Fall and hampered by concupiscence, can still, with grace, pursue the good discerned by the intellect to be true and thus the faculties of the soul can still work in perfect freedom and harmony. Przywara suggested that the 'great difference' between Kant and Aquinas is that Aquinas does not try and conclude the issue between 'cognition as a creative formation of "truth" from the data provided by the senses, "*intellectus agens*", and cognition as pure, intuitive reception of "truth in itself", "*intellectus possibilis*"'. Aquinas leaves the relationship open.

While in the popular imagination Kant is associated with universalism, generated by 'pure reason' detached from all traditions and cultural peculiarities, Przywara nonetheless argued that the tension between this universal dimension of Kantian anthropology and Kantian autonomy gives rise to the 'rage against universal images' that begins to build in the nineteenth century and finds expression in Nietzsche and Max Stirner (author of *The Ego and Its Own*) and also in socialism. Przywara goes so far as to assert that Kant is 'in a true sense the father of socialism'.[46] While Przywara acknowledged that socialism has a strong note of universal legality within itself and signifies the adoption of the Hegelian 'whole', which is merely rebaptised from its being an 'ideative whole' and made into an 'economic whole', nonetheless, he believed that the more active ingredient in the socialist disposition is the 'protest of the "man of work" against the "man of possession", the protest of the man who is, in Marxian idioms, "alienated from his labour" from the person whose labour is a form of self-realisation or exercise of personal autonomy'. In the end Kant's ideas foster both a collectivizing universalism and a de-collectivizing individualism, depending upon which 'wing' or 'dimension' of Kant's anthropology predominates.

Przywara therefore read Kant as someone caught between his own aversion to any reliance of reason upon revelation, and his own Lutheran sensibilities – specifically a Lutheran approach to sin. Far from being 'enlightened' in his own self-understanding of the concept of Enlightenment, Przywara regarded Kant as someone tragically shackled to a Lutheran cosmology. For Przywara there was a contradiction deep

---

45. Ibid., p. 11.
46. Ibid., p. 28.

within the heart and mind of Kant between 'pure reason', that is, the reason of humanity appearing as the light of the world to overcome the darkness caused by an 'obfuscatory supernaturalism', and a 'primal Lutheran element, inextirpable despite all his rationalism, wherein the same world reveals itself as the world of inextirpable original sin and original demonism, which can be so little "enlightened" by "pure reason" that this so-called "pure reason" is but the slenderest expression of its original sin and demonism'.[47] In short, Przywara thought that 'whore reason', to use Luther's idiom, and 'pure reason', to use Kant's idiom, were pretty much the same thing, or, at least, have a tendency to collapse into one another. Przywara described this problem as the 're-awakening of the "aporetic" Kant within the death of the systematic Kant'.[48] Without the *analogia entis* principle, without some both/and understanding of the relationship between nature and grace, we are left with a transcendental subject and an empirical subject, and the problem of how to get from the one to the other. Przywara spoke of the tragedy of the transcendental subject as the tragedy of the Kantian-Nietzschean *'Übermensch'*. At its very foundation the project of promoting an 'enlightened reason' was nothing short of the 'usurpation of the Johannine "God is Light" by and for man'.[49]

This Lutheran undertow in Kant's anthropology manifested itself also in his treatment of the transcendentals: the true, the beautiful and the good. Here Przywara speaks of a 'rigidity' associated with the majesty of an absolute ego. In mounting this case, he called three witnesses to his counsel: George Simmel, Friedrich Schiller and Wolfgang Goethe. In relation to the true, Simmel gives evidence of the 'intolerance of Kantian intellection'. In relation to the good, Schiller speaks of a Kantian 'fanaticism of duty'. In relation to the beautiful, Goethe claims that the 'graces flee' before Kant. Here the contrast with Aquinas is especially stark. Przywara presented the Thomistic alternative in the following paragraph:

> It is clear how fundamentally this [Kantian] subjective pathos and ethos alters within the transcendental theory of Augustine and Thomas Aquinas. God is the *Veritas, Bonitas, Pulchritudo Ipsa*, and consequently the true-good-beautiful is within man to the

---

47. Ibid., p. 32.
48. Ibid.
49. Ibid., p. 33.

extent that he 'lives, moves and is' within God. Truth, goodness and beauty are not dependent upon man, but rather he stands within their resplendence and stands at their service, in the measure that he stands within the resplendence of the majesty of God and stands at its service. Yet, consequently, there is present within all his searching for truth, all this striving after the good, a sense of the humble detachment of a ministering child. For that reason, the form of the actual beauty within this man is precisely: the 'liberated oscillation'. Living from and in the grace of the *Deus-Veritas, Deus-Bonitas, Deus-Pulchritudo* he is pervaded in the most delicate way by this grace: the 'grace' of the *gratia Dei*. His life becomes a grace of the constant intimacy of adoration and adoring intimacy, and such a life knows nothing of the pessimism of a 'radical evil'.[50]

Przywara concluded *Kant Heute* not only with the judgment that Aquinas is to be preferred to Kant but, somewhat surprisingly, that 'amidst the fractured enigmas of present times which do not find their resolution in Kant's solution', the 'voice of wisdom' to whom we should listen is a voice 'that offers Thomistic wisdom in the language of Augustine' – the 'Augustine of our own age, John Henry Cardinal Newman'. Przywara's preferred alternative to Kant is revealed – and it turns out to be Newman.

Przywara noted that Newman confronted many of the same problems of Kant. First, he had to contend with the conflicts between English rationalism in the work of Richard Whateley on the one side and the empiricism of David Hume on the other; and then within Anglicanism he had a further conflict between the rationalist theology of liberal Protestantism – against which he wrote his *Catholicus* letters to the 'Times' – and the religious irrationalism of 'sentimental religion' represented by Samuel Taylor Coleridge and the revivalist sects. As a consequence, Przywara noted, Newman had to tackle the issue of the relationship 'between conceptual thought and its form of certainty (notional thought), and experiential thought and its form of certainty (real thought), and yet equally – in regard to the theological oppositions – the question between a more insightful faith of ideal dogmatic connections and a more lively faith of blind surrender to the omniscient God of inconceivability'.[51] Przywara read Newman's

50. Ibid., p. 87.
51. Ibid., p. 107.

answers to these conflicts in the theory of knowledge as 'a resurrection of the foundational epistemological theory of Thomas Aquinas in modern terms'.[52] He also read Newman's understanding of being and becoming or 'change', as a 'genuine revivification of the "*actus in potentia*" of the moved "becoming" of the metaphysics of Aquinas', and he read Newman's emphasis on the spirit as Newman's agreement with Aquinas that the world is the materialization of the spiritual, from the pure '*actus immaterialis*' of the angelic spirits to the '*formae materiales*' of human bodies.[53] Finally, Przywara noted a concordance between the Thomistic idea of God as '*Deus tamquam ignotus*' and Newman's account of the incomprehensibility of God. The temptation that they both avoid, but Kant could not resist, was to 'somehow exhaust the transcendent universality of God, or even to draw it into the self', thus leading to a form of self-idolatry. In *Polarity*, Przywara also drew attention to a letter Newman wrote to Father Whitty on 28 December 1878, in which, just eight months before the promulgation of *Aeternis Patris*, the encyclical in which Leo XIII exhorted Catholic scholars to return to the study of scholastic philosophy, Newman claimed to be a disciple of Aquinas.[54]

In one of his many poetic observations, Przywara spoke of Augustine, Aquinas and Newman as a trio who found themselves in the 'same autumnal ripeness of old age' – the 'age' being a reference to their historical eras, not their biological ages – 'Augustine on the summit of the ancient world, Aquinas on the crown of the Middle Ages, and Newman in the hey-day of the nineteenth century', reflecting upon the meaning of existence in their time 'as Moses surveyed the Promised Land from the vantage point of Mount Nebo'.[55] While it is common to find Catholic theologians comparing Augustine with Aquinas and speaking of this pair of Church Doctors in hallowed tones, in many of Przywara's publications the name of Newman is added to their illustrious company. Przywara treats Newman as quite the peer of the earlier pair and associates each with a particular ecclesial age: Augustine as the greatest of the Patristics, Aquinas as the greatest of the Scholastics and Newman as the greatest of the moderns.

52. Ibid., p. 108.
53. Ibid., p. 109.
54. Erich Przywara, *Polarity: A German Catholic's Interpretation of Religion*, p. 114.
55. Ibid., p. 116.

In his *Augustinisch: Ur-Haltung des Geistes*, Przywara praised Newman's way of appropriating Augustine's theme of the presence of God within the human soul. Whereas Descartes and Malebranche 'dangerously blur' the distinction between God and the soul, Newman, especially in his *Grammar of Assent*, acknowledged the distance between 'the master and the servant', between holiness and sinfulness, between the judge and the accused, between the immeasurable gift of mercy and the finite condition of the pardoned. Newman's treatment of the conscience 'eliminates all self-satisfaction of the ego in the complete self-abandonment of the ego' to God.[56] In this context, Przywara read Newman as the correct *via media* between Descartes and Hegel on the one side, who do not sufficiently acknowledge the distance and distinction between God and the soul, and Pascal and Kierkegaard on the other side, for whom the distance is so great that another set of problems arise, turning those drawn into the problematic into what Przywara calls 'agnostic Tragedians' (*agnostischen Tragizismus*, literally an agnostic tragicism).

Przywara also regarded Newman's treatment of history in his *Essay on the Development of Christian Doctrine* as overcoming another set of problems common to Descartes and Hegel on the one side and Paschal and Kierkegaard on the other. Hegel, following Descartes's pure spirituality, knows history only as a logical representation of the idea, so that there is no account of merely creaturely history, only the history of the 'becoming' God. Consequently, all history of revelation is naturalized, because natural history as such is already God's history. Kierkegaard, consistent with Pascal's notion of *l'homme, quel chaos* 'cannot open the abyss enough between the never-to-be-understood chaos of history and an ideal sense'.[57] For Kierkegaard, contemporary history is essentially closed against God. Newman, however, overcomes these dilemmas by 'translating the floating tension between "idea" and "real" into history'. For Newman, 'history is the unfolding of an idea, but not in a logical derivation of the real from this idea, but through and in the forces of the real'.[58]

As a third, almost serendipitous, overcoming of the extreme alternatives of the world and history optimism of Descartes–Hegel, and the world and history pessimism of Pascal–Kierkegaard, Przywara

---

56. Erich Przywara, *Augustinisch: Ur-Haltung des Geistes*, p. 68.
57. Ibid., p. 69.
58. Ibid., p. 68.

read Newman as a scholar who offers prophetic insight into the nature of the last battle 'between Christ and the anti-Christ' at the end of modernity. Newman was realistic about the intensity of the battle. He was no example of bourgeois complacency. Przywara declared Newman to be 'the peculiar and unique *Augustinus redivivus* of modern times', because, 'amidst the torrent which bears all things to their doom, his gaze is fixed calmly upon the God of the end. *Deus omnia in omnibus*'.[59] Like Augustine, facing death as the city of Hippo Regius is sacked by Vandals, Newman did not despair. As Augustine managed to save his library from the Vandals, Newman rescued what he could of the high culture of English Christianity.

As a man of the Victorian era, Newman did not live to witness the suicide of Europe in the trenches of the Western front. There is no Newmanian Tract on the Christmas Truce of 1914, the demolition of the Hapsburg Empire, or the incomprehensible situation of Catholic Austria versus Catholic France, or Protestant Germany versus Protestant Britain. However, anyone writing after the First World War needed to attempt some account of what had happened and why. How could 'Christian' Europe go to war against itself and what could be done in the future to ensure that such squandering of human life on an epic scale never occurred again? Such questions were posed again with even greater intensity after August 1945.

Przywara addressed the first of these questions in a collection of four lectures that were published in 1948 under the title *Vier Predigten über das Abendland* – Four Sermons on the West. This collection began with an introduction by Hans Urs von Balthasar in which Balthasar noted that Przywara wrote these lines in an 'apocalyptically blazing Germany, a burning Munich that was sinking more and more into rubble, in which he endured life to the utmost as a comforter, reminder, and helper, until his strength and health collapsed'.[60] At the heart of the collection is a passionate indictment of the intellectual foundations of the Reformation, especially the Lutheran foundations. Balthasar spoke of Przywara competing with Luther's 'dark and immoderate genius', of responding 'to a demand for a duel that could no longer be refused'.[61]

59. Erich Przywara, 'St. Augustine and the Modern World' in *A Monument to St Augustine*, M. C. D'Arcy et al. (ed.) (New York: Dial Press, 1930), pp. 249–87 at p. 286.

60. Hans Urs von Balthasar, Introduction to Erich Przywara, *Vier Predigten über das Abendland*, p. 7.

61. Ibid.

In the first of the lectures, Przywara spoke of four key concepts that gave rise to the 'huge building at the centre of the Christian West' – *Corpus Christi, Civitas Dei, Imperium Sacrum*, and *Théosis Kósmos*: Body of Christ, City of God, Holy Kingdom and Divine Cosmos. He then offers a reading of the Reformation as the 'original revolution' that aimed to destroy each of these four foundation stones and replace them with the concepts: sin alone, conscience alone, word alone and Christ alone. Przywara argued that the Reformation went beyond a corrective as typically found in earlier reforming movements such as the Cluniac, Dominican and Franciscan and instead proffered a total negation. The logical corollary of the 'No' to Corpus Christi was the 'No' to the intrinsic goodness of creation. The world is deemed to be evil and once left to its evil it is secularized. It becomes a world without God, a world as hell. Once this world is under the reign of sin 'there remains only the innermost inside, which is directly related to God, to the God who is himself the *Deus Interior*, the God inside'.[62] Hence there arises the idea of 'conscience alone'. However, this too is no mere corrective but becomes the solvent of any form of visible authority. Similarly, the Lutheran emphasis on the sacred word is read by Przywara as no mere positive successor to earlier Dominican reforms exhorting the importance of the scriptures, but rather as the source of an absolute spiritualism since any objective authority for monitoring the interpretation of scripture has been annihilated by the 'conscience alone' principle. The absolute spiritualism then morphs into an absolute intellectualism and with this, there occurs the birth of German Idealism. Finally, for the Christ alone principle of the Reformation what matters is not the nature of God or the nature of Christ understood in Chalcedonian categories but the question of justification. Christ appears as the divine form of man and from here it is a short distance to the messianic humanity of Hegel and Wilhelm von Humboldt. Thus, the 'conscience alone' principle has led to an extreme egocentrism. The 'word alone' principle has degenerated under the power of secularism to a 'literary-journalistic "conversation" and "talk"'.[63] The 'Christ alone' principle has ended with a neo-promethean man as God while the 'sin alone' principle of the Reformation has become a terrible reality: 'the world as sin and death and curse and hell'.[64] The nineteenth century, Przywara noted, was

62. Erich Przywara, *Vier Predigten über das Abendland*, p. 21.
63. Ibid., p. 34.
64. Ibid., p. 31.

'behind us', a century that 'boasted a distinguished atheism'. It had been replaced by the twentieth century 'that believes in God but hates him'. Przywara concluded that 'the distinguished atheism has turned into a satanic contra-theism, a religiosity that hates God'.[65]

In another essay published in 1948, on the subject of Kierkegaard and Newman, Przywara spoke of the Lutheran dissolution of the Church into a 'Christ alone' pneumatic inwardness, followed by the dissolution of 'Christ alone' to the pure symbol of 'God alone' from the Enlightenment to the nineteenth century, with these two movements followed by a third from the end of the nineteenth century to the middle of the First World War, characterized as a dissolution of the 'God alone' stance to the vision of the 'world alone'. He described the 'myth' of the 'world alone' as the 'last irrationality'.[66] It was, he concluded, 'only when, during World War II, when the bliss of the whole of modernity collapsed into a new chaos, did the question about God, which was the driving and consuming fire in the entire work of Reformation, break out volcanically'.[67] The cumulative result of all of these movements on the chessboard of the German intelligentsia was that the Lord was bringing his flock together 'under the howl of hell in a world without God'.[68]

Przywara approached the second of the above questions – how to avoid a repetition of the carnage of the First and Second World Wars – in a short monograph first published in 1956 as *Idee Europa*. It was reprinted in 2013 in Italian under the title *L'Idea d'Europa: La 'crisi' di ogni politica 'cristiana'*. This work was much less theological than *Vier Predigten über das Abendland* and much less apocalyptic in tone. It was composed after the Second World War had ended rather than in the midst of it. In it Przywara offers a fascinating account of the genesis of the European Union. An 'Idea of Europe' he declared, originated from the French concept of a 'Federation of European peoples' to be opposed to the Holy Roman Empire. According to Cardinal Richelieu and his Capuchin advisor, François Leclerc du Tremblay, who was the original *Éminence grise*, this federation had to be under the effective primacy of France. The idea of a Pan-European federation was then taken up anew at the end of the First World War

65. Ibid., p. 47.
66. Erich Przywara, 'Kierkegaard-Newman', in *Newman Studien*, pp. 77–101 at 85.
67. Ibid., p. 85.
68. Erich Przywara, *Vier Predigten über das Abendland*, p. 36.

by the Austrian Count Richard von Coundenhove-Kalergi (1894–1972), brother of the writer Ida Friederike Görres (1901–1971). After the Second World War, Robert Schuman (1886–1963), who was twice the French prime minister, and Konrad Adenauer (1876–1967), who was the first chancellor of the Federal Republic of Germany (West Germany) from 1949 to 1963, set about promoting this idea. Starting with an agreement between France and Germany, they tried to found a 'European union' with economic, military and finally political ends. Przywara wrote that in all these attempts, the impulse was for a purely instrumental policy, without a search for the foundations of the 'Idea of Europe'.[69] Conversely, he argued that 'an "Idea of Europe", which is not simply the commercial brand of an association of companies operating for economic advantages, must be derived from a reflection on the essence of Europe, for which it is necessary to first question the two great masters of Western thought: Plato and Aristotle'.[70] At the end of his own Platonic and Aristotelian reflections, he concluded that contemporary discussions about Europe show the almost total marginalization of an authentic "Christian Universalism", which until Leibniz had been the basic idea of a "united West", before the prevalence of a purely political and economic consortium. The consequence of this, he thought, was that contemporary attempts to forge a "new West" remain vague and abstract. Like Guardini, he was not enthusiastic about the notion of a new Europe built on nothing deeper than economic interests. There is little or no "dark fire" in economics.

In his Address to the theologians of Germany, delivered at the Marian shrine of Altötting in 1980, a young Pope John Paul II listed Przywara, along with Guardini, Nicholas of Cusa, Matthias Joseph Scheeben, Johann Adam Möhler and St Albert the Great, as one of those outstanding German theologians who 'have not only enriched the church in the German-speaking area, but also the theology and life of the whole church'.[71] Nonetheless, the task of mining the insights of Przywara into cultural polarities and the restoration of the *analogia entis* to the centre of Catholic theology remains a vast work in progress.

69. Erich Przywara, *L'Idea d'Europa: La 'crisi' di ogni politica 'cristiana'*, p. 71.
70. Ibid.
71. John Paul II, Address to Professors of Theology, Altötting, 18 November 1980. Available on Vatican website.

CONCLUSION

Eric Voegelin, who was for a time a professor of political science at the Ludwig Maximilian's Universität (1958–69) in Munich, described ideology as a form of rebellion against God and man – a violation of the First and Tenth Commandments, to use the language of the Old Testament – and *nosos*, the disease of the spirit, to use the language of Aeschylus and Plato.[1] Voegelin juxtaposed philosophy with ideology and asserted that 'ever since Plato, in the disorder of his time, discovered the connection [between the search for truth and man's awareness of his existence in untruth], philosophical inquiry has been one of the means of establishing islands of order in the disorder of the age'.[2]

The authors surveyed in this collection created such an island in the disorder of the Weimar Republic and the years of Nazi tyranny though it was not merely an island where philosophy was practised, but an island where philosophy, theology and literature worked together in a symphonic harmony. This was in stark opposition to the academic practice of building Chinese walls between these disciplines, a practice fostered by the Jesuits in the Baroque era and followed by philosophers of the German Enlightenment a century later. By the time German Catholic scholars attended to the issue during the Weimar Republic and Chairs of the Christian *Weltanschauung* were established, Kant had become, in the memorable phrase of Peter Henrici, a 'secret father of the Church'. As Henrici explained, 'moved by a kind of Christian Pharisaism, Christian existence had become viewed as a meritorious achievement

---

1. Eric Voegelin, *Order and History: Israel and Revelation* (Baton Rouge: Louisiana State University Press, 1956), p. xiv.
2. Ibid.

that God commands and by virtue of which one is able to please him'.[3] For rather too many Catholics, the practice of Christian life consisted largely of duties that were performed because one was obliged to do so. This had become a common element in what was often pejoratively labelled 'bourgeois Christianity'. While Joseph Ratzinger once quipped that 'Kant became the Aristotle of Protestantism, while Schleiermacher became its Thomas', Henrici went further and acknowledged that Catholic scholars had also bought into the Kantian project. This had tragic consequences. As the Italian Thomist Cornelio Fabro remarked, the foreclosure of philosophy to God has two chief results: 'it causes philosophy to "precipitate" as atheistic theology', and it 'necessitates an ultimate appeal on the part of that theology to the principle of immanentism with its insistence on the intrinsic conditioning by the mind of every dimension of being and of the ultimate meaning of truth itself'.[4]

Kant's foreclosure of philosophy to God ended in the despair of the First World War generation. As the Belgian Jesuit Joseph Maréchal noted in an essay published in 1929, 'Poor Kant – the progenitor – is outdated: the unknowable, but real absolute of the Thing in itself, to which he so strongly attached all the objective functions of understanding, is no longer a reality, not even a possibility; worse, it is a flagrant impossibility'.[5] Theodor Haecker succinctly concluded, 'a humanism devoid of theology cannot stand'.[6]

The Kantian emphasis upon duty and the notion of the moral as that which is done out of a sense of duty, rather than for the satisfaction of any affection, or even in accordance with any tradition, shares a logical affinity with the moral theology of Jansenism. Although the two movements, fostered in the first instance by a Belgian Catholic bishop – Cornelius Jansen, Bishop of Ypres (1510–1576) – and in the second instance two centuries later, by a German Lutheran philosopher, may

---

3. Peter Henrici, 'Modernity and Christianity', *Communio: International Catholic Review* (Summer 1990), pp. 150–1.

4. Cornelio Fabro, *God in Exile: Modern Atheism* (Toronto: Newman Press, 1968), p. 1002.

5. Joseph Maréchal, 'Au seuil de la métaphysique: abstraction ou intuition', *Revue néo-scolastique de philosophie*, 31e année, Deuxième série, n°21, 1929, pp. 27–52 at 35. Translation provided by Maddison Reddie-Clifford.

6. Theodor Haecker, *Virgil: Father of the West* (London: Sheed & Ward, 1934), p. 81.

belong to different intellectual genealogies, Henri Bergson's concept of *récoupage* – a dialectical method of reducing two opposite doctrines to a single mistaken tenet – would seem to be applicable in this context.[7] At its surface, Kantian ethics based on a severance of reason and revelation and hence grace and nature appears to be the dialectical opposite of a Jansenist moral theology which holds out no hope at all for ethics and nature without the participation of grace. However, the moral frameworks of both share the property of making duty and obedience to the will of a legislator (even if in Kant's case the legislator is reason itself) the driving force behind moral action. They also share the dialectical affinity of fostering, in the case of Kant, a humanism without religion, while in the case of Jansenius, a religion without humanism.

The authors surveyed in this book did not want a Kantian-Jansenist version of Catholicism – that is, a Catholicism built on conceptions of reason divorced from faith and of duty divorced from love. They eschewed all casuistry for which the Jesuit approach to moral theology had become famous. They wanted a Christian humanism that could meet the criticisms of Nietzsche and appropriate the insights of Kierkegaard. Rather than defending the faith at the bar of the Enlightenment, which would mean relying on only one faculty of the human soul, that of discursive reason or *ratio*, these proponents of a Christian humanism wanted to employ both *ratio* and *intellectus*, discursive reason and intuition, as well as the *memoria* and the *imaginatio*, historical revelation as well as metaphysics, grace as well as nature. In Haecker's words, 'We must fight on sacramental ground!' In Steinbüchel's words, 'We must fight by amplifying the dimension of Christian mystery.' In Guardini's words, 'The answer to sin is not something that takes place within creation, it is not a remedy to be applied, but a new recovery and a new beginning that invest the very roots of being.'[8] On Söhngen's

---

7. For a discussion on this concept see Leszek Kołakowski, *Bergson* (Oxford: Oxford University Press, 1985), pp. 6–7; and Leszek Kołakowski, *God Owes Us Nothing* (Chicago: University of Chicago Press, 1995), p. 115. In *Bergson*, Kołakowski writes, 'When trying to answer a question he [Bergson] confronted two existing solutions embedded in opposite conceptual schemes and then asked at what point they overlapped, that is, what they had in common, whereupon he showed that they shared a false assumption concealed in the very way they phrased the question.'

8. Romano Guardini, *Antropologia cristiana* (Brescia: Morcelliana, 2013), p. 104.

sacramental ground 'the supernatural and natural order do not lie next to each other, but the supernatural order encompasses and also penetrates the natural order'.[9]

Bourgeois Christianity, however, does not fight on sacramental ground. It does not fight at all. It simply goes in search of Christian-friendly elements of the *zeitgeist* with which it might identify and market itself. It views 'sin' therapeutically and bureaucratically. It is either a mental health problem or the misuse of decision-making authority to be countered by better policies and bureaucratic circumscriptions on the exercise of prudential judgment. Within bourgeois Christianity there is no cosmic battle, no demons and no angels. Sacraments, if they appear at all, do so as mere symbols and social-milestone markers. Proponents of a bourgeois Christianity have been, as de Lubac well understood, 'overcome by a desire for conciliation that left them defeated before they had begun'. The ecclesiology that undergirds a bourgeois form of Christianity is inevitably a vision of the Church as a 'People's Republic'. Accommodation to the *zeitgeist* is more important than sanctity. Like Hitler's brand of fascism, it prefers *Gleichschaltung* (a synchronizing equalization) to *Vergöttlichung* (divinization). It rejects Haecker's insight that *Wir sind Hierarchisten* (we are hierarchists). It rejects the idea that only the higher can explain the lower. It kowtows to the nominalist emphasis on the individual. It is ignorant of the *analogia entis*, and from such ignorance it collapses into a state of giving priority to *ethos* over *logos*, to feelings over thinking, to subjectivity over objectivity. There is no holding of these couplets together in a relationship of harmonious integration of polarities. Precisely because it eschews the cosmic battle, bourgeois Christianity can never be prophetic or countercultural. Neither does it take an interest in chivalry. An image of St George killing a dragon makes no sense to the bourgeois Christian for whom there are no dragons. 'Radical aristocrats' like Nietzsche despise it. It is profoundly boring.

The sextet of authors whose publications were 'excavated' in the preceding pages did not, however, despair of Christianity. They understood that the bourgeois Christianity that lacked the power to resist the fascist movement and was the subject of so much opposition from Feuerbach to Marx to Nietzsche is not authentic Christianity, but merely a classic example of what Newman identified as a deformed

---

9. Erich Przywara, foreword to Adam Müller, *Schriften zur Staatsphilosophie* (München: Theatiner, 1923), p. xii.

sort of Christianity that truncates the Christian proclamation to a few *zeitgeist*-friendly elements. The sextet offered hope for those caught in the nihilist cul-de-sac by representing Christianity in a form that transcends all either-or choices, that holds polarities together in a creative tension, and offers a theological anthropology that is both radically aristocratic and inclusive of all humanity. They therefore regarded the cataclysmic death agonies of late modern culture in the three-cornered clash between fascism and communism and liberalism as something that could be the beginning of a hope-filled future. As the publisher Heinrich Wild wrote in a reflection on Theodor Haecker, 'the form of prophetic speech is melancholy illuminated by supernatural hope'.[10] This could describe the genre of all six authors. They were each acutely and painfully aware of the loss of so much of the Christian culture of the West, but they did not despair. The following passage from Przywara is typical of the genre and is offered as the concluding thought of this work:

> If the West is now to die, then it will be commemorated on Good Friday, which already gathers Easter daffodils for an Easter morning all over the world, in which together with the head rises the risen body of Christ, the risen *Civitas Dei*, the risen empire of the whole world, the risen Divine Cosmos. We kneel before the God whom we finally believe in truth, before the God who is the same yesterday and today and forever. The God, 'who called light from darkness, is illuminated in the fact of Jesus Christ in our hearts'; is illuminated from the darkness of our hearts, from the darkness of the body of Christ, from the darkness of the City of God, from the darkness of the *Sacrum Imperium*, from the darkness of the Divine Cosmos ... So today's hour does not sound like hell's cries of despair. A single phrase sounds through them. 'Fiat lux Deus'! Let it be the Light that is God. Amen.[11]

---

10. Heinrich Wild, 'Theodor Haecker's Tag und Nachtbücher', *Hochland* (1946–7), pp. 86–8.

11. Erich Przywara, *Vier Predigten über das Abendland* (Einsiedeln: Johannes-Verlag, 1948), p. 56.

SELECTED BIBLIOGRAPHY

Chapter 1

Bauer, C., 'Carl Muths und des *Hochland* Weg aus dem Kaiserreich in die Weimarer Republik', *Hochland* (1966/7), pp. 234–47.

Dru, A., *The Contribution of German Catholicism* (New York: Hawthorn Books, 1963).

Fuchs, F., 'Die deutschen Katholiken und Die deutsche Kultur im 19. Jahrhundert: Zur geistesgeschichtlichen Einordnung von Karl Muth's Werk', in *Wiederbegegnung von Kirche und Kultur in Deutschland*, Max Ettlinger, Philipp Funk und Friedrich Fuchs (eds) (München: Verlag Josef Kösel & Friedrich Pustet, 1927), pp. 9–59.

Gerl-Falkovitz, H.-B., 'Romano Guardini, Josef Weiger und Carl Muth', in *Carl Muth und das Hochland (1903-1941)*, Thomas Pittrof (Hg.) (Berlin: Rombach Verlag, 2018), pp. 221–35.

Knab, J., 'Carl Muth – Mentor des Widerstands', *Die Tagespost*, 15 December 2017.

Maier, H., 'Wiederbegegnung von Kirche und Kultur in Deutschland: Ein Blick auf die Muth-Festschrift von 1927', in *Carl Muth und das Hochland (1903-1941)*, Thomas Pittrof (Hg.) (Berlin: Rombach Verlag, 2018), pp. 195–205.

Muth, C., 'Bilanz: Eine Umschau aus Anlass des 25 Jahrgangs', *Hochland* XXV (1) (Oktober 1927–April 1928), 1–23.

Muth, C., *Die Wiedergeburt der Dichtung aus dem religiösen Erlebnis* (München: Jos-Kösel'sche Buchhandlung in Kempten, 1909).

Muth, C., 'Ein Rück – und Ausblick zum 20. Jahrgang', *Hochland* XX (1) (Oktober 1922–März 1923), pp. 1–15.

Muth, C., et al. 'Das Gesicht der Zeitschrift *Hochland* (1930): Ein Rundfunkgespräch am Berliner Sender zwischen dem Herausgeber Professor Karl Muth, Dr. Friedrich Fuchs von der Hochland-Redaktion und Dr. Otfried, München', in *Carl Muth und Das Hochland (1903-1941)*, Thomas Pittrof (Hg.) (Freiburg i. Br: Rombach Verlag, 2018), pp. 236–51.

Muth, C., *Schöpfer und Magier* (München: Kösel Verlag, 1953).

Muth, C., *Carl Muth und das Mittelalterbild des Hochland* (München: Neue Schriftenreihe des Stadarchivs, 1974).

Raponi, E., *Antonio Fogazzaro – Carl Muth Carteggio (1903-1910)* (Vincenza: Accademia Olimpica, 2010).

Renz, H., 'Carl Muth und Gertrud von le Fort', in *Carl Muth und das Hochland (1903-1941)*, Thomas Pittrof (Hg.) (Berlin: Rombach Verlag, 2018), pp. 195-205.

Schöningh, J., 'Carl Muth: Ein europäisches Vermächtnis', *Hochland* (1946-7), pp. 1-19.

Chapter 2

Becker, W., 'Der Überschritt von Kierkegaard zu Newman in der Lebensentscheidung Theodors Haeckers', in *Newman Studien: Erste Folge* (1948), pp. 251-71.

Biemer, G., 'Theodor Haecker in the Footsteps of John Henry Newman', *New Blackfriars* 81 (956) (October 2000), pp. 412-31.

Blessing, E., *Theodor Haecker: Gestalt und Werk* (Nürnberg: Glock und Lutz, 1959).

Blessing, E., 'Theodor Haecker: Philosopher', *Philosophy Today* 1 (3) (Fall 1957), pp. 186-94.

Dru A., 'Haecker's Point of View: Notes on the History of Existentialism', in *Downside Review* 67 (209) (1949a), pp. 260-75.

Dru, A., 'On Haecker's *Metaphysik der Gefühle*', *Downside Review* 68 (211) (1949b), pp. 35-45.

Haecker, T., '... dass zu den Grundlagen unserer Kultur das Christentum gehört', in Dieter Thomä (ed.), *Gibt es noch eine Universität?* (Konstanz: Konstanz University Press, 2012), pp. 42-5.

Haecker, T., 'Betrachtungen über Vergil, Vater des Abendlandes', *Der Brenner* 13 (1932), pp. 3-31.

Haecker, T., *Christentum und Kultur* (München und Kempten: Verlag Josef Kösel, 1936).

Haecker, T., 'Das Chaos der Zeit', *Hochland* 30 (1933), pp. 1-23.

Haecker, T., 'Dass zu den Grundlagen unserer Kultur das Christentum gehört', in *Gibt es Noch Eine Universität?*, Dieter Thomä (ed.) (Konstanz: Konstanz University Press, 2012), pp. 42-5.

Haecker, T., *Der Christ und die Geschichte* (Leipzig: Jakob Hegner, 1935).

Haecker, T., *Dialog über Christentum und Kultur, Mit Einem Exkurs über Sprache, Humor und Satire* (Hellerau: Jakob Hegner, 1930).

Haecker, T., *Essays aus den Jahren 1917-1944: Werke 1* (Kempten: Verlag Josef Kösel, 1958).

Haecker, T., *Journal in the Night* (London: Harvill Press, 1949).

Haecker, T., *Kierkegaard the Cripple* (London: Harvill Press, 1948).

Haecker, T., 'Notizen: Die Bestie', *Der Brenner* (Juni 1923), pp. 9-19.

Haecker, T., *Schöpfer und Schöpfung* (München: Jakob Hegner, 1949).

Haecker, T., *Søren Kierkegaard*, trans. Alexander Dru (London: Oxford University Press, 1937).

Haecker, T., 'Theodicy and Tragedy', *The Criterion*, April 1934.

Haecker, T., *Über den Abendländischen Menschen* (Kolmar im Elsass: Alsatia Verlag, 1944).

Haecker, T., *Virgil: Father of the West* (London: Sheed & Ward, 1934).

Haecker, T., *Was ist der Mensch?* (Frankfurt am Mein: Ullstein Bücher, 1959).

Heywood-Thomas, J., and Siefken, H., 'Theodor Haecker and Alexander Dru: A Contribution to the Discovery of Kierkegaard in Britain', *Kierkegaardiana* 6 (1996), pp. 173–90.

Janik, A., 'Haecker, Kierkegaard and the Early *Brenner*: A Contribution to the History of the Reception of *Two Ages* in the German-Speaking World', in *Two Ages*, Robert L. Perkins (ed.), *International Kierkegaard Commentary*, vol. 14 (Macon, Georgia: Mercer University Press, 1984), pp. 189–222.

Kleinert, M., 'Theodor Haecker: The Mobilisation of a Total Author', in Jon Stewart (ed.), *Kierkegaard's Influence on Literature, Criticism and Art, Tome 1: The Germanophone World* (Farnham: Ashgate, 2013), pp. 91–115.

Knab, J., 'Zur Erinnerung an Theodor Haecker', *Die Tagespost*, 7 April 2020.

Munro, G., 'Georg Moenius (1890–1953)', in Jürgen Aretz, Rudolf Morsey and Anton Rauscher (Hrsgb.), *Zeitgeschichte in Lebensbildern: Aus dem deutschen Katholizismus des 19. und 20.Jahrhunderts*, Band 10 (Münster: Aschendorff Verlag, 2001), pp. 131–41.

Munro, G., *Hitler's Bavarian Antagonist: Georg Moenius and the Allgemeine Rundschau of Munich, 1929-1933* (Lewiston: Edwin Mellen Press, 2006).

Munro, G., 'The Holy Roman Empire in German Roman Catholic Thought (1929–1933), *Journal of Religious History* 17 (4) (December 1993), pp. 439–65.

Schmidt, E. A., 'The German Recovery of Vergil in the Early Years of the 20th Century (1900–1938)', *Vergilius* 54 (2008), pp. 124–49.

Tomko, H. M., 'Beyond Exile and Inner Emigration: Rereading Max Horkheimer on Theodor Haecker's *Der Christ und die Geschichte* (1935)', *German Quarterly* (Spring 2017), pp. 157–74.

Tomko, H. M., 'On Dark Nights in Dark Times: Catholic Inner Exile Writing in Hitler's Germany', *Logos: A Journal of Catholic Culture* 22 (3) (Summer 2019), pp. 42–69.

Tomko, H. M., 'The Reluctant Satirist: Theodor Haecker and the Dizzying Swindle of Nazism', *Oxford German Studies* 46 (1) (2017), pp. 42–57.

Tomko, H. M., 'Word Creatures: Theodor Haecker and Walter Benjamin between *Geschwätz* and Pure Language in the Later Weimar Republic', *New German Critique* 45 (1,133) (2018), pp. 23–47.

Wild, H., 'Theodor Haecker's Tag und Nachtbücher', *Hochland* (1946–7), pp. 86–8.

Chapter 3

Lienkamp, A., 'Theodor Steinbüchel', in *Kölner Theologen: Von Rupert von Deutz bis Wilhelm Nyssen*, Sebastian Cüppers (ed.) (Köln: Marzellen Verlag, 2004), pp. 388–412.

Steinbüchel, T., *Annette von Droste-Hülshoff nach hundert Jahren* (Frankfurt am Main: Verlag Josef Knecht, 1950).

Steinbüchel, T., *Die Philosophiesche Grundlegung: Der Katholischen Sittenlehre* (Düsseldorf: Patmos-Verlag, 1947).

Steinbüchel, T., *Der Mensch-Heute* (Stuttgart: Verlag von Ernst Klett, 1947).

Steinbüchel, T., *Die Abstammung des Menschen: Theorie und Theologie* (Frankfurt am Main: Verlag Josef Knecht-Carolusdruckerei, 1951).

Steinbüchel, T., *Europa als Verbundenheit im Geist* (Tübingen: Verlag von J.C.B. Mohr, 1946).

Steinbüchel, T., *Existenzialismus und Christliches Ethos* (Bonn: Verlag des Borromäus-Vereins, 1948).

Steinbüchel, T., *Friedrich Nietzsche: Eine christliche Besinnung* (Stuttgart: Deutsche Verlags-Anstalt, 1946).

Steinbüchel, T., 'Ich und Du: Grundzüge der Anthropologie Ferdinand Ebners', *Kerygma und Dogma* 3 (1957), pp. 208–19.

Steinbüchel, T., *Immanuel Kant: Einführung in seine Welt und den Sinn seiner Philosophie*, Vols. I and II (Düsseldorf: Druck und Verlag von L. Schwann, 1931).

Steinbüchel, T., *Mensch und Gott in Frömmigkeit und Ethos der deutschen Mystik* (Düsseldorf: Patmos Verlag, 1952).

Steinbüchel, T., *Mensch und Wirklichkeit: In Philosophie und Dichtung des 20 Jahrhunderts* (Frankfurt am Main: Verlag Josef Knecht, 1950).

Steinbüchel, T., *Reden bei der Feierlichen Eröffnung des Sommersemesters am 23 April 1947* (Tübingen: Verlag von J.C.B. Mohr, 1947).

Steinbüchel, T., *Religion und Moral: Im Lichte Personaler Christlicher Existenz* (Frankfurt am Main: Verlag Josef Knect, 1951).

Steinbüchel, T., *F. M. Dostojewski: Sein Bild von Menschen und von Christen* (Düsseldorf: Verlag L Schwann, 1947).

Steinbüchel, T., *Vom Menschbild des christlichen Mittelalters* (Darmstadt: Wissenschaftliche Buchgesellschaft, 1951).

Steinbüchel, T., *Zerfall des Christlichen Ethos im XIX. Jahrhundert* (Frankfurt am Main: Verlag Josef Knect, 1951).

Chapter 4

Foley, G., 'The Catholic Critics of Karl Barth in Outline and Analysis', *Scottish Journal of Theology* 14 (1961), pp. 136–55.

Graf, J., 'Gottlieb Söhngen', in *Kölner Theologen: Von Rupert von Deutz bis Wilhelm Nyssen*, Sebastian Cüppers (ed.) (Köln: Marzellen Verlag, 2004), pp. 454–76.

Jall, A., *Erfahrung von Offenbarung: Grundlagen, Quellen und Anwendungen der Erkenntnislehre Joseph Ratzingers* (Regensburg: Verlag Friedrich Pustet, 2019).

Söhngen, G., *Christi Gegenwart in Glaube und Sakrament* (München: Verlag Anton Pustet, 1967).

Söhngen, G., *Der Geist des Glaubens und der Geist der Wissenschaft* (Essen: Verlag Augustin Wibbelt, 1947).

Söhngen, G., *Der Weg der abendländischen Theologie* (München: Verlag Anton Pustet, 1959).

Söhngen, G., 'Die Theologie im Streit der Fakultäten', *Hochland* (1951/2), pp. 225–38.

Söhngen, G., *Grundfragen einer Rechtstheologie* (München: Verlag Anton Pustet, 1962).

Söhngen, G., *Humanität und Christentum* (Essen: Verlag Augustin Wibbelt, 1946).

Söhngen, G., *Kardinal Newman: Sein Gottesgedanke und seine Denkergestalt* (Bonn: Verlag Götz Schwippert, 1946).

Söhngen, G., *Symbol und Wirklichkeit im Kultmysterium* (Bonn: Peter Hanstein Verlagsbuchhandlung, 1937).

Söhngen, G., 'The Analogy of Faith: Likeness to God from Faith Alone?', trans. Kenneth J Oakes, *Pro Ecclesia* 21(1) (2012), pp. 56–76.

Söhngen, G., 'The Analogy of Faith: Unity in the Science of Faith', trans. Kenneth J Oakes, *Pro Ecclesia* 21(2) (2012), pp. 169–94.

Chapter 5

Balthasar, H. U. von, *Romano Guardini: Reform from the Source* (San Francisco: Ignatius, 2010).

Berning-Baldeaux, U., *Person und Bildung im Denken Romano Guardinis* (Würzburg: Echter, 1968).

Fidalgo, J. M., 'El cristocentrismo de Romano Guardini', *Scripta Theologica* 42 (2010), pp. 333–58.

Guardini, R., *Antropologia cristiana* (Brescia: Morcelliana, 2013).

Guardini, R., 'Der Ausgangspunkt der Denkbewegung', *Hochland* 2 (1927), pp. 12–24.

Guardini, R., *Der Gegensatz. Versuche zu einer Philosophie des Lebendig-Konkreten* (Mainz: Matthias-Grüneald-Verlag, 1925).

Guardini, R., *Fede-Religione esperienza: Saggi teologici* (Brescia: Morcelliana, 1995).

Guardini, R., *La conversion di sant'Agostino* (Brescia: Morcelliana, 2002).
Guardini, R., *La coscienza* (Brescia: Morcelliana, 1933).
Guardini, R., *The End of the Modern World* (London: Sheed & Ward, 1957).
Guardini, R., *Gegensatz und Gegensätze. Entwurf eines Systems der Typenlehre* (Freiburg: Caritas-Druckerei, 1914).
Guardini, R., *Mondo e persona* (Brescia: Morcelliana, 2000).
Guardini, R., *Una morale per la vita* (Brescia: Morcelliana, 2009).
Guardini, R., *Nello specchio dell'anima* (Brescia: Morcelliana, 2010).
Guardini, R., *L'opposizione polare: Saggio per una filosofi a del concreto vivente* (Brescia: Morcelliana, 1997).
Guardini, R., *La realtà della Chiesa* (Brescia: Morcelliana, 1967).
Guardini, R., *La Rosa Bianca* (Brescia: Morcelliana, 1994).
Guardini, R., *Il senso della Chiesa* (Brescia: Morcelliana, 2007).
Guardini, R., *Virtù: Temi e prospettive della vita morale* (Brescia: Morcelliana, 1972).
Guardini, R., *La visione cattolica del mondo* (Brescia: Morcelliana, 1994).
Krieg, R. A., 'Romano Guardini's Theology of the Human Person', *Theological Studies* 59 (1998), pp. 457–74.
Kuehn, H. R., *The Essential Guardini: An Anthology of the Writings of Romano Guardini* (Chicago: Liturgy Training Publications, 1997).
Millare, R., 'The Hermeneutic of Continuity and Discontinuity: Between Romano Guardini and Joseph Ratzinger: The Primacy of *Logos*', *Nova et Vetera* 18 (2) (2020), pp. 521–63.
Millare, R., 'The Primacy of Logos over Ethos: The Influence of Romano Guardini on Post-Conciliar Theology', *Heythrop Journal* LVII (2016), pp. 974–83.
Reinhardt, E., 'Romano Guardini, Amigo y maestro de la juventad', *Scripta Theologica* 50 (3) (December 2018), pp. 591–610.
Schlüter-Hermkes, M., 'Die Gegensatzlehre Romano Guardinis', in Karl Muth (Hg.), *Hochland - Monatsschrift für alle Gebiete des Willens/der Literatur und Kunst*, Band 1, 26 Jahrgang (1928/29), pp. 529–39.
Zaborowski, H., 'Contradiction, Liturgy, and Freedom: Romano Guardini's Search for Meaning after the Cataclysm of World War I', *Modern Theology* 35 (1) (January 2019), pp. 43–54.

Chapter 6

Balthasar, H. U. von., *Erich Przywara, in Tendenzen zur Theologie im 20. Jahrhundert. Eine Geschichte in Porträts* (Stuttgart: Olten, 1966).
Barth, K., 'Grusswort an Erich Przywara', in *Der Beständige Aufbruch: Festschrift für Erich Przywara*, Siegfried Behn (ed.) (Nürnberg: Glock und Lutz, 1959), pp. 48–49.

Behn, S., 'Wer ist's?', in *Der Beständige Aufbruch: Festschrift für Erich Przywara*, Siegfried Behn (ed.) (Nürnberg: Glock und Lutz, 1959), pp. 7–18.

Betz, J. R., 'The Analogia entis as a Standard of Catholic Engagement: Erich Przywara's Critique of Phenomenology and Dialectical Theology', *Modern Theology* 35 (1) (January 2019), pp. 81–102.

Ederer, M. F., 'Propaganda Wars: *Stimmen der Zeit* and the Nazis, 1933–1935', *Catholic Historical Review* 90 (3) (July 2004), pp. 456–72.

Gonzales, P. J. P., *Reimagining the Analogia Entis: The Future of Erich Przywara's Christian Vision* (Grand Rapids: Eerdmans, 2019).

Lotz, Johannes B., 'Erich Przywara zum Gedächtnis', *Stimmen der Zeit* 189–90 (1972), pp. 289–90.

McAleer, G., *Erich Przywara and Postmodern Natural Law* (South Bend: University of Notre Dame Press, 2019).

Murphy, F. A., 'The Sound of the *Analogia Entis* Part I', *New Blackfriars* 74 (876) (1993), pp. 508–21.

Murphy, F. A., 'The Sound of the *Analogia Entis* Part II', *New Blackfriars* 74 (877) (1993), pp. 557–65.

Oakes, K., 'Three Themes in Przywara's Early Theology', *The Thomist* 74 (2) (2010), pp. 283–310.

Pidel, A., *Church of the Ever Greater God: The Ecclesiology of Erich Przywara* (South Bend: University of Notre Dame Press, 2020).

Przywara, E., *Augustinisch: Ur-Haltung des Geistes* (Einsiedeln: Johannes Verlag, 1970).

Przywara, E., *Crucis mysterium: das christliche Heute* (Paderborn: F. Schöningh, 1939).

Przywara, E., *Deus semper maior: Theologie der Exerzitien*, vol. 3 (Freiberg im Breisgau: Herder, 1938).

Przywara, E., 'Die Polarität zwischen Individuum und Gemeinschaft', in *Adam Müller: Schriften zur Staatsphilosophie*, Ein Vorwort and Rudolf Kohler (eds) (München: Theatiner-Verlag, 1923).

Przywara, E., 'Forderung des Primates solcher Erziehung', in *Gibt es Noch eine Universität?*, Dieter Thomä (ed.) (Konstanz: Konstanz University Press, 2012), pp. 40–2.

Przywara, E., *Humanitas: Der Mensch gestern und morgen* (Nürnberg: Glock und Lutz, 1952).

Przywara, E., 'Katholizismus', *Hochland* 2 (April–September 1924), pp. 566–74.

Przywara, E., 'Kierkegaard-Newman' in *Newman Studien*, vol. 1 (Nurnberg: Glock & Lotz, 1948), pp. 77–101.

Przywara, E., *Kant Heute* (München und Berlin: Verlag von R. Oldenbourg, 1930).

Przywara, E., *Logos, Abendland, Reich, Commercium* (Düsseldorf: Patmos Verlag, 1964).

Przywara, E., 'Nation, Staat und Kirche', *Stimmen der Zeit* 125 (1934), pp. 371–6.

Przywara, E., *Polarity: A German Catholic's Interpretation of Religion*, trans. A. C. Bouquet (London: Oxford University Press, 1935).

Przywara, E., *Ringen der Gegenwart: Gesammelte Aufsätze 1922–1927*, vol. 2 (Augsburg: Benno-Filser-Verlag, 1929).

Przywara, E., 'St. Augustine and the Modern World', in *A Monument to St Augustine*, M. C. D'Arcy et al. (eds) (New York: Dial Press, 1930), pp. 249–87.

Przywara, E., *Vom Himmelreich der Seele: Christliche Lebensführung, Volume 3, Barmherzigkeit* (Herder & Co: Freiburg im Breisgau, 1922).

Raczyński-Rożek, M., 'Erich Przywara's *Analogia Entis* as a Model of Catholic Thinking in Postmodern Reality', *Teologia w Polsce* 12 (2) (2018), pp. 215–31.

Raczyński-Rożek, M., 'The Church as the Realization of the Nature of Man in *Deus Semper Maior* by Erich Przywara', *Bogoslovni vestnik/Theological Quarterly* 79 (3) (2019), pp. 752–85.

Ratzinger, J., 'Erich Przywara's Alterswerk', *Wort und Wahrheit* 13 (1958), pp. 220–2.

Schel, Kevin M. Vander, 'Erich Przywara on John Henry Newman and the Supernatural'. *Studies in Dogmatic Theology* (3) (2018), pp. 193–214.

Zeitz, J. V., 'Erich Przywara: Visionary Theologian', *Thought: A Review of Culture and Idea* 58 (229) (June 1983), pp. 151–64.

Zimny, L., *Erich Przywara: Sein Schrifttum (1912–1962)* (Einsiedeln: Johannes Verlag, 1963).

AUTHOR INDEX

Abelard, Peter 153
Ackermann, Konrad 21
Adenauer, Konrad 67, 167
Adorno, Theodor 37, 134
Aeschylus 169
Albert the Great 167
Albert of Saxe-Coburg and Gotha, Prince 67
Alighieri, Dante 102, 119, 120, 125
Anselm of Canterbury, saint 91
Aquinas, Thomas, saint 4, 6, 14, 56, 85, 87, 94, 95, 113, 114, 138, 140, 147, 149, 151, 152, 155, 158–60, 162, 170
Aristotle 3, 13, 97, 167
Arrupe, Pedro 157
Auer, Alfons 85
Augustine of Hippo, saint 3, 4, 53, 57, 94, 95, 102, 119, 149–52, 164

Baeumker, Clemens 91
Balthasar, Hans Urs von 3, 5, 8, 11, 29, 32, 51, 52, 115, 120, 129, 130, 133, 144, 147, 164
Bañez, Domingo 14
Barth, Karl 2, 9, 82, 142, 144
Bauer, Clemens 32
Beethoven, Ludwig van 104
Bergengruen, Werner 22
Berlin, Isaiah 144
Bernanos, Georges 62, 129, 130
Bernard of Clairvaux, saint 153
Berning-Baldeaux, Ursula 119
Bertram, Ernst 154
Betz, John R. 2, 3
Bismarck, Otto von 6, 34, 143
Blessing, Eugen 37, 64, 65
Blondel, Maurice 24, 38, 82, 83
Bonaventure, saint 93, 95, 117, 120, 136
Borchardt, Rudolf 46
Borella, Jean 114
Brague, Remi 9, 10
Brémond, Henri 4, 24, 82

Buber, Martin 37, 98, 144
Butler, E. M. 47

Cajetan, Thomas, cardinal 14
Calvin, Jean 156
Camus, Albert 79
Casel, Odo 111–13
Cicero 101
Claudel, Paul 3, 24, 34
Clement of Alexandria 102
Coleridge, Samuel Taylor 161
Comte, Auguste 153
Cortés, Juan Donoso 33, 155, 156
Coundenhove-Kalergi, Richard von 167

Dalberg, Karl von 24
Dawson, Christopher 82
Delp, Alfred 16, 17, 143
Dempf, Alois 23, 87
Descartes, René 149, 163
Deutiger, Martin 148
Dostoevsky, Fyodor 3, 77, 78, 119
Droste-Hülshoff, Annette von 98
Dru, Alexander 36
Dupré, Louis 29, 136

Ebner, Ferdinand 68, 89, 98
Eckehart, Meister 70, 85
Eichendorff, Joseph von 24
Eliot, Thomas Stearns 46
Ern, Vladimir 7, 8, 40
Erschenbach, Wolfram von 85, 87
Esser, Gerhard 117

Faber, Eva-Maria 145
Fabro, Cornelio 170
Falque, Emmanuel 57
Faulhaber, Michael von 38
Fénelon, François 102
Feuerbach, Ludwig 88, 129, 149, 172
Fichte, Johann Gottlieb 9
Ficker, Ludwig von 36

Author Index

Francis de Sales, saint 102
Freud, Sigmund 149
Fuchs, Friedrich 28

Gaál, Emery de 91, 115
Galen, Clemens August Graf von 63
Geiselmann, Josef 108
George, Francis 2
George, Stefan 24
Gerl-Falkovitz, Hannah-Barbara 2
Giacomin, Maria Cristina 24
Gilson, Etienne 14
Goes, Albert 118
Goethe, Johann Wolfgang von 29–32, 44, 67, 68, 104, 148, 160
Gonzales, Philip John Paul 3
Görres, Ida Friederike 142
Graf, Josef 93, 113
Grüzmacher, Richard Heinrich 154

Habermas, Jürgen 67
Hanser, Richard 22
Hart, David Bentley 2
Hart, Kevin 57
Hegel, Georg Wilhelm Friedrich 6, 8, 31, 44, 83, 163
Heidegger, Martin 16, 37, 79, 144
Heine, Heinrich 67
Hemmerle, Klaus 57
Henri, Michel 57
Henrici, Peter 169, 170,
Hildebrand, Dietrich von 16, 17
Hildegard of Bingen, saint 85, 86
Horkheimer, Max 133
Huber-Kempten, Paul 20
Huizinga, Johan 82
Humboldt, Wilhelm von 23, 24, 121, 165
Hume, David 161
Husserl, Edmund 82, 144

Iwanow, Wjatscheslaw 46

Jansen, Cornelius 170, 171
Jaspers, Karl 79, 82
John of St. Thomas 14
John the Baptist, saint 19
John the Evangelist, saint 57, 81, 89, 104
Julian the Apostate 105

Kant, Immanuel 6–9, 23–5, 31, 32, 44, 51, 92, 98, 103, 104, 107–9, 121, 124, 132, 139, 140, 149, 169, 171
Kierkegaard, Søren 3, 4, 6, 15, 36, 41–5, 64, 66, 68, 69, 78, 79, 84, 88, 129, 158–60, 163, 171
Kleinert, Markus 37
Kohle, Rudolf 147
Kraus, Karl 36, 37
Krebs, Engelbert 117
Krieg, Robert A 2, 139, 140
Kołakowski, Leszek 8, 40
Köselitz, Heinrich 155
Kuehn, Heinz, R. 142

Läpple, A. 68, 115
Lavigerie, Charles, cardinal,
Leibniz, Gottfried Wilhelm 167
Leo XIII, pope 162
Lessing, Gotthold Ephraim 104
Lewis, C. S. 46, 62, 75, 89
Lienhard, Friedrich 23
Loyola, Ignatius, saint 4, 155, 156, 158
Lubac, Henri de 5, 12, 13, 15, 38, 43, 83, 157, 172
Lubich, Chiara 57
Lukács, György 79
Luther, Martin 95, 105, 106, 155, 156, 160, 164

MacIntyre, Alasdair 29, 33, 136
Malebranche, Nicolas 163
Marcel, Gabriel 63
Marcuse, Herbert 128
Maréchal, Joseph 170
Marion, Jean-Luc 57
Maritain, Jacques 82
Martin, Alfred von 8
Marx, Karl 67, 78, 84, 88, 129, 149, 172
Maspero, Giulio 57
McAleer, Graham 3
Melanchthon, Philip 102
Merlio, Gilbert 34
Metternich, Klemens von, Prince 67
Millare, Roland 2
Milne, A. A. 62
Moenius, Georg 45
Möhler, Johann Adam 167
Molina, Luis de 4

Author Index

More, Thomas, saint 22, 82
Mozart, Wolfgang Amadeus 104
Muth, Jakob Friedrich 28
Muth, Wulfried 28

Newman, John Henry, saint 3, 4, 10, 15,
  16, 35, 36, 41, 42, 51, 64, 69, 82, 84, 92,
  93, 95–100, 103, 105, 120, 124, 144,
  147, 161–4, 166, 172
Nicholas of Cusa 4, 102, 167
Nietzsche, Friedrich 4, 6, 8, 10, 27, 45,
  51, 63, 64, 69, 79, 72–9, 84, 85, 88, 100,
  105, 121, 126, 127, 129, 137, 144, 146,
  149, 153–8, 171
Novalis, poet 148

Oakes, Kenneth 3, 5
Obenauer, Justus 154
Ockham, William 28
Odenwald, Theodor 154
O'Meara, Thomas F. 3, 138
Ortega y Gasset, José 82
Ouellet, Marc 57

Paul VI, pope 6, 76, 94, 118
Paul of Tarsus, saint 105, 106, 113,
  135, 136
Pascal, Blaise 69, 93, 102, 148, 163
Pasteur, Louis 67
Péguy, Charles 3, 24
Persidok, Andrzej 3
Pidel, Aaron 3, 144, 145
Pieper, Josef 16, 115, 142, 146, 147
Pius XII, pope 96
Plato 3, 4, 36, 95, 101, 104, 119, 167, 169
Pribilla, Max 5
Pseudo-Dionysius 60

Raczyński-Rożek, Maciej 3, 148
Rademacher, Arnold 92, 99, 112
Rahner, Karl 2, 26, 93, 144, 146, 157
Raponi, Elena 27
Ratzinger, Joseph 5, 11, 13, 29, 35, 51, 68,
  73, 81, 89, 94, 95, 115, 130, 139, 141,
  142, 170
Richelieu, Duke and Cardinal 166
Rickert, Heinrich 153
Rilke, Rainer Maria 119
Roscelin of Compiégne 28

Rousseau, Jean Jacques 39, 44
Rowling, J. K. 12

Sailer, Johann Michael 103
Sartre, Jean-Paul 79
Scheeben, Matthias Joseph 111–12, 167
Scheler, Max 10, 153
Schiller, Friedrich 9, 49, 160
Schirnding, Albert von 65
Schlegel, Friedrich 148
Schleiermacher, Friedrich 170
Schmaus, Michael 94
Schmidt, Ernst A. 46
Scholl, Hans 4, 21, 22, 34, 35, 38
Scholl, Sophie 4, 21, 22, 34, 35, 38
Schöningh, Josef 21, 34, 35
Schopenhauer, Arthur 58, 84
Schuman, Robert 67, 167
Seewald, Richard 38
Shrimpton, Paul 2
Simmel, Georg 67, 160
Sokolowski, Robert 57
Spaemann, Robert 133
Spengler, Oswald 8
Spinoza, Baruch 153
Stein, Edith, saint 115, 146
Stenhouse, Paul 17
Stirner, Max 159

Taylor, Charles 29, 136
Thaler, Anna 20
Thérèse of Lisieux, saint 63
Thompson, Francis 36
Tillich, Paul 5
Tillmann, Fritz 68
Tolkien, J. R. R. 62, 89
Tomko, Helena M. 4, 65

Unamono, Miguel de 82

Valéry, Paul 82
Verdi, Giuseppe 49
Virgil, Publius Maro, poet 36, 45–8, 52,
  53, 57, 59, 62, 64, 102, 125
Voegelin, Eric 169
Voltaire, writer 69

Waelhems, Alphonse de 82
Weiger, Josef 118

Weil, Simone 3
Whateley, Richard 161
Wild, Heinrich 172
Wilhelmsen, Frederick, D. 13, 14
William II, Kaiser 108
Windelbrand, Wilhelm 153
Wittgenstein, Ludwig 37

Wojtyła, Karol/John Paul II, pope and saint 115, 135, 167
Wust, Peter 16, 63

Zaborowski, Holger 6
Zeitz, James V. 2, 147
Zucal, Silvano 118, 119, 121, 136

SUBJECT INDEX

Analogia entis 3, 15, 56, 93, 143–5, 149, 152, 158, 159, 167
Analogia fidei 5, 93, 110, 111
Analogia trinitatis 57, 145
angels 60, 61
Aristotelian reason 8
atheism 2, 12, 79, 100, 143, 166
Aufklärung 5
Augustinianism 149–52

bourgeois Christianity 73, 75, 76, 100, 101, 172

Christian existentialism 14
Christian humanism 11, 15, 37, 82, 89, 102–7, 171
Christian personalism 79, 80
Ciceronian tradition 9
Communio: International Catholic Review 5
Communism 12
conscience 4, 35, 38, 97, 98, 121–3, 165
Council of Trent 19
crisis theology 82

Diet of Worms 19

Erasmus Prize 2, 141
exclusive humanism 9, 10
existential Thomists 14
existentialism 79–81
expressivist theory of language 48

fascism 12, 172
First World War 5–7, 20, 68, 78, 89, 124, 134, 164, 166, 170, 171
Frankfurt School 133
French Revolution 49, 55, 137

German Idealism 1, 6, 23, 33, 44, 50, 53, 55, 62, 78, 146, 149, 165
Gleichschaltung 38, 172

Greco-Roman humanitas 46, 62, 92, 101, 103

Habsburg Empire 6, 164
historicism 13
Hitler, Adolf 19, 127, 172
Hochland 5, 16, 17, 19–21, 23–5, 29, 33–5, 38, 63, 107
humanism of the Incarnation 5

Imperium Romanum 59

Kulturkampf 19, 20, 65

Lamed Vav 50
Leonine scholasticism 23, 93
Limes Germanicus 49

magi 67
Marxism 39, 79, 80, 128
mass man 41, 71, 128, 129, 131, 134
Menschenbild 15, 84–9
modernism 26

neo-scholasticism 12, 15, 93, 96, 99
nominalism 148, 172
Nuptial Mystery 4, 81

paideia 101
Petrine Office 28
polarity 119, 120, 143, 162, 167, 148, 152, 153, 173
Prussia 6

Quickborn 2, 117, 118, 146

Radical Orthodoxy 57
Reformation 28, 153, 164, 165
Romantic movement 14, 39, 51, 74, 153

Sapir Whorf hypothesis 48
Schicksal 48

scholasticism 16, 86, 87, 112, 117, 148, 151
Second Vatican Council 1, 12, 15
Second World War 82, 92, 142, 166, 167
secularization 29
Stimmen der Zeit 5, 143, 155

Tricoronatum 67, 91, 106

Weimar Republic 10, 13, 169
Weisswurstäquator 49
Weltanschauung 1, 15, 24, 37, 68, 117, 140, 169
White Rose movement 4, 10, 21, 22, 24, 38, 124

www.ingramcontent.com/pod-product-compliance
Lightning Source LLC
Chambersburg PA
CBHW061832300426
44115CB00013B/2349